OGG & RAY'S

Essentials of

AMERICAN STATE and LOCAL GOVERNMENT

WILLIAM H. YOUNG
The University of Wisconsin

OGG & RAY'S

Essentials of
AMERICAN
STATE and LOCAL
GOVERNMENT

Tenth Edition

New York

APPLETON-CENTURY-CROFTS
EDUCATIONAL DIVISION
MEREDITH CORPORATION

PREFACE

As the national government has increased in size, scope, and complexity, it has perhaps overshadowed the state and local governments of the United States. In the interest of separate consideration of these important elements in the American system, the state and local government sections of *Essentials of American Government* are herewith published separately. In this form, they may be consulted by those interested. The material on the federal system, political parties, voting, and interest groups may be found in the edition dealing with the national government.

William H. Young

CONTENTS

ILLUSTRATIONS

I State Government

1

THE CONSTITUTIONAL BASIS OF STATE GOVERNMENT

THE ROLE OF THE STATES

Robert E. Lee, confronted in 1861 with the choice of serving the central government or serving his state of Virginia, chose Virginia. Such a decision by a major figure in public life today would be unthinkable. The United States is today one people. All the fierce loyalties of nationalism center on our government in Washington, D. C. and on our institutions of production, distribution, communication, religion, and entertainment which transcend state lines. The division of governmental responsibilities between the nation and the states, although rooted in historical necessities, is continued by habit and convenience. The state is a regional unit of government performing highly important functions in the American system but it is not now and is not likely to become a self-contained, politically conscious community in the sense that Belgium or Holland are. No time-worn cliché of American politics is more misleading about the realities of American life than that which refers to the sovereign states. Under the American federal system, it is true, the states are endowed with vast and uncharted reserved powers and in some areas of public policy—but a declining number—the decisions of state officials may not be reviewed or countermanded by any superior. However, as we have observed in chapter 3, the national authority has, through grants-in-aid and judicial review, established its right to review state policies and procedures in many of the important areas of public affairs. *Are the states sovereign?*

Schools of regional writers remind us that our national "oneness" embraces many smaller cultures within it. The patterns of thought and of politics differ widely among New England, the Plains, the Old South, and Middle West. The economic base and the cluster of organized interests associated with it also vary considerably from region to region. In so far *Regional differences among the states*

3

as the states have any identifiable diversities, they arise from these regional affiliations. Probably the most determined loyalties are those of the Old South: Here is the stronghold of states' rights and of regional autonomy. Regional boundaries are far from precise, however, and many states have no clear regional affinity. Some embrace more than one region and several are microcosms of the nation rather than of a particular region. In general, however, our state governments are best understood in terms of the cultural and economic regions within which they are located.

Many efforts have been and will continue to be made to make each state government the focus of a homogeneous local ideology different in some important way from the national culture. School children are, in some cases, required to study the history of their state; local historical societies try to perpetuate "state" traditions; state advertising campaigns designed to attract tourists or industrial facilities describe the "unique" qualities of a state's environment; national political campaign etiquette requires candidates to celebrate the separate traditions or characters of the various states. Few of these efforts are really achieving anything substantial in the way of creating unique systems of law, government, literature, art, or ideology in each of the 50 states. All of them are overborne by the growing impact of national institutions of culture and communication.

The states as national instrumentalities

The American state is indeed a peculiar institution. If it is an institution which tends to perpetuate and, perhaps, even exaggerate, regional loyalties, it is also an institution of national solidarity. In its name, senators are elected to the national Congress, electors are chosen to attest to the selection of the Chief Executive, delegates and committeemen are chosen to sit in national political conventions and conferences, and amendments to the national Constitution are submitted for ratification to its officials. Many interest groups and economic institutions such as chambers of commerce, labor unions, and trade associations which operate nationally are organized by states and our largest industrial corporations are legal "persons" of one or more states. Under the growing grant-in-aid programs of the national government, states are the major administrative units through which program goals are achieved. State labor and industrial departments, public welfare agencies, public health departments, and highway commissions have close and continuing administrative relations with agencies of the national executive. Furthermore, like the national government itself, the states act as softeners and reconcilers of economic, educational, social, and religious antagonisms. Few states are predominantly one class, one culture, or one system of production, and conflicts of interests occur within states as well as within the central organs of power.

The functions of the states

The American state also acts *in loco parentis* to thousands of units of local government. It provides legal authority, funds, advice, commandments for, as well as resolute restraint upon, cities great and small, counties, boroughs, villages, townships, parishes, and school districts. There is a body of opinion and of practice in the United States that supports the idea that our federal system is a three-level affair rather than a two-level one. The local units—primarily cities and counties—are regarded as largely independent of state authority. In many areas local pride is stronger than state loyalty. State legislative apportionment systems in which counties are considered units for representative purposes reflect this attitude. Home-rule provisions in several state constitutions conferring or attempting to confer autonomy upon cities are also examples of this view. The widespread practice of popular election of the officials of these units contributes mightily to their political independence of state officialdom. Thus, there is, in fact, a large measure of power exercised at the local level which cannot easily be reviewed or countermanded by the state government. However, the predominant legal theory is that local units are creatures of the state and must look to its constitution and laws for authority for their every action. Even where home rule has been conferred by constitutional amendment, courts have construed narrowly the power actually granted to the local governments. A substantial and growing volume of local transactions are strongly influenced, if not dominated, by the state governments through the use of grants-in-aid and shared-tax procedures aimed at state support of local functions. The local policy areas of education, welfare, health, and highways are heavily underwritten by the state treasury. State financing normally and inevitably involves state supervision.

INTERSTATE RELATIONS

The states also conduct various relations with one another. They make agreements, extradite fugitives from justice, and participate together in regional and national conferences. If at first view it should appear that in this aspect of their practice the states resemble sovereign nations, we must remember that these relations are controlled by the Constitution of the United States and to a large degree are regulated by congressional enactment.

The Constitution authorizes interstate agreements or compacts pro- *Interstate compacts* vided Congress gives its consent. This device for regulating matters of interest to neighboring states, to states in a single region, or to many states with a common interest has proved increasingly popular. The ever-mounting demand for national action on various problems has been allayed somewhat by the growing use of the interstate agreement. In earlier days the agreement procedure was largely confined to the settlement of boundary disputes, but in this century a growing number of uses have been discovered. More than 120 are now in existence and the device is serving a steadily widening range of interests. Compacts are now used for (1) the development, exploitation, and conservation of interstate water resources; (2) the stabilization and conservation of other natural resources such as petroleum, wildlife, or fish; (3) the control of floods; (4) the development of interstate toll highways; (5) the coordination of higher educational facilities;

(6) mutual protection against forest fires; (7) the coordination of civil defense measures; (8) the reciprocal supervision of probationers and parolees; (9) the coordination of welfare and institutional programs; (10) the administration of particular functions in interstate metropolitan areas; (11) the eradication of air pollution; and, (12) the resolution of interstate tax conflicts, notably in the area of motor licenses receipts and gasoline taxes.

Congressional power over compacts

As the compact has become increasingly popular, if not as yet very effective in many controversial areas of public policy, the nature and extent of congressional interest and authority over it has become a matter of growing concern. The Constitution appears to require that all compacts be approved by Congress. In practice, however, compacts have been entered into without express approval and the courts have held that congressional consent is required only of agreements "tending to increase the political power of the states, which may encroach upon . . . the just supremacy of the United States." Consent need not, furthermore, be given expressly for each agreement. On several occasions, notably in the fields of conservation and highway safety, the Congress has given blanket approval in advance. In recent years, however, the Congress seems to be growing more apprehensive about the effect on its power of the spread of the compact arrangement. On several occasions in the past few years in actions approving particular agreement it has imposed restrictions on the use of supplementary agreements not expressly approved by Congress. It has also sought to limit the powers of interstate commissions created by compacts to those within the purpose of the original agreement. These practices had heretofore been fairly common and unchallenged. In 1960, the Judiciary Committee of the House of Representatives undertook an investigation of the Port of New York Authority (created by compact between New York and New Jersey in 1921) and demanded the production of certain Authority records. The director, acting under instructions from his commission and from the governors of the two states involved, refused to comply with the Committee order in part because the Authority did not come under the lawful powers of Congress. The House promptly voted to cite him for contempt. Although the constitutional question was skillfully avoided by the Court of Appeals in dismissing the contempt action, the Court did say that congressional power over compacts was not plenary.

The participation of the national government as a partner in the compact for the development of the Delaware River Basin (1961) may also establish a new pattern of national participation in areas covered by compacts.

Interstate rendition of fugitives

"A person charged in any state with treason, felony, or other crime," says the Constitution, "who shall flee from justice, and be found in another state, shall, on demand of the executive authority of the state from which he fled, be delivered up, to be removed to the state having jurisdiction of the crime." The object is, of course, to prevent criminals from "beating the law" by taking refuge in areas over which the states they fled from have no jurisdiction and so can execute no processes. An act of Congress specifies that after the accused has been properly indicted, the demand for his return shall be addressed to the executive of the state into which he has fled and by which he has been captured. The governor, if he chooses to honor the request, then returns the fugitive to the police officers of the state making the request. Governors, however, in practice, have not always elected to honor such requests. The reasons advanced for the occasional refusals are that the individual has become a law-abiding citizen of his new state in the meanwhile, or that (in case of Negroes demanded by southern states) he may not expect a fair trial in the state making the request, or that there is not sufficient evidence against him. Despite the mandatory language of the Constitution and the laws of Congress, there is no legal way to compel a reluctant governor to act.

Acting with congressional authorization, more than 40 states have, since 1936, entered into an interstate compact for the mutual rendition of witnesses needed in criminal proceedings and have thus effectively enlarged the scope of their obligations. The Supreme Court has held this arrangement to be valid, asserting that the "Constitution did not purport to exhaust imagination and resourcefulness in devising fruitful interstate relationship."

OBLIGATIONS OF THE STATES TO ONE ANOTHER

The Constitution of the United States imposes certain further obligations on the states in their dealings with one another. "Full faith and credit," says the Constitution, "shall be given in each state to the public acts, records, and judicial proceedings of every other state." This means that transactions of government and commerce which are authenticated by valid legal instruments must be recognized and accepted everywhere in the land, regardless of the state in which they originated. Of course, these legal instruments must be duly authenticated according to forms prescribed by Congress. Thus, the courts in Illinois, for example, must recognize and carry out a decision made by a court in Michigan if invited to do so under proper circumstances. Contracts entered into in New York may be enforced in Florida. Corporations chartered to do business in Delaware, and many of them are, must in general be admitted to do business in North Dakota. It is not possible to evade legal obligation by the simple expedient of moving out of one state into another. Although the effort to make state laws on commercial transactions more uniform throughout the nation has been gaining headway, there is still a large variation from state to state in these matters, and the effect of the constitutional obligation is to require a state to recognize actions properly taken in other states regardless of the fact that such actions may be out of line with the practice in that state.

1. Recognition of legal processes

One aspect of this obligation has, in recent years, proved troublesome: What recognition must be granted by strict states to divorce decrees granted in states like Nevada? Two cases in recent years have arisen over the obli-

Divorce decrees

gation, or lack of it, of North Carolina to recognize Nevada divorce decrees for a couple who took up temporary residence in Reno to obtain the decrees, then married and returned to their home state of North Carolina. The Supreme Court at first held that North Carolina must necessarily recognize the decree, then later said that the parties had not established a bona fide domicile in Nevada and the Nevada court had, therefore, no jurisdiction over them. The latter decision opened the door for states to challenge the validity of divorces granted by other states where the decree had been preceded by only temporary residence on the part of one or both parties. Although in subsequent cases, the Court has appeared somewhat more disposed to enforce Nevada decrees, new decisions involving alimony payments and the custody of children have added to a complex and confused situation. Some groups are proposing a constitutional amendment to resolve the matter.

2. Interstate citizenship

The framers of the Constitution rightly thought that no state should be allowed to discriminate, in favor of its own citizens, against persons coming within its jurisdiction from other states. To do so would jeopardize basic rights common to all of the people and seriously interfere with national unity. Hence it is provided (in a clause carried over almost literally from the Articles of Confederation) that "the citizens of each state shall be entitled to all privileges and immunities of citizens of the several states." In general, this means that citizens of any state may move freely about the country and settle where they like, with the assurance that as newcomers they will not be subjected to discriminative taxation, that they will be permitted to carry on lawful occupations under the same conditions as older residents, and that they will not be prevented from acquiring and using property, or denied the equal protection of the laws, or refused access to the courts. It does not mean that privileges of a political nature, for example, those of voting and holding office, must be extended forthwith. Nor is a state prevented from imposing quarantine or other police regulations which will have the effect of denying free admission or the right to move property in or out. But such restrictions must be justified by provable public necessity. Furthermore, they must be so framed as to fall alike upon the citizens of the given state and those of all other states. It is hardly necessary to add that a citizen of New York, migrating to Pennsylvania, does not carry with him the rights which he enjoyed in New York. The point is rather that he becomes entitled to such rights as the citizens of Pennsylvania enjoy.

3. Peaceful settlement

The history of the Confederation was filled with controversies between states regarding boundaries, commercial regulations, and other matters; and the makers of the Constitution were not so naive as to suppose that under the new frame of government the members of the Union would always live in perfect accord. Among sovereign nations, disputes have traditionally been settled by (1) direct agreements reached through negotiation, (2) arbitration undertaken by some neutral ruler or similar authority, (3) adjudication in an international court, or (4) in the last resort, war. The states of the Union are not supposed to make war on one another, although they did so from 1861–1865. They may, and do, reach agreements through direct negotiation. But the method of settlement chiefly contemplated by the Constitution's authors was that of judicial determination. In pursuance of this intent, the judicial power of the United States is extended to all "controversies between two or more states," with the further provision that in all cases in which a state is a party (regardless of the identity of the opposing party) the Supreme Court shall have original jurisdiction. The road to amicable adjustment of interstate differences by regular judicial process is thus always open, and many troublesome disputes over boundaries, water diversions, fishing rights, and other matters have been cleared up by resorting to it. A good illustration of this is the 1963 decision of the Court in the 40-year-old dispute between Arizona and California over the distribution of water from the lower Colorado River Basin under the terms of the Boulder Canyon Project Act of 1928. Years of effort to resolve the matter through interstate compact had failed. The Court decision upheld the distribution under the Act of 1928 but opened the door for subsequent modification by Congress.

FRAMEWORK OF STATE GOVERNMENT: THE STATE CONSTITUTION

To a student of political institutions, the most striking thing about the American states is not their regional peculiarities but their great and abiding uniformities. The government of every one of the 50 states is based upon a written constitution and these are strikingly similar. The first written instruments of government in this country were established at the time of independence by the original 13 states. The national Constitution leans heavily on those of New York and Massachusetts. The constitutions later enacted by the other 37 states closely parallel the national document and those of the original states. The frame of government provided by these fundamental laws in every case follows the American pattern of limited, representative government organized around three separate and mutually restraining organs of power. Every state constitution contains a bill of rights guaranteeing to the inhabitants the basic American freedoms in much the same language and to much the same purpose as those added to the national Constitution and discussed in an earlier chapter. Major differences center on the character of the guarantees of separation of church and state and the protection, or lack of it, afforded to Negroes, Mexicans, and other minority groups. Every state has a single chief executive, the governor, elected by popular vote, and a representative legislature also directly elected and, in every state but Nebraska composed of two equal bodies. An elaborate system of courts is also characteristic of the states. Many of the judges of these

Similarities among the states

General Status of State Constitutions
1967

STATE	NO. OF CONST.	EFFECTIVE DATE OF PRESENT CONST.	NO. OF AMENDMENTS PROPOSED	APPROVED
Alabama	6	1901	408	266
Alaska	1	1959	43	1
Arizona	1	1912	116	56
Arkansas	5	1874	(Not Available)	52
California	2	1879	600	350
Colorado	1	1876	(Not Available)	70
Connecticut	2	1965	(Not Available)	(Not Available)
Delaware	4	1897	(Not Available)	80
Florida	5	1887	205	142
Georgia	8	1945	730	549
Hawaii	1	1959	11	9
Idaho	1	1890	105	70
Illinois	3	1870	33	13
Indiana	2	1851	612	22
Iowa	2	1857	(Not Available)	24
Kansas	1	1861	81	54
Kentucky	4	1891	42	18
Louisiana	10	1921	607	460
Maine	1	1820	111	101
Maryland	4	1867	169	133
Massachusetts	1	1780	102	85
Michigan	4	1964	0	0
Minnesota	1	1858	180	90
Mississippi	4	1890	104	35
Missouri	4	1945	33	19
Montana	1	1889	50	35
Nebraska	2	1875	165	106
Nevada	1	1864	98	57
New Hampshire	2	1784	121	52
New Jersey	3	1947	14	11
New Mexico	1	1912	149	66
New York	6	1894	182	139
North Carolina	2	1868	(Not Available)	(Not Available)
North Dakota	1	1889	(Not Available)	84
Ohio	2	1851	169	92
Oklahoma	1	1907	161	67
Oregon	1	1859	249	124
Pennsylvania	4	1873	103	73
Rhode Island	1	1843	70	36
South Carolina	6	1895	364	251
South Dakota	1	1889	142	73
Tennessee	3	1870	34	19
Texas	5	1876	281	178
Utah	1	1896	76	50
Vermont	3	1793	200	44
Virginia	5	1902	154	95
Washington	1	1889	87	48
West Virginia	2	1872	64	37
Wisconsin	1	1848	131	87
Wyoming	1	1890	54	30

SOURCE: Council of State Governments, *Book of the States*, *1968–1969* (Chicago, 1968), 15.

tribunals are, however, elected. Each of these main branches of government is endowed with some power to check or restrain the other two, much as they are in the national government. Unlike the national Constitution, which makes no important provisions for the organs of state government, the state constitutions universally provide in some detail for a system of local government and an assignment of powers to the various types. The states also impose numerous and detailed restraints upon the lawmaking powers of their legislatures resulting from a long history of abuses and not duplicated in the national Constitution by any comparable restraints upon the powers of Congress. Furthermore, the politics of the states typically involve contests within and between the two major political parties. Every state also has numerous organized interest groups, which seek to influence the conduct of public affairs at the state and local levels. In every state but Louisiana the whole system of civil and criminal law is based on the English Common Law brought here by our forefathers.

There has probably been no more extensive exercise in making constitutions in the history of self-government than that represented by the 50 American states. Considering this experience one can only be deeply impressed with the skill of the framers of the Constitution of the United States. Together, the states have installed more than 130 constitutions and have amended the 50 now in effect more than 3,000 times. Almost every state has scrapped one or two constitutions since 1789, frequently after amending them many times. Only two states are now operating under constitutions of the late eighteenth century and these have been extensively altered. *State constitutions versus national Constitution*

The typical state constitution is divided into articles and like the national Constitution contains (1) a bill of rights; (2) a section on the organization, powers, and duties of the legislature; (3) a section on the mode of selection and the powers of the governor and other executive officers; (4) a section on the court system and (5) a section on the amending process. Unlike the national document, in addition to these features, many state constitutions provide sections dealing with (1) the structure and powers of local units of government; (2) the organization and financing of the state system of public education; (3) the qualifications for voting and the conduct of elections; (4) the procedures governing and the regulations imposed upon the chartering of corporations; (5) the organization and operation of programs of public health and welfare; and (6) the levying of taxes and the conduct of the state's fiscal affairs. Partly in consequence of this last list of provisions, most state constitutions are considerably longer than the national Constitution. Partly, however, this is due to the greater penchant of state politicians and voters to load up the fundamental law with details of state policy, such as highway location or the rate of a particular tax. Frustrated by state executive or legislative inaction, interested citizens in several states are able to rush into the constitution by popular initiative details of policy and administration which later prove to be wholly *Contents of a typical constitution* inappropriate, and new amendments have to be drafted to get rid of them. Legislatures, too, are prone to solidify into constitutional prescription public policies which they hope to place thereafter beyond legislative tinkering. State politicians have been generally unable or unwilling to follow the path of the national framers and avoid minutious wisdom. The constitution of Florida, for example, not only provides for a two cent per gallon gasoline tax but specifies in detail the formula by which the proceeds are to be distributed. Texas levies a property tax for the benefit of certain public colleges and specifies to the fifth decimal place how much each is to receive. Louisiana, in a constitution of 200,000 words declares Huey Long's birthday a legal holiday forever and names two bridges after him!

The national Constitution is a grant of power to a new central government; the state constitutions, by contrast, are largely restraints upon power. Rarely is the allegedly broad authority of the state spelled out. Since we live in an age of mounting governmental activities, constitutional prescriptions of restraints are likely to prove more fragile than the reverse.

MAKING AND REVISING THE STATE CONSTITUTION

No serious effort has been made since 1787 to rewrite completely the national Constitution although it prescribes a procedure by which this might be done. No comparable myth of sanctity surrounds our state constitutions and in most states they have been rewritten two or three times. All but ten of the present state constitutions prescribe the assembling of a special convention for this purpose and in seven of the ten, by judicial or legislative determination, the power to do so has been established. It is generally supposed that regardless of constitutional prescription the power to rewrite it by convention is inherent in the people.

Calling a convention   The first formal step toward holding a convention is, generally, a decision by the legislature to submit to the voters the question of whether they want one. In a few states this question may be placed on the ballot by popular initiative petition. Several state constitutions require the periodic submission of this question to the voters: in Alaska, Hawaii, New Hampshire, and Iowa every ten years; in Michigan every 16 years; and in Maryland, Missouri, New York, Ohio, and Oklahoma every 20 years. In most of these states, but not all, the question may also be submitted at other times. After popular approval has been gained—in several states this is made difficult by requiring extraordinary popular majorities—the legislature by statute fixes the time, place, and delegate apportionment of the convention. The convention is thus likely to be a mirror of the legislature and, at least up to this decade, to reflect the lack of equality as between the urban and the rural and small-town populations. Once assembled, the convention normally functions very much like a legislature with officers, committees, hearings, and debate.

There is a growing disposition to provide technical assistance to conventions through advance preparation of materials on the major questions confronting them. This work is usually done by specialists in these fields. The convention for Illinois in 1920–1922 was aided by 15 bulletins prepared for its consideration; 12 volumes were prepared for the New York convention of 1938 and several more for that of 1967; 30 monographs were prepared for the New Jersey convention of 1947; and several studies were made for the Alaska convention in 1955–1956. In many cases the advance staff work is done under the direction of an advisory or preparatory commission appointed by the governor or by the legislature for this purpose. *Technical assistance*

There is also a developing trend to use preparatory commissions to inquire into whether and to what extent constitutions need revising and even to prepare drafts of proposed new sections for consideration by a convention or by the legislature and electorate if it is decided to attempt amendment rather than revision. Such commissions have been recently established in Florida (1955, 1958, and 1965), Kentucky (1957 and 1964), North Carolina (1957), Pennsylvania (1957), Texas (1957), West Virginia (1957), Wisconsin (1960 and 1965), Kansas (1957 and 1961), Maine (1961), Oregon (1961), Massachusetts (1962), Georgia (1963), California (1963), Idaho and Maryland (1965), Washington (1966), and Louisiana, Arkansas and Texas (1967). Those commissions which have proposed amendments have had some success. Those proposing a convention or wholesale revision by amendments have not as yet made much headway. These commissions are easier to establish, less expensive to assemble, and better prepared to analyze and consider various proposals than most conventions are likely to be. The trend toward their use as a substitute for conventions will probably continue. *Use of preparatory commissions*

Constitutional conventions have the primary function of drafting new fundamental laws or formulating amendments to existing ones. Some conventions, like that in Illinois in 1862, have gone farther and assumed actual management of state government, displacing existing officers, substituting others chosen by the convention, and attempting to supersede the legislature in various respects. Occasionally the legislature, in making provision for the meeting of a convention, has attempted to impose limitations upon its work which the convention has wholly or in part disregarded. Several times, conflicts have resulted as to the proper powers of a convention; and out of them three theories have developed. According to the first, the legislature is supreme, and in the act of calling the convention may limit the powers of that body by excluding from its consideration amendments to certain sections of the constitution, by requiring it to propose amendments to certain sections of the constitution, by prescribing the manner in which its work shall be submitted to popular vote, and by various other methods. Those who take this view hold that the convention has no right to disregard or to deviate from any of these statutory restrictions. According to a second theory, the convention has all the sovereign powers of the people, and accordingly, is during its period of existence the supreme body in the state. It is superior to the legislature and to all other branches of the state govern- *Power of conventions* ment, and may disregard any or all limitations which the legislature seeks to impose upon its activity, and may, indeed, legally exercise whatever governmental functions it cares to assume—as the Illinois convention of 1862 tried to do.

Prevalent view of convention powers

Each of these two theories has some support in convention precedents and judicial opinion. But the view now most generally held is that a convention is neither sovereign nor wholly subject to the legislature; that, on the contrary, the two are coordinate bodies, each supreme within its proper sphere and bound by the provisions of the existing constitution and statutes. If the constitution authorizes the legislature to impose restrictions on the convention, the latter is bound to respect such limitations; on the other hand, if such authorization is lacking, the legislature cannot bind the convention as to what shall be placed in the revised constitution, or lay other restrictions upon it. The convention, furthermore, may neither supersede any existing organs or agents of state government nor exercise any of the powers assigned to them. Its functions are limited to proposing a new constitution or amendments to the existing one. In practice, however, several conventions, notably that of New Jersey in 1947, have accepted limitations imposed by the legislature on the apportionment system of the legislative seats.

Ratification of a convention's work

Although a minority of state constitutions require it, the almost universal practice among the states is to submit the results of the convention's deliberations to the voters for approval. The vote required for approval is typically a majority of those voting on the question but several states require approval by a majority of those voting in the election.

Method of submittal

A convention may submit its work in one of three different forms. It may, for example, present it as a series of specific amendments to be voted on separately, as was done in New York in 1938, in Tennessee in 1953, in Connecticut in 1965, and in Pennsylvania and Hawaii in 1968. This is practicable only when a comparatively small number of amendments are proposed. Or it may submit a complete new or revised constitution, to be accepted or rejected as a whole, as in Illinois in 1922, in Georgia and Missouri in 1945, in New Jersey in 1947, in Michigan in 1964, in New York in 1967, and Rhode Island and Maryland in 1968. This method has the disadvantage of compelling articles or clauses not widely opposed to suffer the same fate as others stirring controversy. Opposition to some change in the system of taxation, for example, may be so strong that, rather than see a proposal of the kind adopted, its opponents will vote against the entire document, although everything else may be satisfactory. The sum total of such fractional opposition may mean the entire constitution's defeat. In this cumulative fashion, the proposed new constitution for New York was wrecked in 1915; that for Illinois in 1922; that for Florida in 1958; and those for New York, Rhode Island, and Maryland in 1967 and 1968.

The third method is a compromise between the two mentioned. A substantially complete revision may be submitted for ratification or rejection as a whole, with at the same time one or more especially controversial articles or sections submitted separately, thus enabling the electorate, if so inclined, to approve the convention's work in general while yet disapproving specific features.

CONSTITUTIONAL AMENDMENT

The constitutional convention is a drastic method of updating constitutions. It is, however, responsible for relatively few alterations. By far the most common method of state constitutional revision is simple amendment. Every state constitution provides a procedure by which particular provisions may be changed. In every state amendments may be proposed by the state legislature. In 37, affirmative action may be taken at one legislative sitting. However, a majority of these states require an unusual majority vote to do so—a two-thirds vote in 19 states and a three-fifths vote in 8 states. In the remaining states (13), affirmative action by two distinct sessions of the legislature is required. In Delaware the action of two legislatures completes the process but in all the other states, an amendment proposed by the legislature must be placed before the voters for ratification. Typically, legislatures may propose any number of amendments at any time but a few states, where the framers were so taken with their product that they wanted it modified only slightly if at all, limit the legislature to two or three amendments at a time—Arkansas, Kansas, Kentucky, and Montana, for example. Vermont's constitution may not be amended at all except at ten-year intervals. Occasionally, legislatures have proposed wholesale revision rather than isolated amendment. The New Jersey legislature did this in 1944 on the authority of a referendum but its handiwork was rejected by the voters. An attempt in 1911 by the Indiana legislature to do this was invalidated by the courts.

Amendment by legislative proposal

An alternative method of laying amendments before the voters is now authorized in 13 states. This is *popular initiative,* which originated in Oregon in 1902 and rapidly gained favor over the next two decades. It has attracted little favorable notice since 1920. By this procedure a proposal may be drafted by any person or group and then if a sufficient number of voters' signatures can be obtained on a petition demanding it, the proposal must be placed before the voters for ratification at an early election. Support for the popular initiative stemmed from distrust of or disgust with the behavior of state legislatures in blocking reforms. Experience with it suggests that the only effective alternative over the long run to a corrupt or incompetent legislature is to elect a better legislature. Little is really gained, except increased voter weariness, by running to the electorate with new duties every time a legislature misbehaves.

Proposing amendments by popular initiative

In the vast majority of states, the popular vote required to ratify a

Popular vote on amendments

proposed amendment is a majority of those voting on the question. Several of the state constitutions, however, make adoption more difficult to obtain by requiring a majority of those voting in the election. Experience indicates that rarely do more than 60 percent of those who participate in an election pay any attention to referred proposals which may appear on the ballot. Thus, a large portion of those who do not vote on the question at all are, in effect, counted as if they voted No. Other requirements of unusual majorities are imposed in a few states.

Elaboration of the constitution

The frequent use of the amending and revising processes in order to keep state governments abreast of the times does not mean that state constitutions are not elaborated, embellished, and greatly modified by legislation, executive order, judicial construction, and unwritten custom. Just as in Washington, every act of officials in state capitals subtly interprets, enlarges, supplements, or changes the basic framework of government provided by the constitutions. Furthermore, many institutions of American political life have grown up and flourished outside the constitutional prescriptions. The whole system of political parties, the activities of organized interest groups, the character of voter participation, and many other practices and institutions are rarely mentioned in state constitutions.

State constitutions too detailed

Constitutions which are frequently amended or revised lose much of their value and a great deal of their prestige. The precepts underlying our system of government are few and can be set forth in a few carefully written paragraphs. The statesmen of one generation are rarely successful in compelling their successors to achieve these ends only by certain well-defined paths. State political leaders and jurists have shown rare ingenuity in circumventing constitutional provisions which they could not or would not alter. The world will not stand still despite the perfection it may be thought to have reached in one moment of time. If, as some fear, the central government may come ultimately to dominate our polity to the extent that the states are no longer significant, our failure to apply in the states the constitutional wisdom of the nation may bear part of the blame. A national commission appointed in 1953 to examine our modern federal system and, if possible, to halt the trend toward centralization reported: ". . . most states would benefit from a fundamental review and revision of their constitutions to make sure that they provide for vigorous and responsible government, not forbid it." This advice was again strongly urged upon the American people in 1967 by the Chamber of Commerce, the Committee for Economic Development, and other organizations interested in halting the flow of functions to Washington.

REFERENCES

The following textbooks are devoted to state and local government and cover in greater detail the material in this and subsequent chapters.

W. Anderson, C. Penniman, E. W. Weidner, *Government in the Fifty States* (New York, 1960).

F. G. Bates, O. P. Field, *et al., State Government* (4th ed., New York, 1954).

Council of State Governments, *Book of the States* (Chicago) Sec. 1, published biennially and containing tables on state constitutional matters and summaries of developments.

R. B. Dishman, *State Constitutions: The Shape of the Document* (New York, 1960).

D. R. Grant and H. C. Nixon, *State and Local Government in America* (Boston, 1963).

W. B. Graves, *American Intergovernmental Relations* (New York, 1964).

————, *American State Government* (4th ed., Boston, 1953).

H. Kaufman, *Politics and Policies in State and Local Government* (Englewood Cliffs, N. J., 1963).

D. Lockard, *The Politics of State and Local Government* (New York, 1963).

A. F. Macdonald, *American State Government and Administration* (5th ed., New York, 1955).

G. T. Mitau, *State and Local Government: Politics and Processes* (New York, 1966).

National Municipal League, *A Model State Constitution* (New York, 1963).

T. Sanford, *Storm over the State* (New York, 1968).

C. F. Snider, *American State and Local Government* (2nd ed., New York, 1965).

2

THE STATE LEGISLATURE

Impor-
tance

The major center of democratic policy-making at the state level in the United States is the state legislature. It occupies a position in both structure and ideology closely akin to that of Congress at the national level. Many of the conflicts of the body politic are here resolved and the entire machinery of state government provided with purpose and method. Unlike the Congress vis-à-vis the states, the state legislature exercises wide control over the structures and policies of local governments. State political interest groups concentrate their energies on efforts to influence the legislative process. For all of the activities within the scope of their concern, the legislatures of the states are the main centers of decision.

The
decline of
the state
legislature

In the beginning of our national history the state legislatures were the major centers of political power in the nation and they remained so until well into the nineteenth century. Their importance and prestige, however, suffered several sharp declines and today they are nowhere near as important as they once were. The first major setback to the power of the state legislature was, of course, the Constitution of 1787. It was designed to curb the power of state legislatures and was drafted by men who were deeply disturbed by the policies and personnel of the state assemblies. During the Jeffersonian era, however, the national power was in the hands of men friendly to state power and some of the ground was recaptured. The more serious decline in state legislative power and influence was a product of the American Industrial Revolution. The development of a national economy linking farm and factory by means of the railroads created problems with which the state legislators were unable to cope. Caught up in the ruthless push of greedy land speculators, railroad promoters, currency manipulators, and corporate minions, the lawmakers succumbed to temptation or fought vainly against wealth and power which were too big to be contained. Scandal after scandal rocked one state capital after another as legislatures buckled beneath the irresistible forces of industrialization. Public confidence in the honesty and wisdom of the legislators sagged sharply. The solution (typically American) to this state of affairs was to prevent evil-doing by restraining the powers of the doer. If a public body is restrained from doing evil, it is usually at the same time restrained from doing good, so to the humiliation of lack of confidence was added the frustration of lack of valid power. Into state constitutions from 1865 onward for two or three generations were written a growing list of inhibitions and restrictions on state legislative power under which most legislatures labor even today. Meanwhile, the growth of a genuinely national economy effectively placed beyond the competence of states a large number of problems which have required national attention in this century. It is ironic to observe that many of those who have complained so bitterly over the "unwarranted" rise of the power and prestige of the national government have also helped to forge the fetters which constrain the states.

There are some signs—increased pay and more frequent sessions, for example—that public confidence in our state lawmakers is slowly rising. Most of the state assemblies, however, bear the scars of the blows rained upon them in the last half of the nineteenth century.

Functions of State Legislatures

Like the national Congress, the state legislatures perform a wide variety of functions. Many of these are not, strictly speaking, legislative. In the first place, the legislature of every state is the major, if not the sole, originator of constitutional amendments as described in the previous chapter. The upper houses of our state legislatures also universally share the appointing power of the governor. The scope of the executive power is, typically, more limited at the state than at the national level because of the widespread practice of electing several of the major state administrative officials. In a few states and for a few officers, state senators are relatively more powerful than their counterparts in Washington because of their participation in the governor's removal power. In a few states, also, the legislature has an independent appointing power: Judges, for example, are named by the legislatures in Connecticut, South Carolina, Vermont, and Virginia. State legislatures, like the Congress, also have an important hand in supervising state administration. They create administrative machinery, prescribe the procedures to be followed, and review the conduct of the executive branch in connection with appropriation enactments. They may and do conduct investigations of administrative behavior much as the Congress does. In a few states, legislative control over administration is limited by unnecessarily detailed constitutional prescriptions of administrative structure and procedures.

The lower house of virtually every state is endowed with impeachment authority over state officials and the upper house, with the power to try impeached officers. Several states authorize their legislatures to oust judges

Functions:
1. Constituent

2. Executive

3. Judicial

by a procedure which does not involve a trial but may require a special vote of the two houses.

4. Representative

The state legislator spends a good part of his time, just like the congressman, in representing his constituents before administrative agencies and intervening, if he can, in their behalf.

5. Legislative

The typical activity of the state legislature, however, is lawmaking and to it lawmakers devote most of their time and energy. Apart from the vast differences of power as between the state and the nation, the most significant legislative difference arises from the time and attention which state lawmakers must give to the problems, structures, powers, and procedures of the thousands of local and special units of government which they must regulate. Congress, although exercising a profound influence upon states through the grant-in-aid procedure, does not enact the comprehensive and detailed prescriptions for the states that the states do for their local subdivisions.

STATE LEGISLATIVE POWER

Powers are restricted and unenumerated

Speaking broadly, a state legislature has the power to enact laws relating to any aspect of our society unless it is forbidden by the Constitution of the United States expressly or by implication, or by the constitution of the state. Under the American federal system, the states are entrusted with all the residue of powers not specifically delegated to the nation and, therefore, a precise delineation of the scope of state legislative power is impossible. A casual perusal of the statute books of an American state reveals that legislatures deal with a vast array of topics of wide social concern. The most important of these are elections, natural resources, education, veterans' benefits, crime and correctional administration, health, welfare, local government powers and structures, highways, bridges, and airports, agriculture, weights and measures, trade practices, industrial safety, labor–management relations, aeronautics, banking, interest, sales, partnerships, corporations, real estate, domestic relations, judicial organization and procedure, inheritance, trusts, and professions. In almost every matter, however, state legislative authority is confined and restricted in various ways.

Limitations on state power arising from the federal system

One significant source of limitation on the power of the states is, of course, the federal system. The delegation of power to the national government has placed many subjects beyond the power of state officials and the Congress and courts have broadened and deepened these restraints.

1. Foreign and interstate relations

The national government is plainly intended to conduct all official relations with foreign nations and states are consequently forbidden to enter into any "treaty, alliance, or confederation." A state may enter into a "compact or agreement" with a foreign state with the consent of Congress, but only if the agreement does not create a political relationship such as an alliance. Except for an agreement between New York and Canada concerning an international bridge, no such agreements have been concluded.

In general, defense, like foreign relations, is a national rather than a state function. Without the consent of Congress no state may keep troops or ships of war, or "engage in war unless actually invaded or in such imminent danger as will not admit of delay." The restriction, however, does not preclude the states from maintaining organized militia for use primarily in repressing domestic disorder. Such militia have, however, long since been assimilated to the armed establishment of the nation. The governors are still fairly free to direct their use inside the state boundaries.

2. National defense

The most important limitation imposed on the power of the states by the Constitution, excluding only the Fourteenth Amendment, is the grant of power to Congress to regulate commerce among the states. In the first place, the national courts have defined "commerce" to include virtually every type of movement of persons or things and every type of communication or negotiation whether for business purposes or not. They have defined "interstate" to embrace any such movement across state lines at any stage of a transaction. They have defined the total regulatory power of Congress to embrace any operation or transaction which might affect the "commerce" they have so broadly defined. There are, in consequence, relatively few business transactions in modern America which do not come within the purview of congressional power. Furthermore, all of the navigable or potentially navigable rivers of the country come under national authority by a series of interpretations.

3. Commerce

The power of the states to levy and collect taxes for revenue or regulatory purposes is limited expressly by the Constitution and also by judicial inference from its provisions. In order to assure uniform national impositions on interstate and foreign trade, the Constitution forbids any state, without the consent of Congress, to levy any duty on imports or exports, except for the purpose of financing inspection at terminals or harbors. Such duties, if laid by a state, are subject to validation, revision, or control by the Congress and net proceeds must be turned over to the national Treasury. State duties of this type, while collected for a time in the early days of the nation, are now virtually unused. States are also forbidden without congressional approval to levy "tonnage duties," that is, taxes on the cargo or carrying capacity of ships.

4. Taxation

a. Export and Import duties

b. Tonnage

State taxing power is also bound by the general limitations on states such as those forbidding them to impair the obligation of contracts or to deprive any person of property without due process of law, or to deny to anyone the equal protection of the laws.

c. General limitations

One of the most significant limitations on state taxing power stems from a decision of the Supreme Court in 1819 written by Chief Justice Marshall in which he asserted that a state could not levy a tax on a national instrumentality. The power to tax, he said, involves the power to destroy, and the federal system prescribed by the Constitution did not intend the

d. Exemption of instrumentalities"

states to be able to hamper the national government by burdening its agents or functions. Under this general doctrine, the property of the national government has been immune from any type of state or local taxation. In some instances this is true even though the property may be leased to private interests for profitable purposes, but the Court has recently been narrowing the exemption of goods in private possession. This policy has worked some hardship in areas where national holdings are vast, such as the Tennessee Valley. Congress has, therefore, on occasion authorized cash contributions by national agencies to local units of government in lieu of tax revenues lost to the unit by national ownership. The doctrine of national tax immunity also shelters fiscal institutions chartered by Congress and their shares, unless Congress authorizes state or local taxation. Congress has so authorized the taxation of national bank stock and bank property but only under conditions which it imposes. For a time, the Marshall doctrine was construed as protecting the salaries of national employees from state income taxation, but the Congress in 1939 authorized such taxation and the Supreme Court reversed its earlier position and concurred. The income from national securities, even when issued to finance farm or business loans, is still exempt from state taxation despite several recent efforts to procure congressional authorization for such taxation.

State immunity from national taxation

The states, it should be added, long enjoyed a similar, but not identical, immunity for their instrumentalities from national taxation. Congress and the courts have, however, been steadily narrowing the allowable exemptions from national taxes. And the national government may now tax salaries of state and local employees, state or local property when used for business purposes, and many other state activities. The Court still insists that some immunity remains to the states, but it is not nearly so broad as that remaining to the national government.

5. Currency

One of the advantages the framers hoped to derive from the Union was a common currency system. Hence the Constitution gives the national government full control over the country's currency and forbids the states to coin money, to emit bills of credit (any evidences of indebtedness intended to circulate as money), or to "make anything but gold and silver coin a tender in payment of debts." Under their reserved powers, the states can charter banks; and banking institutions so created exist beside and compete with national banks in all of the states. Furthermore, the states can authorize these banks and banking associations to issue notes for circulation as currency, although not as legal tender. In 1865, however, this latter power was stripped of all practical significance by an act of Congress laying taxes up to ten percent on such notes and thereby making it unprofitable to issue them. The Supreme Court upheld the measure, and as a result state bank currency has passed entirely out of existence.

6. Contracts

Frightened by Shays' Rebellion and by the continuing threat to creditor interests of the agrarian-debtor–dominated state legislatures, the framers were determined to place the sanctity of contracts beyond the power of states to diminish. The Constitution, in consequence, forbids any state to pass any law impairing the obligation of contracts. This clause has been almost from its inception one of the most fruitful in litigation and in pleas for the Supreme Court to overturn state legislation. Early in our history, in two celebrated cases (Fletcher *v.* Peck, 1810, and Dartmouth College *v.* Woodward, 1819), the Court held that the contracts protected by the Constitution included public grants of land or privilege, including charters or franchises granted to corporations. The effect of this broad interpretation has been mitigated subsequently by judicial exclusion of charters to public corporations such as municipalities, by state legislation reserving the right to alter or amend charters granted by the state, and by judicial acceptance of the idea that the needs of public health, safety, and welfare may override the sanctity of some types of contractual relations. Since 1900 there has been a growing area of judicially accepted state power over contracts and a consequent diminution in the protection to vested interests prescribed by this constitutional prohibition. Even creditor–debtor relationships have been invaded by state legislation during the depression of the nineteen thirties— with the approval of the Court. The clause, nevertheless, continues to provide a basis for judicial review of the justification for the exercise of state power. It also stands as a strong bulwark protecting many rights of creditors.

The Fourteenth Amendment forbids any state to make or enforce any law abridging the privileges and immunities of citizens of the United States. Designed to protect the freed Negroes against discriminatory treatment by southern state governments, this clause was early construed to add little or nothing to the existent system of protection of personal rights. The Supreme Court has stated that the privileges here protected are only those expressly conferred by the Constitution and laws, and are manifestly attributes of national rather than state citizenship. This particular provision of the Constitution has not, thus, imposed·any serious limitation on state power. *7. Privileges of citizens of the United States*

A second source of limitation on state power is the American dedication to constitutionally recognized civil rights. In considering the American system of rights in chapter 4, we noted that the due-process and equal-protection clauses of the Fourteenth Amendment provide the legal foundation for a national system of rights, uniformly applied and judicially enforced upon the states and their officers and agencies. The Constitution of the United States also expressly prohibits states from passing ex post facto laws or bills of attainder, from impairing the obligations of contract, and from depriving citizens of the vote on account of race, color, sex, or failure to pay a tax. Every state constitution also guarantees certain rights to its citizens and restrains legislatures, executives, and courts from impairing or infringing these guarantees. Every person in this country is, therefore, protected in the exercise of certain rights and from arbitrary governmental procedures by a double guarantee in state and nation. However, there are many variations from state to state in the detailed guarantees of state constitutions. For example, several state constitutions define religious freedom so as to prohibit state appropriations for parochial or seminary instruc- *Limitations arising from guarantees of civil rights* tion. The Supreme Court of the United States does not so define the religious freedom guaranteed by the Fourteenth Amendment nor do the constitutions of several other states. Some state constitutions, further, forbid imprisonment for debt, some forbid distinctions as to property rights between citizens and aliens, and many do not now require indictment by grand jury nor unanimity of decision by trial juries in all cases. Even where guarantees are cast in identical language, "due process of law," for example, courts in different states have given various meanings to these words. The rights of citizens are, therefore, somewhat differently stated and applied in the states.

Limitations imposed by states on themselves

1. Prohibition of local and private laws

A third group of limitations on state legislative power was imposed by the voters or by the legislators themselves and accompanied the decline in legislative prestige in the period 1860–1910. Hundreds of constitutional changes were adopted in this period which confined legislative authority. These may be summarized under a few main headings. One large class of restrictions has to do with special, local, or private laws. Many state legislatures are forbidden to pass such enactments dealing with one or more of the following subjects: municipal corporation charters, business corporation charters, particularly in the fields of banking and public utilities; divorce; county government structure and powers; location of seats of local government. There is no doubt that legislative efforts to deal with problems peculiar to one person, corporation, city, or country were frequently incompetent, occasionally corrupt, and rarely discriminating. The prohibitions, strictly applied however, have prevented wise action also in cases where account must be taken of unique circumstances. Moreover, clever lawmakers find ingenious methods of evading the spirit if not the letter of the constitution. A common method in dealing with cities, for example, is to classify them according to size, making quite sure that the larger are each in a class by themselves. Classification schemes are subject to court review of their "reasonableness" in the light of the object sought. While many have been overthrown, few judges have ever thought that putting New York, Chicago, Pittsburgh, Cleveland, or San Francisco each in a class by itself was "unreasonable." An even more ingenious evasion is to word a statute, ostensibly applicable generally, in such a way that in reality it fits only one or two cases. In many situations, it must be said, these evasions are both wise and desirable. Large cities, particular associations, or corporations do have peculiar problems and it is highly desirable on occasion to deal with them without disturbing all the cities, associations, or corporations.

2. Regulations of legislative procedure and sessions

Another group of constitutional restrictions deals with legislative sessions and procedures. Among such are requirements that (1) all bills be printed in advance of final action; (2) statutes not be amended by cross reference but that all amended portions be included in full; (3) all bills be given three readings; (4) roll call votes be taken on final passage; (5) sessions of the legislature not last longer than a specified time—usually 60 days. Legislatures have found ways of living with these rules although there are few that are not evaded or ignored on occasion. The attempt to get short sessions by constitutional fiat is little short of absurd in these days of growing government.

Still another category of restrictions on legislative authority are those dealing with taxes, appropriations, and debts. Most states forbid the loan or pledge of public credit to private ventures or to local units of government. Many forbid appropriations except for a "public purpose." Many forbid extra compensation for public officers or contractors. Many states are required to tax property only at a uniform rate based on valuation. In some, like Illinois, such a clause has been interpreted to forbid a graduated income tax. A large number but not a majority forbid borrowing except to suppress insurrection or repel invasion. Another large number require popular approval by referendum on each borrowing operation proposed by the legislature. *3. Restrictions on taxes, loans, and appropriations*

To restrictions expressly imposed by constitutions have been added others evolved by state courts: such principles as (1) that any clause empowering the legislature to act in a particular manner is to be regarded as a denial of its rights to act in any other manner; and (2) that every pertinent provision of a constitution is to be construed as limiting legislative power *to the greatest possible extent*. In several states, the upshot of these remarkable interpretations is that, whereas in theory the legislature has all legislative power not denied to it by terms of the national and state constitutions, in practice it has tended to become a body with delegated powers. Few factors have contributed more to deaden popular interest in the work of the legislature, and to deprive the state of the services of its best citizens, than the shriveling of legislative power under express constitutional restrictions, reinforced by narrow judicial canons of interpretation. *Implied or resulting limitations*

THE STATUTORY INITIATIVE AND REFERENDUM

Of all the restrictions upon legislative freedom enacted in the period of popular distrust of state lawmakers none was more sweeping than the statutory initiative and referendum. These two devices, usually associated, are designed, in part at least, to vest lawmaking directly in the hands of the electorate. The referendum allows the voters to disallow laws passed by the legislature and the initiative allows them to place on the statute books measures which the legislature has been unable or unwilling to enact. Starting in South Dakota in 1898, the movement for popular legislation swept through the nation but made most headway in the Plains states and in the Far West. In the next two decades, constitutions were amended to provide for the initiative and referendum in 18 states and for the referendum only in two other states (Maryland and New Mexico). The movement came to an abrupt halt and has made no converts since that time.

Initiative and referendum arrangements although varied in detail are similar in essentials. One form, the *optional referendum,* takes place when *Forms of the referendum* the legislature, desiring an expression of popular sentiment upon an act that it has passed, specifies that the measure shall not go into effect until it shall have been approved by the voters at an election. The legislature may also leave districts or counties to determine for themselves whether a certain law (licensing of liquor sales, for example) shall apply to them. In this form, referenda may be and are used all over the nation. The referendum under consideration, however, is the mandatory type, and independent of the legislature. Where it prevails, provision is usually made for suspending of all general legislative enactments for a certain period (usually 90 days) in order to give the people of the state an opportunity to pass judgment on the work of their lawmakers. If during the interval a prescribed number or percentage of the voters (most commonly 5 percent) decide that a given measure is undesirable, they can, by filing a petition, prevent it from taking effect until it has been submitted at the polls and approved by the electorate.

Procedure under the initiative

The initiative may be invoked whenever any considerable number of people believe that the legislature has failed to enact necessary or desirable laws. A citizen or group of citizens, usually a political–interest group, may then draw up a bill. This done, the next step is to obtain the signatures of a specified proportion of the voters (usually 5 or 10 percent of the number of votes cast at the last election for governor or some other specified office) on a petition requesting that the bill be enacted into law. The petition is filed with the secretary of state and then either of two courses may be taken, as the law prescribes. One is called the *direct initiative;* the other, the *indirect initiative*. Under the direct form, the measure is submitted to the people at the next regular election or at a special election, with the popular verdict final and the legislature entirely passive. Under the indirect form, the bill must be submitted to the legislature at its next session; and if that body acts upon it favorably, it becomes law without any popular vote. If, however, the legislature fails to act favorably, the bill is referred to the people and becomes law if approved by the required majority. In most states, the legislature is not permitted to amend any bill originating under the popular initiative. In some, it may put before the people a rival or substitute measure. The governor may in no case veto a measure enacted by initiative and referendum.

Results

Popular lawmaking has not accomplished most of the expectations of its sponsors. In some states it has rarely, if ever, been used. In others, notably those on the west coast, it has been used excessively. Where it is used, voters in large numbers have shown a great lack of interest in propositions placed before them. In a few cases laws which were difficult to administer and impossible to finance have been placed on the statute books. In one case (Missouri in 1921–1922) the devices were used by a minority party to prevent laws enacted by the majority from taking effect. Interest groups, some of whose ambitions the devices were designed to thwart, have been as effective in "selling" the people as the legislators. There is little evidence that the legislative process has been improved by inviting the voters to take a direct hand in the matter.

STRUCTURE OF STATE LEGISLATURES

The states are firmly wedded to a two-house legislature. Nebraska enjoyed a moment of national fame in 1937 when it established a single-chambered body after a vigorous and stirring campaign led by the late Senator George Norris. None of the disasters pictured by the supporters of the old two-house system has occurred, but neither have some of the glowing hopes of the proponents been realized. For a time, the question of one house or two was debated up and down the land, and the Model State Constitution continues to recommend the one-house system; but interest has subsided and almost nowhere is this "reform" getting serious consideration. There is really no compelling reason for two houses in the state legislature such as that which created the Senate and the House in Washington. Local governments are not like states in any legal sense. They had no separate existence before, during, or after the Revolution and there was not then and is not now any good reason for representing them as such. Our continued use of the two-house system in states indicates how much we are influenced by habit and tradition. It also indicates that there is nothing so bad about the bicameral plan as to encourage vigorous efforts to change it.

The two-house legislature

In most states, the major differences between the two houses are that (1) the upper-house member serves a longer term than the lower-house member—usually four years as opposed to two years; (2) the upper houses are smaller and, therefore, the constituencies of the members are larger— usually from two to three times as large; (3) in one house greater weight has in the past been given to area considerations in fixing the district boundaries than in the other; and (4) the terms of members of upper houses are usually staggered so they do not expire at the same time. The same electorate selects the membership of both houses.

Differences between the two houses

The major controversy over the structure of legislatures today is that dealing with the basis of representation. Should legislatures represent people, counting each as one or should they also represent area or predetermined units of government? Or should people be represented in one house, and area or governmental unit in the other? In most states the legislature itself determines how large each house will be and draws the district boundary lines for the seats. In many, however, this decision is controlled, or at least influenced by constitutional prescriptions of three types: (1) those fixing an upper limit on the size of one or both houses; (2) those requiring the districts to be redrawn after each census; (3) those modifying a strict population basis for representation by requiring, for example, that each county have at least one member in one of the houses or by forbidding one

Basis of representation

county to have more than a specified proportion of the total seats in one house or by prescribing equal representation of towns or counties.

Urban underrepresentation

The result of past legislative and constitutional decisions is that in virtually every state the sparsely populated regions have been overrepresented and the growing urban and suburban areas underrepresented in the legislature. Typically, the rapidly growing great metropolitan areas of the United States are discriminated against in the state systems of apportioning legislative seats, just as in Congress many districts are also gerrymandered for partisan advantage. Why is this so? In the first place, the national example suggests to many people that population should be recognized as a basis of representation in only one house and governmental jurisdictions (counties mainly) regardless of size should be represented in the other. This argument would have greater weight if the jurisdictions had any recognizable separate identity but most of them were created by and remain creatures of the state legislature. Secondly, adjusting districts to population requires that legislators in stable or declining areas give up seats and this they are usually reluctant to do. Thirdly, our great cities have on many occasions been dominated by highly organized, corrupt, and ruthless machines which the rural and small-town people fear and despise. Then too in many large cities organized labor is quite powerful if not decisive politically, and the merchants, bankers and farmers of the rural areas and small towns are implacably opposed to increasing its influence. In many cases also, one party (usually the Democratic) is in power in the city and another (usually the Republican) in the small towns and farming areas. Since for a century the flow of people has been from farm to small town to city, the burden of change is one the city people and inertia or deadlock serves the cause of the overrepresented. Finally, there is some evidence to suggest that the city voters do not take their representation in the state legislature seriously. Many political posts—councilman, magistrate, mayor —in our cities are more lucrative and more honorific than the post of legislator. In the countryside, the legislator is relatively more important and the post more widely sought. Our state legislatures, in consequence, have been commonly dominated by the outlook—economic, political, and social—of the small town while our society is metropolitan. The typical state legislator is a county seat lawyer, a prosperous farmer, or a small-town merchant. Frustrated in the state legislature, powerful urban groups like organized labor carry their demands to Washington and lend support to the growing influence of the central government.

Reapportionment by commissions

A few states have tried to remove reapportionment from the legislative arena by entrusting all or part of the responsibility for adjusting districts to changing population patterns to some other agency. In Arizona, the secretary of state certifies to each county the number of members of the lower house it is entitled to elect. This certification occurs every two years on the basis of the vote cast for governor. California has a reapportionment commission consisting of the lieutenant governor, attorney general, secretary

State Legislatures
Size, Term, and Sessions
August 1, 1967

| STATE | LOWER HOUSE | | UPPER HOUSE | | FREQUENCY OF REGULAR SESSIONS |
	SIZE	TERM (YEARS)	SIZE	TERM (YEARS)	
Alabama	106	4	35	4	Biennial
Alaska	40	2	20	4	Annual
Arizona	60	2	30	2	A
Arkansas	100	2	35	4	B
California	80	2	40	4	A
Colorado	65	2	35	4	A
Connecticut	177	2	36	2	B
Delaware	35	2	18	4	A
Florida	119	2	48	4	B
Georgia	205	2	54	2	A
Hawaii	51	2	25	4	A
Idaho	70	2	35	2	B
Illinois	177	2	58	4	B
Indiana	100	2	50	4	B
Iowa	124	2	61	4	B
Kansas	125	2	40	4	A
Kentucky	100	2	38	4	B
Louisiana	105	4	39	4	A
Maine	151	2	34	2	B
Maryland	142	4	43	4	A
Massachusetts	240	2	40	2	A
Michigan	110	2	38	4	A
Minnesota	135	2	67	4	B
Mississippi	122	4	52	4	B
Missouri	163	2	34	4	B
Montana	104	2	55	4	B
Nebraska	—	—	49	2	B
Nevada	40	2	20	4	B
New Hampshire	400	2	24	2	B
New Jersey	60	2	29	2	A
New Mexico	70	2	42	4	A
New York	150	2	57	2	A
North Carolina	120	2	50	2	B
North Dakota	98	2	40	4	B
Ohio	99	2	33	4	B
Oklahoma	99	2	48	4	A
Oregon	60	2	30	4	B
Pennsylvania	203	2	50	4	A
Rhode Island	100	2	50	2	A
South Carolina	124	2	50	4	A
South Dakota	75	2	35	2	A
Tennessee	99	2	33	4	B
Texas	150	2	31	4	B
Utah	69	2	28	4	B
Vermont	150	2	30	2	B
Virginia	100	2	40	4	B
Washington	99	2	49	4	B
West Virginia	100	2	34	4	A
Wisconsin	100	2	33	4	A
Wyoming	61	2	30	4	B

SOURCE: Council of State Governments, *Book of the States*, *1968–1969* (Chicago, 1968), pp. 49, 50, 51.

of state, controller, and superintendent of education. These officers are charged with reapportioning if the legislature fails to do its duty. Similar bodies with slightly different powers and members are provided in South Dakota, Texas, and Ohio. Missouri, in the constitution of 1945, provided a commission of 10 members selected by the governor from lists submitted by the central organs of the two major parties. This body is charged with redistricting the Senate, and if it should fail to do so in good time, the whole Senate must be elected at large. The secretary of state reapportions the lower house in Missouri on the basis of a formula expressly provided in the constitution. Illinois for a time had a system for both houses much like the Missouri system. Hawaii and Alaska entrust the responsibility to the governor with the help of an advisory board and allow any voter to seek a court order to compel the governor to act properly. Michigan, in its new constitution, provides for a reapportionment agency made up of eight legislators named by their parties—two each from four regions into which the state is divided. Pennsylvania in 1968 approved a commission of five: the party leaders of each house plus a chairman selected by them.

Reapportionment by the courts

Since inequalities in systems of apportioning seats are in many instances contrary to the letter and spirit of state constitutional prescriptions, state courts have been invited on numerous occasions to intervene. Typically, they have refused to do so and have justified their position on the grounds of want of effective power to compel another branch of the government to act. Until 1962, the Supreme Court of the United States also declined to intervene. However, in one of the most controversial and epoch-making decisions in its history, it held in May, 1962, that the system of allocating seats in state legislatures could and would be reviewed by national courts for compliance with the equal-protection clause of the Fourteenth Amendment. Failure of the state of Tennessee to reapportion for 61 years, the Court held, was a justiciable action worthy of being adjudicated on its merits and in the light of the possible debasement of voting rights arising from unequal representation. This decision encouraged challenges to the apportionment system of most of the states and the Court was finally brought to declare that the equal-protection clause requires both houses of state legislatures to be apportioned on a population basis so that insofar as possible each voter equals every other—"one man, one vote." Since that decision 45 states have adopted new apportionment plans, some of which are still under attack before the courts. Five states had already reapportioned on a population basis before the decision. The case law on what constitutes "equality" is developing very rapidly in view of the wide variety of practices under review and it is, therefore, not possible to state precisely what amount of deviation from strict mathematical equality will be tolerated. It is clear, however, that some will. Meanwhile, several groups have organized a concerted drive to halt or reverse the trend toward judicially imposed equality in districting. Some are pushing for an amendment to the Constitution to deprive the national courts of jurisdiction in state legislative apportionment cases;

others, led by Senator Dirksen of Illinois, for an amendment which would authorize the states to apportion one house of a bicameral legislature on the basis of factors other than population if such an apportionment was approved by the state voters in a referendum. The Dirksen proposal was narrowly defeated in the Senate in mid-1965 but is far from dead: Very nearly two-thirds of the states have petitioned Congress for a convention to consider an amendment of this type.

State legislatures are not addicted to the single-member district system *Single-* of representation—a system widely believed to be closely tied to our two- *member* party system. A majority of states use multimember districts to some extent *district* and several (Washington, Maryland, and Illinois, for example) use it ex- *system* clusively for their lower houses. In fact, until the latest round of reapportionments very nearly half of all members of lower houses were elected in districts assigned two or more representatives. In Illinois, the multimember district system in the lower house has been geared to a unique system of cumulative voting which assigns each voter three votes to allocate as he wishes among the candidates for the three seats in each district. This system is intended to guarantee minority representation and it apparently has done so. In the other states the multimember district system has resulted from other but related considerations.

ORGANIZATION OF THE STATE LEGISLATURE

The officers, committees, rules, and party apparatus of state legislatures are, without major exception, patterned very closely after those of Congress. Leadership is provided through the party system; the real work is done largely in the standing committees; the rules are based largely on Jefferson's manual modified by constitutional prescription; the lobby is filled with energetic spokesmen for the major economic, religious, and social groups of our society. Let us, therefore, concentrate our gaze upon significant differences from the national pattern.

The speaker of the lower house of state legislatures is nearly every- *Officers* where relatively more powerful than his counterpart in Washington. In the vast majority of states, the speaker appoints the members of the standing committees, as he did in Congress until 1910. Further, his control over the procedure is not shared, typically, with a powerful Rules Committee. In some states where the Rules Committee is powerful the speaker is likely to be its chairman. Since the body he dominates is usually much smaller than that in the Congress his dealings with his colleagues are more direct, personal, and informal than is possible in Washington. Only the majority floor leader closely approaches him in ability to shape the product of his branch of the legislature.

A number of states have abandoned the office of lieutenant governor and replaced it, in part, by a presiding officer elected by the Senate itself.

Where this has occurred, this official resembles the speaker in power and influence rather than the Vice-President. In some states where the national scheme of electing a president *pro tempore* is used, this official appoints the standing committees. In many, however, a small Committee on Committees elected by the Senate does this job.

Committees   Standing committees in each house in every state act very much like those in the Congress. In general, however, it is safe to say that the committees do not constitute as important or as independent sources of influence over the legislative product as their counterparts in Washington. Sessions are shorter and less frequent, turnover is somewhat higher, and seniority is not quite so rigidly adhered to. Thus expertness is less readily acquired by the state legislators. In an effort to avoid the duplications and deadlocks of the two-house system, several states make much greater use of joint committees (including members of both houses) than is done in Washington. Massachusetts, Connecticut, and Maine conduct most of the legislative business through joint committees and several states outside New England use joint committees to shape appropriations and taxation measures. Many observers and students of the legislative process believe the joint-committee system has real advantages over the traditional arrangements.

Interim   State legislatures also make use of special committees meeting between
committees sessions to conduct studies, carry on investigations, and shape legislation for the future. Whereas in Congress the trend has been to have more investigating and research done by the regular standing committees and to rely relatively less often on special or select committees, in the state capitols the trend is toward consolidating special interim committees, into one grand legislative council or research commission supervising all interim inquiries and generally preparing a program of legislation for the next session. Little investigating or systematic research is performed by standing committees of state legislatures. Typically, only the major interim study commissions or councils are equipped with expert staff assistants. Few regular committees at the state level have anything more than clerical aid. California has been developing a staff of budget analysts for its appropriations committee but elsewhere the congressional staffing program has not been imitated by the states.

The reorganization by Congress in 1946 of its committee system reducing the number of committees and of assignments has stimulated many of the states to do the same and the average number of such committees has dropped from 39 to 22 in lower houses and from 31 to 20 in Senates. Still the typical legislature has far too many standing committees and the typical legislator too many committee assignments.

Secrecy   In a great many states the committees' activities are neither reported nor recorded and the rules and traditions encourage a great amount of secrecy in the legislative process. In a few, however, the process is surrounded by openness unknown even in Washington. Wisconsin, for example, requires that committee meetings be open to the public, that due advance notice be given of hearings on proposed bills, that all bills be reported out of the committees before the session ends, and in other ways attempts to open its deliberations to public view. Part of the problem everywhere stems from the fact that legislative sessions are not nearly so well nor so expertly covered by reporters as are the sessions of Congress.

Every state legislative body has developed an elaborate and complex *Rules* set of rules. There are among these many thousands of rare and exotic specimens. In the main, however, the states follow the congressional precedents. Typically, debate is not quite so closely limited as in the House of Representatives nor so open to filibuster as in the Senate. A two-thirds majority in either house can usually ride roughshod over the normal procedure but this is rarely obtained by any faction or party. Most of the states have made little effort to modernize their rules or to adjust them to the growing volume of legislative business. In this respect, however, they are aping Washington quite skillfully. The most striking thing about state legislative procedure is the almost complete lack of documentation. Only a handful of states keep any kind of record of the debate either in committee or on the floor. A journal or record of votes and actions taken is about all the record available to a student of the legislative process. There is thus little guidance for the courts in determining legislative intent or for the citizen trying to understand either the process or the result.

In the states as in Congress the two major political parties claim the *The party* loyalties of an overwhelming majority of all the legislators. Party affiliation *apparatus* produces also an informal structure of leadership operating through caucuses, floor leaders, and policy committees. This structure is, in general, extremely important in determining committee assignments, in determining the holders of the official positions of speaker and president of the Senate and in determining the nature of the output. The patterns of party politics in the states, however, differ so strikingly one from another that few generalizations about the party in the legislature can safely be attempted. There are, in the first place, a large group of states (perhaps as many as 14, including most of those in the Old South and some in New England) where one party so completely dominates the state government that its influence in the legislative process is impossible to assess. In these states, factions within the dominant party vie with one another for control of the elected officers and influence on the conduct of the government. These factions act very much as parties act elsewhere except that they are much less formal in organization and much less stable and enduring. Party caucuses and formally designated leaders are virtually unknown in most of these one-party states. There is another smaller group of states where one party normally has a majority in both houses but where the other party has some representation. In these also, factionalism in the majority party is quite common and the institutions of party government in the legislature are not highly developed. The closest parallel to the situation in Congress exists in those remaining states (perhaps 23, including most of the large states like New Jersey, Ohio, Pennsylvania, Illinois, California) where the two parties are more closely matched and engage in vigorous and continuing competition. Even in some of these, however, the party is less influential than the interest group in legislative decision-making. In many of the two-party states the instrumentalities of party government are more active than in Congress. In several the caucus meets every day that the legislature is in session and considers all the major matters on the calendar. Less reliance is thus placed on the floor leaders and speakers for carrying out party policy. In many of the states also one or another of the parties may consistently control at least one house, but the governorship tends to be captured by one party and then by another. In these states, party influence through the governor's office is an important factor in the legislative process.

Finally, in two states, Nebraska and Minnesota, party affiliation is prohibited by law to members of the state legislature. All of them are elected on a nonpartisan ballot. In these, factions tend to form and to act like parties do in the other states. This effort to rid the legislature of the "evils" of party politics has not, thus far, been imitated elsewhere.

In summary, it appears that the influence of party affiliation on state legislative decision-making is clearly related to the state party patterns. It is greater where genuine two-party competition exists. Nowhere, not even in Congress, is it decisive. It should be noted further that the party organizations in many of the states take less interest in the selection and financing of state legislators than they do in Congressmen and that even the successful candidates are unlikely to feel so strong an obligation to the state party.

THE LEGISLATIVE PROCESS

The effect of limited sessions

One of the great differences between state legislative and national legislative operations arises from the limits placed by many states on the amount of time the legislature may be in session. Most state legislatures meet regularly only once every two years. About half the state constitutions limit even these sessions to a specified number of days (36, 40, 60, 90, or 120 days with 60 the most common) or limit the number of days for which legislators may be paid. Congress meets each year for as long as its leaders feel is necessary to realize the possibilities of that session. The national procedure is, therefore, relatively deliberate and even leisurely. State legislatures faced with several hundred bills and resolutions in a session of 60 days every other year must abandon deliberation and the chance of careful second thoughts. Since legislative business is growing increasingly complex and voluminous, artificial time limitations play havoc with the careful, studied, and unhurried processes contemplated by the rules and traditions of American legislative bodies. Initiative in legislation passes to state executives, dominant interest groups, or powerful party leaders and measures are either passed or defeated. There is little time for debate, amendment, conference, or research.

One particular manifestation of efforts by law or custom to restrict legislative activities is the "end of the session rush." In many states, the last few days of a session are confused and hectic with hundreds of bills taken up and passed or rejected in a few short hours. On occasion no member nor any presiding officer or floor leader is fully in command of the proceedings and certain as to what has been done and what left undone. In part this has been traced to the legislative habit of beginning each session in the leisurely and deliberate manner specified by the rules and then sprinting to the finish under the lash of the constitutional deadline, a determined governor, and the majority leaders. Various states have experimented, as Congress has not, with devices for abating the storm. Several forbid new measures to be introduced after a certain period without the support of an unusual majority or the scrutiny of a special committee for the purpose. A few have tried the split session. In the first part of the session bills are introduced and referred to committees for study then after a recess the bills are debated and decisions on them reached. California made the most use of this plan but finally dropped it in 1959. West Virginia and New Mexico tried it and abandoned it. Massachusetts is authorized by its constitution to use it but has never done so. A great many states have sought to expedite the consideration of measures by the use of electronic voting devices by which roll calls can be completed and votes recorded in a few seconds as compared to the time taken in Congress for this purpose.

"End of the session rush"

Massachusetts has perhaps done as much as any state to improve the uneven flow of legislative traffic. The joint-committee system already described has helped materially. Committees are required, with some exceptions, to report all matters referred to them not later than early March and in many cases within three days of their receipt. None of these has been wholly successful in helping legislatures avoid the confusion of the last few days of the session.

The imprint of the activities of political interest groups on the state legislative process has been deep and continuous for several generations. Public concern was earlier attracted to the problems at the state level and has been more widely aroused for a longer period than at the national level. In many states the result of this concern has been to fasten shackles on the legislature so that it can do less harm if corrupted by the "interests." A few have grappled directly with lobbying and the lobbyist and have tried to bring the practice and the practitioner under regulation. In fact some of the experience of these states was incorporated in the national effort at regulation. Outstanding efforts have been made by California, New York, Wisconsin, and Massachusetts. The general pattern or regulation now widespread among the states includes (1) requiring all lobbyists to register with a state official their names, employers, and the scope and character of their legislative interests; (2) requiring lobbyists to file at intervals or at the close

Lobbying

of the session a statement of their expenditures for lobbying purposes; (3) forbidding employment of lobbyists on a contingent fee basis. Where honestly and capably administered, these regulations have made it possible to publicize the extent and character of lobbying and have accomplished little else. Wisconsin, in 1957, took the latest and most drastic step to "purify" the lobby by forbidding any lobbyist to buy or give any legislator anything of value (meal, drink, or even a cigar).

The "enemy" in all of these efforts is the paid lobbyist acting directly on the legislature. Few laws deal with the interest group itself and fewer still with efforts to influence public opinion (indirect lobbying) or to bring indirect pressure on legislators or administrators.

Uniform state laws   Americans are, on the whole, proud of the diversity of methods and policies for dealing with the problems of our society that 50 separate state governments encourage. There are some areas of state legislative interest, not as yet controlled or standardized by national programs, which invite if they do not require greater uniformity of treatment, state to state, than results from our federal pattern. Many examples could be cited in the fields of commercial law, crime, highway rules and others. Since 1892 a National Conference of Commissioners of Uniform State Laws has been actively promoting such uniformity. This voluntary agency composed of representative lawyers and professors of law from each state designs and recommends such laws to each state for adoption. More than 115 of these have been prepared and offered to the states on such subjects as negotiable instruments, bills of lading, declaratory judgments, narcotics, criminal extradition, rules of criminal procedure, divorce, reciprocal enforcement of support. Thirty or more have been adopted in a vast majority of states, several more in a sizable number of states, and many in a few states.

TECHNICAL ASSISTANCE FOR LEGISLATORS

One of the most notable changes of the past decades in the state legislative process has been the growth of technical and expert aid for the legislators. Few subjects demanding the attention of modern legislators can be dealt with intelligently without knowledge of the problems or without aid in casting the proposed solutions into appropriate legal language. The movement from pioneer frontier to complex urban industrial environment has increased the difficulty of legislative problem-solving many times over. The hearing given to bills might be supposed to elicit all the relevant data needed by the legislator to make a wise decision, but unfortunately this is not always the case. Much of the testimony is special pleading, and large segments of the public, although concerned, may be inarticulate.

1. Legislative reference bureaus   One of the oldest and most useful aids is the legislative reference bureau. Such an adjunct was first introduced in New York and Massachusetts in 1890 as a function of the central state library and in Wisconsin in 1901 as a permanent agency and nowadays, under some form or name, is found in virtually every state. Two main purposes are served: (1) assembling, shelving, or filing and indexing for ready use the statutes of the various states; judicial decisions interpreting and applying such statutes in concrete cases; administrative reports and other materials throwing light on the workings of various laws; governors' messages; and a wealth of miscellaneous materials on all manner of subjects—taxation, transportation, labor, public utilities, insurance, pensions, agriculture, corporations, and education—likely to come up during a session; and (2) providing special research service to legislators to compile in ready form information on any selected topic.

Originally, many of the reference bureaus also provided bill drafting assistance to help legislators put their ideas into proper statutory form. A few continue to do so. Generally, however, the bill drafting function has been detached and separately organized. In many states, it has been joined to the long-standing function of statutory revision—continuous revision of the state laws to eliminate with legislative approval, anachronistic, contradictory and inconsistent provisions.

Beginning in Kansas in 1933 a movement for central, bipartisan research commissions spread through the nation. These agencies are usually called legislative councils and, in general, are designed to aid legislatures by making extensive studies of the major state problems and by developing suggested legislation for dealing with these problems. Many of the councils or commissions do most of their work in the interim between sessions and are aided by research assistants regularly employed on the staff of the council. The hope of the sponsors of this development that a self-produced program of major legislation might be prepared at leisure by the leaders of the legislature and that by this method some of the leadership in legislation lost to the executive branch might be recaptured has not been fully realized in most of the states that have created such agencies. A few have been outstandingly successful. Many councils, however, have been obliged to spread their efforts over too many subjects, or have been denied funds to hire competent staff, or have become embroiled in party or factional contests. Several have aroused the animosity and suspicion of the members of the legislature not selected to participate in their deliberations. *2. Legislative councils*

The growth of state expenditures in recent years has stimulated increasing legislative concern for more effective fiscal review and postaudit practices. In the past decades, several states have created and staffed agencies responsible solely to the legislature which conduct continuous review either of executive agency spending proposals and practices or of the actual expenditures made. The California Joint Legislative Budget Committee established in 1941 is the best and one of the earliest examples of this type of legislative service agency. *3. Fiscal review agencies*

REFERENCES

General

The American Assembly, *State Legislatures in American Politics* (New York, 1966).

J. D. Barber, *The Lawmakers, Recruitment and Adaptation to Legislative Life* (New Haven, 1965).

A. E. Buck, *Modernizing Our State Legislatures* (Pamphlet, Philadelphia, 1956).

A. B. Coigne, *Statute Making* (New York, 1948).

Council of State Governments, *Our State Legislatures* (Chicago, 1946).

————, *American State Legislatures: Their Structure and Procedures* (Chicago, 1950).

Council of State Governments, *Book of the States,* biennially, Sec. II (Chicago).

Alexander Heard (ed.), *State Legislatures in American Politics* (Englewood Cliffs, N. J., 1966).

M. E. Jewell, *Legislative Representation in the Contemporary South* (Durham, N. C., 1967).

————, *The State Legislature—Politics and Practice* (New York, 1962).

R. Luce, *Legislative Assemblies* (Boston, 1924).

————, *Legislative Problems* (Boston, 1922).

————, *Legislative Procedure* (Boston, 1935).

J. C. Wahlke and H. Eulau (eds.), *Legislative Behavior* (Glencoe, Ill., 1959).

H. Walker, *The Legislative Process* (New York, 1948).

B. Zeller (ed.), *American State Legislatures* (New York, 1954).

Particular Problems

G. E. Baker, *Rural Versus Urban Political Power* (New York, 1960).

H. W. Davey, "The Legislative Council Movement in the United States, 1933–1953," *Amer. Pol. Sci. Rev.,* XLVII, 785–797 (Sept., 1953).

P. T. David and R. Eisenburg, *State Legislative Redistricting: Major Issues in the Wake of Judicial Decision* (Chicago, 1962).

Interim Report of the New York State Joint Legislative Committee on Legislative Methods, Practices, Procedures, and Expenditures, Legislative Doc. No. 35 (Albany, 1945). *Final Report,* etc., Legislative Doc. No. 31 (Albany, 1946).

C. O. Johnson, "The Adoption of the Initiative and Referendum in Washington," *Pacific Northwest Quar.,* XXXV, 291–303 (Oct., 1944), and "The Initiative and Referendum in Washington," *ibid.,* XXXVI, 29–53 (Jan., 1945).

Oklahoma State Legislative Council, *Constitutional Study* No. 4, "Strengthening the Legislative Process"; No. 7, "Legislative Organization and Procedure" (Oklahoma City, 1948).

O. D. Weeks, *Research in the American State Legislative Process* (Ann Arbor, Mich., 1947).

3

THE GOVERNOR AND THE EXECUTIVE BRANCH

The principal political officer of each state is the governor. He is also the *Impor-tance of the office* chief executive, a major lawmaker, an important party leader, and the ceremonial head of the commonwealth. His major task is to devise a program for the conduct of the affairs of his state and then to seek appropriate legislation, necessary financing, and popular support to carry it out. To the public he is the state and they expect him to find a remedy for every ill of the body politic. He is rarely, however, able to work his will by command. Exhortation is his most widely used method and close bargaining with those whom he cannot dominate his daily exercise. The governorship in America is a miniature Presidency but without many of the President's most powerful tools. Unlike the Presidency, however, the governorship is not the summit of a public career but rather a small hill on which to learn the art of mountain climbing. The governor's office is the testing grounds for statesmen and the men who occupy it usually expect to go on to the Senate, the Cabinet, or the Presidency itself.

In every state the governor is today elected by popular vote on a partisan ballot for a term of two or four years. The office was not originally so conceived. In only two colonies (Connecticut and Rhode Island) was the governor chosen by the people and in 11 of the 13 original states he was selected by the legislature. Popular election gradually won its way during the early half of the past century and prepared the ground for the emergence of the popular and powerful leader of the present era. The general trend has been toward lengthening the governor's term and whereas several decades ago two years was typical now the governor serves four years in all but 11 states. Fear of unrestricted tenure, as in the case of the Presidency, has led in a number of states to constitutional restrictions on continued eligibility. In 11 states, the governor may not succeed himself and in 12 states he may serve no more than two consecutive terms. Many of the great industrial states which have produced so many strong presidential aspirants (for example, Ohio, Illinois, California, New York) have four year terms without restrictions of this type. New York, for example, has had only six different governors in four decades. In these states, furthermore, party competition is unusually keen. Many of those with eligibility restrictions are one-party states. In summary, the trend everywhere is toward creating a more powerful position manned by more experienced leaders.

Nomina-
tion and
election

In every state the governor is now selected under party auspices in a partisan election. In a few states candidates for the major parties are nominated by statewide conventions (for example, New York until 1967) of locally elected delegates. The typical method is by popular voice in statewide direct primaries. In several of the states where primaries are used, however, the party seeks through official conventions or semiofficial and informal caucuses and conventions to present to the voters aspirants bearing the approval of the organization. In many of the southern states, the primary is more important than the election since Democratic nominees virtually always win in November. In an effort to secure majority choice, many of these states have two primaries with the two candidates finishing at the top in the first heat contesting in a second or "run-off" primary election. Three states have used a modified electoral college system weighted somewhat in favor of the rural and small-town populations in connection with the gubernatorial election. In Mississippi a legislative-district, electoral-vote system has been used in the election and the winner must obtain both popular and electoral majorities. In Georgia and Maryland a system based on counties was used in the nominating procedure but not in the final election. The Supreme Court has recently declared these schemes invalid as contrary to the equal-protection clause. The character of the procedure for entering the gubernatorial sweepstakes is to a large degree influenced by the existence of real two-party competition. In general, the more competitive the parties the more nearly the process resembles that for the Presidency. But in the numerous one-party states the contest is really an intraparty affair and many kinds of informal organizational and campaign patterns exist. Whatever the method of reaching this high office, in every state there are numerous practices, customs, and traditions which influence selection and are collectively of greater consequence than the qualifications as to age and length of residency written into the constitutions.

Removal

The governor, as well as other major state officials, may be removed by impeachment and conviction on the national pattern in every state except Oregon. As in Washington, this procedure is rarely used: Only 13 governors have ever been impeached and of these only 6 were convicted and removed from office. In a dozen states governors may be recalled by popular petition and vote. Only one governor (Frazier of North Dakota in 1921) has been ousted by this method. Typically, the lieutenant governor succeeds to the office on the death, resignation, or removal of the governor. Several states without this office, place the secretary of state, president of the Senate, or speaker of the lower house next in line.

THE GOVERNOR AND LEGISLATION

The modern governor invests a large part of his energy in procuring the legislation and fiscal resources to carry out his program. Popular election, the organization of political parties, the limitations of legislators' pay and of the length of sessions, and partisan campaigning have all contributed to the emergence, in most states, of the governor as a major influence in law-making. This development closely parallels that of the office of President and is supported in large measure by factors outside the formal constitutional assignment of powers and duties. Many of the newer state constitutions and amendments, however, reflect the increasing importance of executive leadership in the legislative process and provide to the governors a more extensive and more compelling set of legislative powers than the President can command. *Constitutional position and powers:*

State legislatures, typically, meet less frequently than does Congress, and the sessions are, in many states, rigidly limited as to length. The power of the governor to call the legislature into special session is relatively of greater importance, therefore, than that of the President. Typically, the governor by declaring the purposes of the session, may bar consideration of other subjects. Of course, the governor cannot compel the legislature to agree with his proposals. *1. Special sessions*

Like the President, the governor is obliged by constitutional prescription to inform the legislature on the condition of the state's affairs. Ordinarily the major message which opens the regular session is delivered orally and attracts a wide audience. This "state of the state" message is commonly followed by numerous messages on particular subjects from time to time during the session. Bills exactly designed to achieve the governor's suggestions also flow from the executive office in a steady stream. In many of our large and consequential states his is the principal initiative in law-making. *2. Messages*

Year in and year out the most important set of executive recommendations are those embraced in the budget. Virtually every state has since 1910 adopted the executive budget system which places the governor in the leading role in preparing and recommending a fiscal program for his state. In discharging this responsibility, the governor gains, probably, his greatest influence over the conduct of the state administration and, at the same time, initiates the most important bill or set of bills in each regular legislative session. *3. Budget proposals*

Originally the states bestowed the veto power grudgingly or not at *4. Veto power* all (Massachusetts and South Carolina made the only provision for it among the original thirteen states). As popular election gradually freed the governor from his early dependence on the legislature, the veto became an important adjunct to his position. It is authorized in every state except North Carolina. Furthermore, in all but a handful of states, the veto extends to items in appropriation bills (a power for which several recent Presidents have pled vainly). In Washington the item veto extends to all measures and in Oregon to bills declaring an emergency. The item veto equips the governor with power to deal with riders and with the expenditures outside his budget suggestions and tends to enhance his influence in legislation. In a few states, Massachusetts, Tennessee, Pennsylvania and California, for example, the item veto has been construed to permit the governor not only to strike out particular appropriations but reduce the amounts. This places him in an even more powerful position to determine the character and scope of the state's fiscal commitments. It also encourages legislative extravagance and irresponsibility. The legislators rely on the governor to whittle the appropriations back down to the limit of the state's income and, of course, to accept whatever onus attaches to this procedure.

Like the Congress, state legislatures may override a veto but the vote necessary to do so varies from a mere majority in Connecticut and a few other states to two-thirds of the full membership in each house in almost half of the states. Most states allow the governor five days to consider a bill after he receives it when the legislature is in session. After adjournment, many states give the governor more time. Some give him a pocket veto—i.e., vetoing a bill by inaction—but in others he must actually veto the bill to prevent its becoming law. New Jersey provided in its recent constitution for a practice which, in fact, had been used increasingly in several states of reassembling the legislature at a specified time after adjournment to consider the governor's vetoes of measures passed in the closing days of the session. This has the effect of eliminating the pocket veto.

All things considered, the typical governor has a stronger and more effective negative on legislation than does the President. At both levels of government, however, vetoes are rarely overridden and largely occur after the legislature has adjourned. At best, however, the veto is a negative influence and can be transformed into positive leadership only by skillful bargaining.

The governor's influence over legislation, and it is usually considerable, really arises like that of the President from his posture as the leader of his party, his superior ability to gain public interest and support for his program, his near monopoly on the creation of statehouse news, his ability to dispense favors large and small to legislators who follow his lead, and his power to punish by veto, refusal of appointment, or publicity those who obstruct his programs.

THE GOVERNOR AS EXECUTIVE

If as legislator, party leader, and popular hero, the modern governor closely resembles the modern President, as an executive and as manager of the administrative machinery the two are poles apart. The President's towering and lonely position as director of a huge and complex administrative apparatus, as commander of great military forces, and as devisor of the foreign relations of the nation is unmatched at the state level. *Weaker than the President in:*

In the first place, few state constitutions assign executive authority to governors in clear and unambiguous terms. Some say that he shall take care that the laws be faithfully executed but rarely is he assigned any agencies of law enforcement under his direct control. Some say that he shall be chief executive but on several occasions state courts have held that this endows him with little or no inherent executive authority. Many grant to him certain power of appointment and removal but this too is in many states hedged around with inhibitions. *1. Constitutional power*

Further, in every state one or more officials of the state administration are directly elected by the voters and are in no sense subordinates to the chief executive. Most commonly, the offices of attorney general, secretary of state, treasurer, auditor, and superintendent of public instruction are filled in this way. Each presides over an important agency which is thus largely removed from oversight by the governor. In many of the new constitutions, notably those of New Jersey, Alaska, and Michigan, this group of independently elected state executives is either sharply reduced or eliminated. In many states, other major departments or agencies are controlled by lay boards appointed for long and staggered terms. Such boards usually select the executive officer of the department and serve as screens between him and the chief executive. These arrangements blur, if they do not obliterate, any sense of subordination by the agency directors. A movement inaugurated in Illinois in 1920 by Governor Lowden and subsequently spreading to many other states has sought to sweep away the board system of department management and, to some extent, the elected department head system and replace it with single, governor-appointed heads along the lines of the national executive branch. Several of the largest and most important states have adopted what has come to be called "the strong executive" plan but a large number cling to the system described earlier in this paragraph. *2. Control over departments*

The President's appointing and, by inference, his directing authority is limited, as we have noted earlier, by the spread of the civil service merit system throughout the national administration. The same thing on a small scale has happened in the statehouses. In general, however, the merit system has made relatively less progress among state employes and thus executive patronage is somewhat more extensive. It may be argued that patronage

"WEAK" EXECUTIVE TYPE OF STATE ADMINISTRATIVE ORGANIZATION

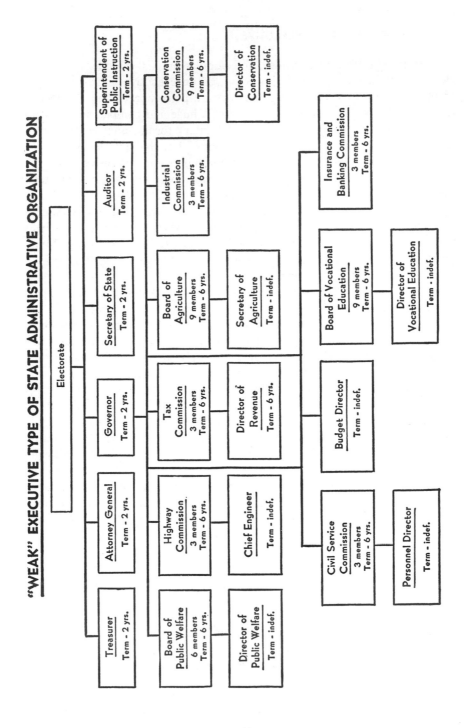

"STRONG" EXECUTIVE TYPE OF STATE ADMINISTRATIVE ORGANIZATION

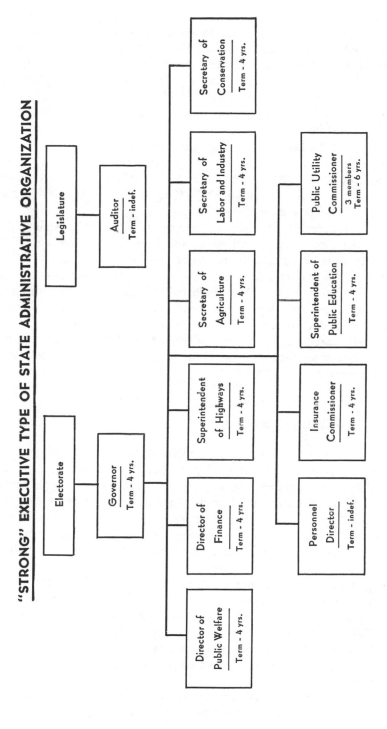

strengthens the governor's hand in party affairs and in dealing with the legislature; it does not improve his position as an effective state executive.

3. Requirements of confirmation

As in Washington, D. C., executive appointments, typically, must be confirmed by the upper houses of the state legislatures. In a few states, notably North Carolina, Massachusetts, New Hampshire, and Maine, some appointing authority is shared with an executive council or council of state.

4. Reliance on local officials

Finally, the state executive everywhere must rely heavily for law enforcement and the provision of some state services on locally elected and locally controlled officials such as mayors, sheriffs, and prosecuting attorneys. Except that the governor is empowered in several states to remove these officials for sufficient cause, they are largely beyond the reach of his direction and owe him no particular loyalty or deference. Presidents, as a result of the decision made in 1787–1788, suffer no comparable disadvantage in discharging their responsibilities.

It is apparent that few governors are in as commanding positions over their state administrations as the President is over his. The trend everywhere is to improve the governor's position in this regard. The movements for the four-year term, the elimination of many independent agencies, the reduction of the number of elected administrators, the substitution of governor-appointed department heads for boards or commissions, the executive budget system all are designed to achieve this end. In many of our great states giant steps have already been taken and some steps have been taken in almost every state, but the typical governor is still not a powerful executive.

THE EXECUTIVE BRANCH

Importance of administration

The growing services of modern state governments are provided through numerous agencies, departments, commissions, and bureaus grouped, usually rather loosely, into the executive or the administrative branch. Administration at all levels of government in the United States has been growing at a phenomenal rate for many decades. In total effort, however, the states are still far behind the government at Washington. Our local governments, in fact, spend more than the states. Nevertheless, administering governmental programs at the state level is a tremendous enterprise and occupies the time and energy of more than 2.2 million persons and an annual expenditure in excess of $51 billion. The typical state will employ 90,000 people organized into 20 to 30 separate agencies at an annual cost of $700 to $800 million. All of the problems of effective and responsible administration of public policies which have been discussed in connection with the central government are also present, albeit on a smaller scale, in the states.

Organization:

In comparing the administrative machinery at the national and state levels, it is well to recall the comparatively feeble sweep of the typical governor's directing influence. There is, for example, nothing at Washington quite comparable to the autonomous executive departments found in nearly every state headed by elected officials. The most important of these by far are the departments of public instruction or education which regulate the provision of public education throughout the state. The other autonomous departments, treasury, state, attorney general's, are relatively less important in most states but nevertheless constitute separate, single-headed, executive departments responsible only to the electorate.

1. The use of autonomous departments

The general use of any type of single-headed department responsible to the chief executive is a relatively new phenomenon among the states and may be found as the predominant mode of administrative organization only in those states like New York, Illinois, New Jersey, Michigan, which have undergone extensive overhauling since about 1920. In many states, the provision of major services, such as highway planning and construction, the care of the needy and unfortunate, the operation of institutions of healing, correction, or rehabilitation, is carried on by a commission, or board of plural membership and part-time service. Most of these boards employ full-time directors to manage the service, retaining, however, power over general policy and program.

2. The use of single-headed departments

The board system of administrative direction was the preferred system in most states for many decades and developed particularly in the field of institutional management. As state responsibilities for prisoners and the mentally ill and defective developed in the last century, a board of trustees to oversee the warden or director seemed to many the most appropriate method. As the number of institutions expanded and as states sought by parole, probation, mental hygiene programs, and public assistance to keep people out of the institutions, the board system became cumbersome and inappropriate and demands for its abolition became more insistent and gradually more compelling. The board system, however, was never confined to institutional management and has been and is being widely used for the regulation of agriculture, the conservation of resources, the promotion of business, the administration of labor laws, and many other purposes.

3. Continued reliance on boards and commissions

In the delicate area of regulation of the rates and profits of public utilities the states have almost uniformly followed the national pattern of adjudication through the independent regulatory commission. In general, these are staffed by full-time, relatively well paid, commissioners appointed by the governor and serving staggered terms of six to nine years. In more than a dozen states, however, the public utility or railroad commission members are elected by popular vote and, in at least one state (North Carolina) are selected by the legislature. It is not uncommon to require that members on such commissions be drawn from more than one political party.

4. The regulatory commission

The government corporation may also be found in several states but nowhere is it used as extensively as in the national government. The most widely used state corporations are those for the administration of toll roads or turnpikes, liquor stores, building construction, and power distribution.

5. The corporation

Commonly the state corporations have relatively greater freedom to arrange their finances than do the other types of agencies.

Growth of manage-ment services

Modern state administration is characterized by the rapid growth of management services. In fact many services such as central purchasing, consolidated budgeting, pre- and post-auditing, maintaining buildings, and procuring personnel were tried out initially in state and city governments. The success there attained commended them to other state capitals and city halls, and to the central government in Washington. Whereas in Washington, all of these management agencies are ultimately responsible to a single executive head, the President, in many, if not most, states this is not the case. Almost everywhere, for example, legal advisement is provided to the departments or agencies and to the governor by the attorney general's department and this official is separately elected in all but a handful of states. Auditors, treasurers, and controllers charged with prescribing systems of accounts, keeping track of cash, and reviewing fiscal transactions either before or after the incurring of the obligation are also almost universally elected in the states. Typically, purchasing, building construction and maintenance, budget preparation, and central printing are closely associated with the executive office and, therefore, more directly subject to executive authority but there are numerous exceptions among the 50 states. In several states, administrators of service functions are insulated against executive direction by long terms or merit selection with tenure.

Manage-ment services in "weak-" executive states

As in Washington, the growth of centralized management services has accompanied the demand for more efficiency and economy in governmental administration. The controls exercised by such agencies arose, however, in response to charges of "spoils" and "boodle." The problems of responsibility for the accomplishment of public policies raised by the growth of management services are many and have been discussed in connection with the national government. A different and additional set of difficulties characterizes the growth of these services in states without strong executive direction and without a coordinated executive branch. In many cases, the purchasers, auditors, accountants, legal advisors, printers, engineers, architects, and personnel administrators may, in fact, be responsible to no one in the entire executive establishment. On the other hand, governors lacking direct and specific directional authority over state departments and agencies have on many occasions sought to achieve influence through the management services attached to their offices or under their direction. When this has occurred, the management services have become instruments of control and direction over state affairs in a way that may also threaten the position of the line administrators. The most sweeping moves in the direction of strengthening the executive through management controls have occurred in Minnesota, Wisconsin, Alaska, Vermont, Indiana, and a few other states where the major management functions have been gathered into Departments of Administration and placed directly under the governor.

The administrative apparatus of the states, like that in Washington,

D. C., can never be fully and finally organized. New services, new methods, new ideas make change both inevitable and necessary. Reorganization is, therefore, a continuing concern in the states. Initiated in this century largely by Governor Lowden of Illinois and Governor Smith of New York sweeping changes have been made in the direction of strengthening the governorship and streamlining a hodgepodge of agencies and services. No sooner had this set of reforms swept through many states than new demands for change occurred. The Hoover Commission, for example, stimulated many states to follow the national lead and from 1949 to the present one state after the other has established study commissions—in some cases several—to review administrative organization and procedure and to make suitable recommendations for reform. It would be hard to picture the net impact of all these studies. Many have been abortive and without substantial result; others have led to far-reaching changes. In general, the greater changes seem to have been made in states that had avoided or resisted the reforms of the twenties. Most state legislatures have proved unwilling to go as far as the Congress in implementing reorganization studies by endowing the executive with the authority to make changes by executive order subject to legislative veto. New Hampshire in 1949, Pennsylvania in 1955, Michigan in 1958 and Oregon in 1959 are the only states that have, with various limitations, endowed their governors with this power. The new state of Alaska grants this authority in its constitution. In many states, also, administrative organization is prescribed for part or all of the executive branch in the state constitution and effective reorganization may require changing the constitution as well as the statutes. The principal beneficiary of most of the studies and most of the successful reform efforts has been the governor and thus reorganization efforts may be classed with other developments already described as part of a general movement to strengthen the governor as chief executive of the state.

Continuing efforts at reorganization

STATE PERSONNEL ADMINISTRATION

No administrative organization can be very much better than the quality of the people who service it. To the states the problem of recruiting and maintaining an able body of public servants is one of continuing importance and difficulty. The civil service reform movement which led to the growth of the merit system of personnel administration in the national executive branch also sought comparable results in the statehouses. A few states, notably Wisconsin in 1905, adopted sweeping merit system laws and a few others (New York in 1883, Massachusetts in 1884, for example) adopted merit systems for some employes but most resisted the removal of partisan appointment and by the mid-thirties only a small minority of states had very effective merit systems for a majority of their employes. The great expansion in state merit systems occurred after 1936 as a result of

Importance of personnel policies

Spread of state merit systems

the requirement of the Social Security Act of that year that states participating in national grants under that law must install merit system selection and protection for employes in the various assistance, insurance, and health programs. Thus by national compulsion a large number of state employes in every state were brought under an approved merit system. Since that time gains have been made in Indiana, Oregon, North Carolina, Vermont, Montana, Nevada, Oklahoma, Kentucky, Alaska, Hawaii, Iowa, Idaho, Nebraska, California, and a few other states. There remain, however, a large minority of states without statewide merit systems of personnel administration.

Continuing state personnel problems
The adoption of the merit system has by no means solved all the personnel problems of the states. There is a persistent tendency for merit systems to become routine, mechanical, and unimaginatively directed. Much more positive efforts at recruiting talent, maintaining attractive wage and benefit schedules, encouraging public careers, and overcoming the undue rigidities of classification schemes are necessary even in states most widely committed to merit selection. The three-man civil service commissions, so widely used for enforcing merit rules, have scores of critics. Many reorganization studies have suggested single-headed personnel departments as more appropriate under modern conditions and many have sought to enlarge the power of the governor to influence personnel administration. In general, states without extensive merit systems, however, continue to lag far behind the others in the national search for talent to man the services of the states, but none of the states is long on talent. Unionization of state employes has also extended widely and sharp challenges have occurred recently to state laws forbidding strikes or work stoppages by public employes.

REFERENCES

The Governor

M. L. Faust, *Manual of the Executive Article for the Missouri Constitutional Convention of 1943* (Columbia, Mo., 1943).

V. O. Key, *American State Politics: An Introduction* (New York, 1956).

L. Lipson, *The American Governor: From Figurehead to Leader* (Chicago, 1939).

C. B. Ransome, Jr., *The Office of Governor in the South* (University, Ala., 1951).

———, *The Office of Governor in the United States* (University, Ala., 1956).

J. A. Schlesinger, "The Politics of the Executive," in H. Jacobs and K. Vines, *Politics in the American States: A Comparative Analysis* (Boston, 1965).

Administrative Organization

J. C. Bollens, *Administrative Reorganization in the States Since 1939* (Berkeley, Calif., 1947).

A. E. Buck, *The Reorganization of State Governments in the United States* (New York, 1938).

Council of State Governments, *Book of the States,* biennially, Sec. IV (Chicago).

———, *Reorganizing State Government* (Chicago, 1950).

J. W. Fesler, *The Independence of State Regulatory Agencies* (Chicago, 1942).

O. P. Field, *Civil Service Law* (Minneapolis, 1939).

W. V. Holloway, *Personnel Administration in the States* (Oklahoma City, 1948).

National Civil Service League, *Model State Civil Service Law* (New York, 1946).

O. G. Stahl, *Public Personnel Administration* (5th ed., New York, 1962).

K. O. Warner and M. L. Hennessy, *Public Management at the Bargaining Table* (Chicago, 1957).

M. Yates and M. Gilchrist, *Administrative Reorganization of State Governments; A Bibliography* (Mimeo., Chicago, 1948).

4

STATE FUNCTIONS AND SERVICES

*Growing
list of
state
services*

Recalling for a moment the enormous array of national services and controls, we might well ask if there is anything left for the states to do. The answer is: a great deal. States have never been so active, spent so much money, or provided such comprehensive services as they do today. There is scarcely an aspect of our society untouched by the state. The states and their local government units are the primary protectors of life and property; they are deeply engaged in regulating and stimulating economic activities inside their boundaries; they provide the most extensive system of public education for their young people ever known; they succor, rehabilitate, and care for the sick, the poor, the handicapped, the veteran, the neglected, the criminal, the aged; they engage in many kinds of internal improvements including particularly the most complex and elaborate system of highways and airports in the world; they act to protect consumers, preserve resources, and manage elections. The list could be extended for several pages. More than two-thirds of the states' fiscal resources, however, are expended on three programs: public education; highway construction and maintenance; and public health and welfare.

PUBLIC EDUCATION

The greatest single public enterprise of the states and their local subdivisions is the provision of education to the youth of the nation. In the numbers of persons involved and, probably, in social consequences this is the greatest public effort at any level. It is topped in dollars spent only by the huge national defense effort of the nuclear age, the Cold War, and Viet Nam. In 1967, more than 43 million pupils attended public primary and secondary educational facilities; they were taught by more than 1.9 million teachers; and the expenditures on their behalf exceeded $22.4 billion.

From the earliest days of this nation the provision for free public education has been considered a cornerstone of the American way of life. Even before the adoption of our present Constitution, the Congress had required that public lands in the territories be set aside for the support of schools (Northwest Ordinance of 1787). Throughout our history, however, education has been regarded as a state rather than a national responsibility. Certainly, throughout the last century the national government was concerned only slightly and mainly at the college level. In the states the main burden of building, staffing, and managing the schools was carried for generations by the localities with the state governments concerned largely with providing a legal framework for the local discharge of these responsibilities. Administratively and financially the state involvement was modest. Largely to avoid partisan, political influences on the school system, separate units of local government—the school districts—have been the principal agencies for managing education. These districts—usually coterminous with some other local political unit—were operated by elected boards and were financed almost exclusively by levies on property.

Education a state and local responsibility

At the turn of the century the typical rural school district operated one school building with one teacher and offered instruction through 6 or occasionally 8 grades to 15–20 pupils. City school systems had already widely substituted the multiple-teacher platoon system or the grade and subject specialist system for the one teacher per school arrangement. The high school was also becoming increasingly common in the cities. About 17 million young people were enrolled in 1900 and the typical American youth might average 6–8 years of school at public expense.

The schools in 1900

As this century progressed the demand for educational services and opportunities grew rapidly. The high school became well-nigh universal, kindergartens and nursery schools reached preschool-aged children, vocational courses were developed on a large scale both inside and outside the regular school organization, recreational programs during and after school hours were begun, libraries in the schools and in the communities were established, evening classes for adults were started, efforts were made to reach out to the handicapped, the abnormal, and other categories of children unsuited to the normal classroom situation. By 1945, the school systems were reaching more than 23 million young people and more than 60 percent of those of high school age were actually in school. All of these developments added greatly to the costs of education and brought sharply into focus the remarkably unequal abilities of local school units to finance these programs from levies on local property. During this period, therefore, the state governments came to play an increasingly active role in financing and supervising the school program. State educational departments, heretofore largely hortatory in method and limited in function, were professionalized and given more active supervisory responsibilities. One state after another (1) established minimum standards of teacher training, curriculum coverage, and adequacy of physical facilities below which impecunious or incom-

Rapid expansion of educational programs

State responsibilities

petent local management might not sink; (2) brought to the aid of hard pressed local units fiscal resources gathered from a broader tax base; (3) developed public teacher training institutions to supply the growing need for competent teachers; (4) assumed full responsibility for special educational programs for handicapped, neglected or abnormal children; (5) expanded the coverage and stiffened the enforcement of compulsory school attendance laws; and (6) during the depression made numerous special grants to succor distressed districts and to aid school construction.

Impact of birth rate rise on schools

The last twenty-five years have seen greater demands on the school system than ever before. The rapid rise in the birth rate—from 18.4 per 1000 in 1936 to 27.0 per 1000 in 1947—launched a period of unprecedented growth in school enrollments. First the elementary schools were flooded; then the high schools; and now the colleges. Enrollments have been growing at the rate of almost 1 million a year for over a decade. The decline in the birth rate since the mid-fifties suggests that this growth phase is temporarily over. Second, the heavy migration of population from farm to city and from central city to suburb has left many old schools without pupils and brought together hundreds of thousands of children without adequate schools. Third, the continuation of early trends toward lengthening schooling has kept these new millions of youngsters in schools longer than their fathers. Fourth, the tremendous scientific and technological advances of the past few decades have sharply increased the need for competent instruction while many of the potential instructors have been lured into industry, government and institutions of higher learning by better pay and greater social recognition.

The upshot of all of this is that the states are more deeply involved—legislatively, financially, and administratively—in the provision of schooling from kindergarten through university than ever before. The major controversy today is the extent to which the national government, since it entered the field of public education finance in 1965, should exercise some control over the policies and practices.

School district reorganization

A major effort of modern educational statesmanship, despite the growing power and influence of the state governments and the nation, has been to strengthen the local district by vastly enlarging its size so that it might through a broad enough tax base and a large enough child population be able efficiently to provide an adequate educational program. The number of districts has declined from 127,000 in 1932 to 23,000 in 1967. A dozen states have made the county the smallest unit for school administration and Delaware has a statewide school unit. The number of one-teacher schools has fallen from 149 thousand in 1930 to fewer than 18,000. Nevertheless, many experts believe there is much yet to be done. They cite the 1,600 districts which operate no schools at all, the 17,000 districts with fewer than 50 pupils, and the continued sharp inequities in the burden of taxes required to support adequate programs. On the other hand some of the great metropolitan systems have become such giants that effective management is well-nigh out of the question and New York City, at least, prodded by the state is moving somewhat reluctantly to decentralize its operations. No doubt these developments have strengthened many local districts that have survived reorganization and consolidation. They have been achieved, however, largely by stern state control and by heavy commitments from the state treasury. Perhaps the most difficult and most important of the remaining problems of district organization is the small high school. Most experts believe that it is financially prohibitive and administratively wasteful to attempt to offer modern education in a school of fewer than 450–500 pupils. Nevertheless, of the 25,000 high schools in America only 4,000 are as large or larger. Almost one-third of the nation's high school pupils attend schools of inadequate size, and therefore, of inadequate depth or breadth of subject matter. The high school, however, is the center of the social life of many small communities; without one the possibilities of growth are thought to be small. The residents, therefore, tend to cling to these outworn facilities with desperate and bitter determination.

States heavy fiscal commitments

The major source of continuing and expanding state influence in American education is the growing reliance on the states' fiscal resources to finance it. In 1930, about 16 percent of the cost of public education through high school was provided from state tax funds and virtually all the rest from locally assessed taxes on property. Today (1968) 40 percent comes from state taxes, another 8 percent from the national government and only 52 percent from local sources. The major aim of state participation is, of course, to equalize educational opportunities by supplementing inadequate local means. However, the state appropriations are also widely used to encourage district consolidation, for example, by paying a large share of the costs of bus transportation essential to the enlargement of the pupil-service area. As has been true of the national grant-in-aid system, state grants have typically increased the regulatory and supervisory power of state departments of education. Typically, money is distributed to local districts on the basis of formulae established by law. These commonly take into account: (1) local ability to pay measured by the value of taxable property per pupil or per school unit; (2) the number of pupils in attendance or the number of teacher–pupil units; (3) the amount of tax actually levied. Compliance with certain minimal standards is usually required of units receiving state money. These may relate to number of days or hours of schooling, the qualification, pay, and tenure of teachers, the variety of the courses offered, and the characteristics of the physical plant. State subsidies are also used to stimulate the development of special services such as libraries, medical and dental services, vocational guidance and to finance school lunch programs, special services to handicapped children, and building planning.

The state legislature and education

The chief battleground in the development of state educational policy is the legislature. Here the whole pattern of state aids has been hammered out in countless long and difficult sessions. Virtually the whole code of laws governing the provision of public education has, of course, been enacted and revised by the legislature. All local school units are, legally, creatures of the state and their organization, management, powers, and functions are spelled out in the state law in considerable detail. Underlying the states' school program is in every state a compulsory school attendance law requiring, typically, young people from age 6–16 to be in regular attendance at some school and authorizing employment for youths 14 or over only under carefully regulated conditions. The movement for consolidation, the elimination of the one-room school, the attack on the small high schools, the demand for better paid and more broadly trained teachers, and many other struggles occur in the legislative halls of every state and at every session. Taxpayer groups, chambers of commerce, labor unions, and educational associations of every type may be found pressing their respective and differing views on state legislatures throughout the nation.

State educational administration

The administration of the states' growing educational commitments is entrusted everywhere to a department of education or instruction insulated in most cases from gubernatorial influence. In about half the states today and in nearly all of them a few decades ago the chief of this department (commissioner or superintendent) is or was elected by the voters for two or four years and in many cases on a nonpartisan ballot. In the past few years, however, a movement to replace popular election by selection by a state board of education has gained momentum and this is now the mode of selection in 23 states. All but a handful of states, now, associate a board of education with the chief educational officer. Typically these boards are appointed by the governor, although in some of the states the members are elected and in a few states are selected by the legislature. The state board commonly has broad policy-making functions and, in some cases, authority to utter detailed rules and regulations governing various aspects of school administration. However selected, the chief educational officer presides over a department with professional and clerical assistants and through them administers school aids, inspects facilities and curricula to enforce state standards, certifies as teachers properly qualified persons, collects and correlates statistical material on expenditures, teachers, attendance, and in other ways discharges state responsibilities.

Vocational education

The concentration of the early high schools on college preparatory courses not entirely suited to the 90 percent of the graduates who did not attend college, the demands for skilled workers caused by rapid technological advances, and the stimulus of national subsidy begun in 1917 combined to foster the development in every state of a more or less elaborate system of vocational education at the high school and post-high school level. In most states vocational programs and schools are managed at the local level through the regular school organization. At the state level, however, it is not uncommon to find vocational and adult education separately organized and financed. There may be, as in Wisconsin, a state board of vocational education with a subordinate director and staff administering state aids and exercising supervision or there may be separate bureaus or offices within the state department of education. Commonly there is a pattern of financing and a code of laws unique to the vocational system. Until quite recently, in fact, state supervision of vocational education was more detailed and more elaborate than that for the regular schools.

Virtually every state maintains a state library or libraries serving the *State library services* needs of lawyers, historians, legislators, and citizens at the capital and in many instances providing some statewide library services. A growing number of states—30 in 1967—now also provide financial aids to local public libraries. Usually these aids are based on population or area or both served by the library and involve some imposition of standards of library management. Congress, since 1956, has also been appropriating national grants to states for library services largely in the rural areas and this has stimulated greater state participation in the development of local library programs.

Every state now includes as part of its system of education one or *State colleges and universities* more institutions of higher learning supported in large measure by public funds. Although there were a few public colleges and universities—mainly in the Midwest—established prior to 1862, the famous Land Grant College (Morrill) Act of that year marks the beginning of the era of rapid growth of public colleges. This famous law set aside public lands for each state, the proceeds from the sale of which were to be used to endow and maintain at least one college in each state for the purpose of providing instruction particularly in agriculture and mechanical arts. A few states (Massachusetts, New York, New Jersey, and Pennsylvania) arranged for existing private institutions to carry out this purpose of the law but all the rest established or assigned to existing public institutions the responsibilities indicated. Thus grew our great American land-grant or public universities. In the Midwest, Plains, Far West, and South these are in most states the major institutions of higher learning. State legislatures subsequently matched many times over the national grants and the state universities and colleges gradually expanded to their present importance. To these, most states subsequently added normal schools for teacher training and these then grew into teachers colleges and finally into general colleges with diverse curricula. In recent years, as the demand for college education has grown, locally sponsored junior or community colleges have been added to the school system of several states. These, although locally managed, are, typically, heavily supported by state aids.

The famous G.I. Bill which sent veterans of World War II to college *Rise of college enrollments* at government expense coupled with the rising demand for more and more technical and professional training have in the postwar era started a trend toward college-going of surprising dimensions. Whereas in 1920 perhaps one high school graduate in ten went on to college, today more than 40 percent do so (six out of ten in California). This rise in the proportion of 18-year-olds seeking further education and the sharp upturn in the birth rate described above are flooding our colleges (public and private) and causing heavier and heavier demands upon state financial resources. Although originally it was hoped that the public institutions would be free to natives of the various states, the great pressure for adequate income has caused most states to impose higher and higher tuition charges on the public university student. The state schools have also, over the years, greatly expanded their research programs not only in the fields of agriculture and engineering but throughout the subject matter disciplines. Led by Wisconsin they have also undertaken wide programs of service to the citizens of the states bringing to farm, factory, union meeting hall, professional office, governmental headquarters, and private home the knowledge and technical competence developed on the various campuses. In this decade the national government has moved in with research contracts, fellowships, facilities grants, and dormitory loans to augment greatly the aids long provided to the colleges. The national treasury has thus become a growing source of support for the public—and private—institutions of the land.

Government of public colleges

Public institutions of higher learning are almost universally governed by lay boards of trustees appointed by the governor, elected by the voters, or, in a few cases, selected by the legislature. Usually there is one board for each institution but a few states (Oklahoma, New York, New Mexico, and Oregon, for example) have placed all or most of the institutions under a single governing body. These boards select the president, deans, and other administrative officers and through them direct the institution. In many states (Michigan and Minnesota are good examples) the government of the state university is provided for in the constitution and the institution occupies a position of administrative and fiscal autonomy somewhat different from the typical state department.

PUBLIC HEALTH AND WELFARE

The attack on communicable diseases

In the long struggle against contagion, plague, and infectious diseases, a struggle which has wiped out one after another of the death-dealing epidemics, the states and their local subdivisions have borne the major responsibilities. By the support of local hospitals, the administration of vaccination, the distribution of sera, the imposition of quarantine, the purification of water, the regulation of food handling, the administration of tests and check-ups and countless other procedures local officials have helped to eradicate the great scourges of the past. The states began to assume responsibilities for disease control in the last quarter of the nineteenth century. Massachusetts created the first state department of health in 1869 and within 50 years every state followed suit. State activities were early designed to supplement and strengthen the local programs by the distribution of aids, the imposition of standards, the stimulation of lagging areas, and by the financing of institutional care for certain illnesses, mainly tuberculosis and insanity. Although ceaseless vigilance and the maintenance of support for preventive inoculations are still essential, the major battle against contagion has been largely won in the United States. To be sure, some of the germ-caused diseases continue to resist efforts to suppress them. Tuberculosis continues to require state and local diagnostic programs and the maintenance of sanatoria. The death toll, however, has been gradually falling and many states find their facilities only half used. Venereal diseases also present continuing problems. After a sharp decline from 1937–1953 the incidence is once again on the rise. Rheumatic fever continues to take its toll but a major effort has yet to be made to deal with this crippler. The major health problems of modern Americans, however, are of a far different sort. The chronic and degenerative diseases are the great killers and cripplers of the mid-twentieth century.

As was noted in discussing the national health programs, cancer and heart and circulatory disorders are the leading causes of death today and chronic disabilities such as arthritis, mental illness, cerebral palsy, epilepsy, and muscular dystrophy are the main incapacitators. None of these responds to the methods used to fight germs. State programs, thus far, are largely educational and are designed to promote early diagnosis, better diet, and proper living habits. A few successes have been achieved, for example in the early detection of uterine cancer by the widespread administration of the Papanicolaou testing procedure. In general, however, major advances must await the discoveries by research scientists of causes and then perhaps of cures. Meanwhile, every state carries a heavy load of institutional care and relief grants for the poverty-stricken disabled.

The attack on degenerative diseases

Of all the chronic cripplers none presents the states with more baffling and more expensive responsibilities than mental illness. Every state maintains one or more institutions for the custody and treatment of the mentally disturbed and in New Jersey, Wisconsin, Iowa, and Michigan these are supplemented by county hospitals or asylums. On the average, more than 500,000 patients occupy these facilities at an annual cost of nearly $1 billion. For decades the major concern of the states was to protect and preserve family and community welfare by the removal and incarceration of those who were dangerous or unmanageable. The story of the long struggle to free these hapless sufferers from chains, strait jackets, rocking chairs, and cells, not to say the occasional brutality of their keepers has been well told. Staggering problems remain however. Despite the widespread provision for voluntary admission and the growing emphasis on prompt diagnosis and intensive treatment, far too many people come to the state hospitals only in advanced stages of mental breakdown when rehabilitation has become nearly hopeless. Every effort at accelerated and intensive treatment has been embarrassed by the very short supply of qualified psychiatrists and by the inability or unwillingness of the states to offer sufficiently attractive financial rewards. A growing number of senile persons (accompanying the lengthening life span of our people) for whose illness there is little hope, is filling the beds of the state institutions. Enormous obstacles remain to

Mental illness

recruiting and maintaining an adequate staff of nurses and attendants. There is still much to be learned about the types, causes, and pathologies of mental diseases. The modern state efforts, therefore, are directed to (1) formation of community clinics and local hospital programs aimed at early diagnosis and prompt treatment; (2) encouragement of specialized facilities for the senile, the emotionally disturbed child, the violent, and other categories; (3) development of more widespread public understanding of the nature and symptoms of mental breakdown; and (4) in collaboration with the national government, stimulation of research. Of course, many states have a long way to go to bring their institutions up to the level of those in the more progressive states.

Mental deficiency

The institutional care offered by the states also includes facilities for those who are born hopelessly, and, in the state of present knowledge, incurably defective. About 126,000 mentally retarded children are born every year. Modern practice is to encourage the early and lifelong institutionalization of those who are hopelessly defective rather than to leave them amidst family and community. The result of this and of the higher birth rate has been to throw an increasing load on the already hard-pressed facilities in most states. Also, the effectiveness of the antibiotics in curing germ diseases has kept these unfortunates alive longer. Most state institutions for the mentally defective or retarded provide training in simple laboring skills for those able to profit by it and are likely thus to send some into gainful employment.

The care of the aged

The rapid rise in the number of persons over 65 in our society has had far-reaching implications. Not the least of these is the increasing number of persons suffering from the degenerative ills of age and for whom until the enactment of Medicare public assistance or old age insurance payments were scarcely adequate to pay for protracted medical care. In most states, old age assistance payments for the medically indigent have continued to rise to help cover these costs and Congress has finally provided extensive medical cost coverage under the old age and survivors insurance programs. Many states also are introducing licensing, regulation, and inspection for the growing number of private nursing homes catering to these aging citizens. Colorado is experimenting in state-provided homes for the aged. Connecticut, New Jersey, New York, Massachusetts, and Minnesota are encouraging local construction of low rent housing projects designed particularly for the aged. A White House Conference on Aging held in 1961 sponsored by Congress encouraged the states to reconsider their programs to give priority to constructing special geriatric institutions, to encourage more community housing projects, to seek wider employment opportunities, to improve home-nursing services and, in other ways, to bring the best knowledge and experience to the aid of those in the sunset of life.

Health administration

The health department through which most of these programs are carried on is, in most states, headed by a director or health officer appointed by the governor. Usually a lay board of health is associated with the director for policy-making and in a dozen states this board appoints the health officer. In most states, these departments are woefully understaffed due, in part, to the acute shortage of qualified doctors, nurses, and technicians available for public employment. It is not uncommon for states to separate the administration of institutions, such as those for the mentally ill, from the educational and regulatory health functions and to provide a separate agency, board, or department for institutional management. Typically, state health programs are largely achieved through local health offices and departments, especially in the cities, and the state staff provides technical aid and assistance. In addition to the more costly programs already described, state health services commonly include (1) collection, analysis, and publication of vital statistics; (2) regulation and testing of public and private water supplies and administration of controls over pollution and sewage disposal; (3) inspection of food handling and food processing; (4) development and promulgation of regulations aimed at improving industrial hygiene and at alleviating disability arising from poisonous, noxious, or disease-causing industrial processes; (5) promoting better maternal and infant hygiene; (6) administration of national and state grants for hospital construction; (7) provision of laboratory diagnostic services to physicians and hospitals not serviced by local facilities; and (8) in a growing number of states, development of controls over air pollution.

Although illness or disability may be a big factor in producing poverty, improvements in the nation's health have not eliminated, as yet at least, the need for elaborate programs for the care of the needy. We have noted that beginning in 1935 the national government has played a major role in financing public assistance and that state–local responsibility has thus been greatly diminished from the days of the poorhouse and the soup kitchen. Nevertheless the principal burden of administration and a substantial part of the financing still falls upon the states and their local units. In general the determination of who is to receive aid and, within broad limits, the amount of aid each is to receive is determined by local welfare agencies through professionally trained social workers. The state welfare departments keep the books, prescribe standards, coordinate local efforts, and assist local units that cannot carry their part of the financing. Everywhere, under the present national–state–local arrangements, the states and the local units are jointly or separately wholly responsible for the relief of all those who cannot qualify for categorical assistance or whose payments under the national programs are inadequate to the exigencies of their situations. This "general relief" responsibility embraced in 1967, more than 660,000 persons. *Public assistance*

Despite the heavy emphasis in modern public assistance on cash grants to individuals, there remains a residue of "indoor" or institutional care provided, mainly by counties, to the unfortunate. County poorhouses, homes for the aged, and hospitals for the infirm continue to serve those *"Indoor relief"* who are unable to look after themselves in the community. Many states, in fact, are encouraging by aids or grants the expansion of county or city institutional facilities especially for the aged who require nursing care.

The care of offenders

It is not uncommon for states to include among the responsibilities of departments of public welfare, the incarceration and rehabilitation of offenders against the criminal laws of society. Some states, of course, organize this function separately in a department of correction. Modern penology is based on the idea that criminals are largely so because they are sick or poor or underprivileged and that correctional programs should place greater stress on treatment, education, and rehabilitation than upon discipline, isolation, and spiritual regeneration. For this reason many of the procedures and policies suited to care of the mentally ill, relief of the poverty stricken, and education of the neglected are, with appropriate modifications, the basis of correctional programs and are administered by agencies with these other responsibilities.

Developing role of the state

The role of the state in correctional administration has been a slowly developing one. Counties and cities had in the beginning the major responsibility for keeping in their jails or lockups those convicted of criminal offenses. Early in the nineteenth century, movements for prison reform swept through much of Europe, the British Isles, and the United States. The reformers demanded, among other things, that hardened or habitual offenders and those convicted of grave offenses be removed from local facilities where, mixed with those awaiting trial, witnesses, and minor offenders of all ages, they tended to spread their malevolent influence and to require costly security measures not suited or needed by the other occupants. States began to build penitentiaries where those guilty of felonies—as distinguished from misdemeanors—would be guarded and cared for at state expense. Later as studies revealed the desirability of further classification of offenders, states built and operated separate institutions for female offenders, for juveniles, and for those not really requiring maximum security incarceration. By the end of the century most of the states operated several correctional institutions. In many cases each was directed by a warden and a separate board of trustees.

State programs in this century

In this century, dissatisfaction with the results of penitentiary administration arose from (1) high rates of recidivism; (2) high costs of construction and management of maximum security programs; (3) continued high incidence of crime; and (4) the belief that, in some way as yet scarcely tried, a large number of criminals could be made socially useful citizens. Further classification of offenders was proposed and the supervision of a large portion of the prison population in medium and minimum security camps, farms, and training schools was widely adopted. Parole was introduced as a method for supervising the return of the offender to society, cushioning the shock of freedom, and restoring to useful labor those who should no longer be locked up. Under the same kind of extramural supervision by welfare agents, systems of probation were developed for those who might be harmed rather than helped by incarceration, provided, of course, the dangers to society from their freedom were minimal. Within the institutions greater and greater stress has been placed on vocational training, regular education for those who had not received much schooling on the outside, and physical and psychological therapy based on prompt and extensive physical and mental examinations. Working more and more with the courts, state correctional agents have sought more flexible sentencing—relating the sentence to the needs of the criminal rather than to the nature of the crime—more supervision before and after and even in lieu of incarceration.

No one is yet entirely satisfied with results. The states vary widely in the degree to which they have accepted and put into practice the theories of modern penologists. Although most of the newer programs such as probation and parole are considerably cheaper per offender than immuration in a maximum security penitentiary, the penitentiaries are still used and appropriations for correctional programs are everywhere rising. There are still not enough specialized minimum security installations in most states according to the experts and the case loads of parole and probation agents are usually excessive. Juvenile and sex offenders and narcotics addicts continue to present troubling problems. Putting prisoners at useful labor, especially manufacturing, has everywhere attracted the opposition of organized labor. Few states are able or willing to afford the kind of medical and psychiatric attention for prisoners that some experts demand. The century-long debate over the value of capital punishment continues almost unabated especially in the 42 states that have not abolished it.

HIGHWAY CONSTRUCTION AND MAINTENANCE

States as builders

Every state must, of course, provide itself with public buildings, a capitol, a state office building, university and other educational structures, hospitals, asylums, and what not. All have built airports; a few have constructed harbor works (as at San Francisco, New Orleans, and Mobile); and New York built, owned, and operated the Erie Canal. Dams and reservoirs have been constructed for flood control; and parks and forest preserves have been laid out and provided with suitable buildings and other facilities. By all odds the most important public works with which any state has to do, however, are highways. These are increasingly the life blood of the state economy, bringing food and fibers from farm to market and supporting village industry and merchandising everywhere. There is no more persistent drive for larger and larger state expenditures in any field of state service than that for wider, thicker, smoother highways.

Highways become a state concern

The record of highway construction, financing, and administration in this country is a story of progressive shifting of activities from smaller areas to larger ones, until finally the states came to occupy a predominant role.

Originally, roads were built and repaired wholly by towns, townships, villages, and cities. With the advent of the automobile and the resultant demand for paved roads linking up various mercantile and manufacturing centers, the county became involved. Finally, in the early nineties, Massachusetts and New Jersey led the way to substantial management by the state. Legislatures began giving financial aid to local highway authorities to be expended under state supervision and with the advice and assistance of state officials. Then they started taking over main roads, often to the great advantage of counties financially unable to provide the thoroughfares everywhere demanded by the modern motorist. With the advent of national subsidy in 1916, state authority was increased and systems of state trunk highways were established linked up by national influence into a system of interregional roads for the whole nation. Typically, however, no unit ever completely abandoned its interest in or control over some portion of the highways. Today we find township roads administered, frequently with state aid, by townships, village and city streets maintained by those units, county trunks, and state highways.

The highway situation today County and township roads still comprise some 75 percent (2.3 million miles) of the country's total highway mileage. The city motorist usually tries to avoid them, because only about two-thirds of this mileage has hard surfacing and most of this is gravel or crushed stone. Altogether they carry less than 15 percent of the nation's total traffic. As farm-to-market roads and as feeders to the state system, they, however, are indispensable. Farm-to-market roads are controlled in some states mainly by towns or townships, in others by counties; while roads of a little more importance, often described as "secondary" and linking up county seats and other such centers, usually are chiefly county-controlled. Heavily traveled main thoroughfares are everywhere parts of the state system and in many states most of the feeder roads are also. Thus (1) four—Delaware, Virginia, West Virginia, and North Carolina—have centralized the management and financing of *all* roads in the state government; (2) four New England states divide responsibility for farm-to-market and secondary roads between the state and the towns; (3) 27 states divide it between the state and the counties; and (4) the remaining states apportion it three ways: among state, counties, and towns or townships. In all cases in which local units function, funds come in considerable measure as aids from the state treasury. Primary roads, comprising the *state* system, constitute only a quarter of total mileage (520,000 miles), but link up the principal cities, usually are well paved, and carry 85 percent of the traffic. All primary and some secondary roads are heavily subsidized by the national government and are built and maintained in close cooperation with the supervising Federal Highway Administration in the Department of Transportation at Washington. Particularly significant is a trunk-line network of some 41,000 miles constituting a National Interstate Highway System planned during recent war and postwar years by state highway departments and the Federal Highway Administration, and linking up 42 of the 50 state capitals and indeed all but a few of the country's cities of over 50,000 population. On this system more than 70 percent of the current aids paid to states is being spent.

All states administer their highway programs through either a separate highway department or a highway division of a public works department, usually the former (by national requirement they must have one or the other if they are to qualify for grants-in-aid). In more than one-third of the number, the department head is a full-time, salaried highway commissioner or a director of highways; in the remainder, a part-time highway commission of from three to seven members, functions through a director. All are commonly appointed by the governor, although in some instances they are elected. In counties, highway functions sometimes are kept immediately in the hands of the county board or one of its committees but often are entrusted to an appointive or elective highway commissioner or supervisor. In New York, New Jersey, and Pennsylvania, and in 22 other states one or more state roads have been placed in the charge of a turnpike or toll road authority. The toll road authority is a popular device for constructing very expensive, multi-laned, grade-separated, limited access superhighways for through traffic and levying a special charge on that traffic for these unusual facilities. In this way, the state highway income is reserved for providing less adequate but more widely distributed highway service to the state motorists. The standards of construction on the new national interstate system are so closely parallel to those of the toll roads that it is doubtful if new roads in any numbers will hereafter be built by this procedure.

Adminis- trative arrange- ments

If the simple and rather straightforward description of state highway developments set forth in the previous paragraphs suggests that all is going smoothly in highway matters, such is far from the case. We now have almost 95 million motor vehicles registered in the United States traveling more than 900 million miles per year. In addition to the increasing rate of obsolescence of our highways which the rapid growth of vehicular traffic and the vastly increased driving speeds have brought about, there are 53,000 persons killed annually in auto accidents and perhaps 1 million seriously injured. By 1955, in fact the number of persons killed on our highways in this century surpassed the numbers killed in all the wars thus far fought by our soldiers. This terrible and continuing toll of life and limb has meant increased costs of insurance and increased costs of safety enforcement programs. A growing portion of our uniformed police forces, state, county, and municipal is assigned to regulating traffic and is not available for protection of persons and property against criminals. Then too there is the question of who should pay for the highways and streets and the relative contribution of each: the abutting property owner, the municipal resident, the passenger car operator, the trucker, the farmer, the merchant. In general, the abutting property owner in municipalities pays on the front-foot basis for original paving and for curbs and gutters. The property taxpayer pays for much of the cost of maintenance and reconstruction of most city streets, and some town roads. The state and national treasuries pay from gas tax or other taxes on autos or drivers for through streets connecting state trunks, state and many county trunks. Many experts feel that the trucking industry pays less than its share of the cost of the highways since trucks contribute most to serious maintenance and reconstruction costs. Urban residents feel that they get too small a share of highway user taxes in view of the fact that such a large part of the vehicular mileage is on city streets. The farmers feel that urban interests are the major beneficiaries of the state and national road systems. The railroad owners and workers, of course, argue that the highway program is subsidizing their demise. Finally, there are the troublesome questions of highway planning: which roads should be surfaced and when; what kinds of surfacing should be used; what controls should be exercised over the development of signs, taverns, and other commercial enterprises along the roads?

PROMOTION AND REGULATION OF PRIMARY ECONOMIC INTERESTS

Business

Basis of state control

By virtue of its police power, a state is entitled to regulate all business activities within its borders except those instituted by the national government or those involving transactions in foreign or interstate commerce. A good while ago, the courts developed a category of businesses, including public utilities, banks, and insurance companies, regarded as of particular concern to the public, and hence specially "affected with a public interest." These have been held to require more intensive regulation than business in general. Few forms of business, however, are not now of concern to the public in one way or another. While the "public interest" concept has by no means been discarded, the present tendency is to look upon all businesses as subject to whatever regulation may be required for protecting public health, safety, morals, and welfare—so long as there is no deprivation of life, liberty, or property without due process of law, or denial of equal protection of the laws.

Corporations: 1. Status

Many people engage in business (usually on a modest scale) requiring no government authorization. Most medium-sized and larger businesses, however, are carried on by partnerships or corporations fully subject to state control. The formation and dissolution of partnerships and the rights and liabilities of partners are amply covered by state law. A corporation cannot operate, or even exist, without a charter issued by a government. Certain corporations, for example, national banks, are chartered by Congress but the overwhelming majority of business corporations are chartered by the states. Originally, corporations were chartered individually by special legislative act. From this, however, arose so much favoritism and corruption that even before the Civil War most states substituted a general corporation statute under which any responsible group of persons desiring to incorporate may do so by meeting prescribed conditions and applying to the proper administrative authority, usually the secretary of state. Today nearly all state constitutions either forbid incorporation by special act or severely restrict it. A corporation chartered in one state may do business in other states, but only as a "foreign corporation" subject not only to the same regulations as "home" corporations, but also to any special requirements that may be imposed upon it or its class.

With charters easy to obtain and operation under them commonly advantageous, the corporate method of doing business has become general. The most comprehensive regulation of the business community as a whole arises in most states, thus, in connection with the initial granting of corporate charters. Certain types of business operations, however, have been selected for special attention by state legislatures. Among these are financial institutions (banks, savings and loan companies, insurance companies), utilities, stock brokers, milk distributors, and manufacturers. Certain practices of the business community have also been subjected to regulation, for example, monopolistic price fixing. *2. Regulation*

Early in the history of corporate enterprise, concern was stirred by the rise of business combinations prone to squeeze or drive out competitors, control prices, and indulge in other monopolistic practices. Much legislation aimed at curbing "trusts" was enacted. With business, however, taking on an increasingly interstate aspect, the problem outgrew the capacities of the states; and in 1890 the Sherman Antitrust Act started a long but even yet by no means wholly effective program of national action. Virtually all the states, however, still have copious antitrust laws (applicable, of course, only to strictly intrastate situations and actions) and codes of fair business practices similar, within their spheres, to the national laws enforced by the Federal Trade Commission. As on the national level, enforcement is, typically, left to the attorney general who has neither the means nor time to do much. A few states have launched successful suits against undertaking combines, gasoline dealers, milk distributors, and other local enterprises. On the whole, the state record in this field is, if anything, less successful than that of the national government. Furthermore, in recent years several states have partially reversed the traditional concepts of competitive enterprise and have authorized price-fixing agreements of certain types between manufacturers and dealers. These acts have been underwritten by a national law of 1937 (amended in 1952) authorizing such price agreements wherever state laws support them. All but a handful of states have enacted these Fair Trade Acts, but the highest state courts in 21 states have declared all or part of such laws unconstitutional. The fair trade program is, therefore, in decline. *Antimonopoly regulations*

Two commercial banking systems exist side by side in the United States—national and state. National banks, of course, are chartered and

Regulation of financial institutions

regulated by the national government, but state banks by the several states. State control, within its field, extends to bank organization and management, capital stock, liabilities of stockholders and directors, assets and investments, loans, reserves, other forms of protection for depositors and customers, and arrangements for periodic inspection of records and accounts by representatives of the state banking department or other designated agency. Trust companies, building and loan associations, and similar financial institutions are regulated in the same general manner. Any bank or other such concern becoming insolvent or otherwise embarrassed may be taken over by state authorities and operated until it can either be put on its feet or liquidated. Most state banks are, however, members of the federal reserve system and this brings them under the scrutiny of the Federal Reserve Board and all savings institutions are members of and inspected by the Federal Deposit Insurance Corporation. A large amount of needless duplication of examining of banks and savings institutions is avoided in many states only by administrative arrangements among the national and state examiners. Small loan companies and pawnbrokers continue to be regulated, more or less effectively, by the states alone.

Every state also regulates all forms of insurance, with a view to protecting the public against exorbitant rates, requiring companies to honor valid claims for insured losses, and, in the case of life insurance, maintaining the security of invested savings. General laws prescribe the conditions which a corporation must meet in order to engage in insurance business in the state. Usually each company and all of its agents must be licensed by an insurance department or other authority; detailed regulations cover forms of policies, reasonableness of rates, types of securities in which funds may be invested, and volume of reserves that must be held for covering policies as they become payable; and full provision always is made for periodic reports and for official inspections as in the case of banks. As pointed out earlier, the Supreme Court, in 1944, reversed an earlier ruling by holding that insurance is interstate commerce. While this opened a way for national regulation under the commerce clause, Congress has thus far been content to leave the matter to the states. Many states in late years have been strengthening their regulatory statutes in the hope of staving off such intervention. A few states, such as Wisconsin, have actually entered the business of providing some types of insurance in competition with private companies. In recent years also a few states, led by New York, have expanded the scope of their state insurance agencies to embrace inspection of labor-union welfare and pension funds.

Regulation of public utilities

The most stringent, steady, and effective state regulation is reserved for public utilities—businesses which although as a rule owned and operated by private persons and concerns, are preeminently "affected with a public interest," enjoy special privileges (such as the use of streets and highways and the right of eminent domain), and either are or tend to become "natural monopolies." Included are all public transportation facilities such as railroads, street railways, air transport, bus and cab lines, and all enterprises providing electric light and power, water, gas, and telephone and telegraph services. All of these are subject to state (and in varying degrees also local) control, except that the interstate aspects fall within the jurisdiction of the Interstate Commerce Commission, the Federal Communications Commission, and the Federal Power Commission. State regulation, under a multitude of laws, and in every state except Delaware through a public utilities commission (or its equivalent), touches such matters as permits and franchises, financial structures, securities issues, accounting and reporting, quality of services, rates, and general safety and convenience for the public. Since 1900, too, the basis of action has largely shifted from municipal franchise regulation under the contract power to direct state regulation under the police power.

All of the states' interests in the business community are not repressive and regulatory. Many states spend generously to promote industrial development within their boundaries. Departments of Commerce, Bureaus of Industrial Development, Planning and Development Commissions have been springing up all over the nation in the past two decades and each of them is dedicated to attracting more industry and to facilitating expansion of the industry already established. The resort business is the only business, apart from those identified with agriculture, that has been selected for special support through state advertising in many states. *Promotion of business*

Labor

For many years regulatory legislation to protect factory workers from the abuses of industrialization was left almost entirely to the states. But as the national economy continued expanding, with more and more employment connected in some way with interstate and foreign commerce, inadequacies of state control stimulated national activity. As shown in an earlier chapter, labor legislation and the enforcement of labor regulations have developed, especially since 1933, into one of the principal functional sectors of our national government. Even yet, nevertheless, millions of workers produce only for intrastate commerce, and accordingly, as workers, are subject only, or at least primarily, to state authority. Half a dozen ways in which states meet their obligations may be mentioned.

Springing in part from pressures exerted by organized labor, in part from voluntary legislative recognition of the obligation to promote general well-being, laws protecting health and safety of workers—in some instances dating back 60 or 70 years—have multiplied on state statute books. Aimed especially at health are, for example, laws restricting the hours of continuous work for women in industries, stores, and hotels, forbidding employment of women in mines, regulating the labor of children not covered by the national Fair Labor Standards Act, requiring proper heating, lighting, and ventilation and the removal of dust and noxious fumes in factories, *1. Health and safety* and fixing standards of sanitation. Directed at safety are measures designed to avert or mitigate the effects of industrial accidents and diseases by requiring safeguards for dangerous machinery, exits, fire escapes, equipment of street cars and local trains with safety appliances, and by providing for the safety of laborers on buildings, bridges, and other public works, together with periodic inspection of factories, workshops, and mines. Laws in this comprehensive category often are necessarily rather broad and general, with appropriate administrative authorities, usually commissioners, left to prescribe more detailed rules and regulations. Undoubtedly the frequency and severity of industrial accidents have been reduced by these state efforts.

2. Work-men's compen-sation   Closely related to safety and health regulations are the elaborate systems of workmen's compensation insurance established by the states. Occupational accidents are, by these programs now treated as a proper charge upon industry. Some of the systems are compulsory and some optional; some apply to all accidents of the kind and others only to those in the more hazardous occupations. Most grant compensation for some or all occupational diseases. Employers in every state are required to procure insurance either from the state or from private firms providing coverage for their employees in case of on-the-job accidents. State agencies of various types closely supervise the program to assure prompt and adequate recompense to the injured worker. Coverage, however, is almost everywhere confined to manufacturing. Construction, transportation and agricultural workers are frequently not protected. Benefit schedules also have hardly kept pace with postwar inflation. With the related problem of sickness among wage-earners, little has been done, although New York is pioneering in the development of a state program of insurance for nonoccupational illness. Since Congress passed the Vocational Rehabilitation Act of 1920, state and national governments have cooperated in restoring to self-supporting capacity persons who have been disabled in industry, or in any legitimate occupation, or by disease; and thousands have been refitted to earn a livelihood.

3. Labor standards and relations   Much of the early effort of several progressive states in establishing by law standards of employment, including maximum hours, minimum wages, and special protection and prohibitions for working women and children, has now been overshadowed by the national effort in these fields. The national laws, however, still leave a numerous working population over whom the states may and do claim jurisdiction. Most states, therefore, have some kind of regulating agency in these fields. The touchy and controversial field of labor–management relations is also characterized by state activity. Most of the states which have enacted labor relations laws have done so in the past 15 years and most of their laws follow rather closely the National Labor Management (Taft–Hartley) Act of 1947 rather than the earlier act of 1935. They impose restrictions on unions as well as on employers. A growing stream of state legislation in the past decade has been directed against the practices of labor unions and their leaders. Much of it is aimed at the closed or union shops, boycotting, jurisdictional disputes, and work stoppages in public utilities. So-called right-to-work laws aimed at the closed or union shop have been passed by several states in recent years. The jurisdiction of state labor–management agencies is not yet completely settled but on any definition of national power, some workers and employers are under control of the state. The Eisenhower Administration attempted with some success to narrow the national activities in the field and to allow state agencies to operate in borderline cases.

Little more need to be said here of the elaborate state programs of public employment service and unemployment compensation which have been established under national supervision in the past two decades. *4. Unemployment compensation*

A number of state legislatures have declared discrimination against Negroes and other minority groups in matters of employment to be contrary to public policy. A few states have also provided educational agencies and conciliatory procedures to achieve this policy, for example, Colorado, Indiana, Kansas, and Wisconsin. Since World War II four (those of New York and New Jersey in 1945, Massachusetts in 1946, and Connecticut in 1947) have gone even farther by enacting penal statutes forbidding any employer of more than six persons (five in Connecticut) to refuse to hire any applicant, or to discharge or discriminate against any employe, because of race, creed, color, or national origin, and also forbidding labor unions to exclude, expel, or discriminate against any person for such reasons. New Mexico, Oregon, Rhode Island, and Washington more recently have enacted compulsory laws of this type. In the first two and one-half years of New York's experience, the Fair-Employment–Practices Commission set up for purposes of enforcement was able to dispose of over 1,000 complaints received without resorting in a single instance to criminal proceedings, or even to formal hearings. *5. Fair employment practices*

Agriculture and Conservation

Agriculture and natural resources are important in the economy of every state and, in most instances, basic. Furthermore, the rural members dominate a large number of state legislatures. Every state, therefore, has an active and well-supported program of benevolent aid to farmers and farming. Ample constitutional authority is supplied both by the police power and by the power to levy taxes and spend money for general-welfare purposes.

Every state maintains an agricultural college and in connection therewith an agricultural experiment station and an agricultural extension service. In these institutions scientific studies are carried on relating to soils and fertilizers, land use, the breeding and care of plants and livestock, agricultural marketing, and indeed every resource, operation, and activity of concern to the farmer. Bracketed with research also is education in the form *1. Research and education* not only of agricultural training at the college level in classrooms and laboratories, but wide circulation of bulletins and reports, extension courses bringing new ideas to people on the farm, and counseling and demonstration work carried on by county agricultural agents and (for the benefit of the farmer's wife) home demonstration agents as well. All of this, as we have observed, is supported in part by national subsidy.

2. Suppression of diseases and pests

Aside from bad weather and adverse marketing conditions, the principal agricultural hazard is a legion of plant and animal diseases and pests— boll-weevil, corn borer, Mexican fruit fly, Japanese beetle, and other insects in the case of plants; hoof-and-mouth disease, hog cholera, brucellosis, bovine tuberculosis, and the like, in animals. In every state, means of eradicating or curbing the ravages of these scourges are objects of study; and inspections, quarantines, and other controls are provided both through legislation and by administrative action. Weed eradication receives attention also; and in sparsely-settled western areas, protection of flocks and herds against predatory animals.

3. Marketing

Because so largely interstate, agricultural marketing falls mainly within national jurisdiction. Room remains, however, for state (1) regulation of the grading, packaging, and labeling of products, (2) control of marketing through commission merchants, (3) encouragement of farm cooperatives (for buying as well as selling and shipping), (4) assistance to state and local agricultural fairs, and (5) countrywide advertising of the state's products—the citrus fruits of Florida, the dairy products of Wisconsin, the wines of California, Washington apples, and Idaho potatoes.

4. Conservation

Closely related to promotion of agriculture is the mapping, development, and conservation of natural resources. On the legal theory that wildlife is owned by the state and held in trust for the people, virtually every state licenses and otherwise controls hunting and fishing, and also carries on propagation activities at game farms and fish hatcheries. Forest lands are protected against fire; private owners are encouraged and aided in forest development, in some states by forest crop laws deferring taxation of growing timber; three-fourths of the states maintain state forests; and others (notably Wisconsin) develop and protect county or other local forests for both conservational and recreational purposes. For 50 years, states having important oil and gas resources have combatted waste, first with regulations designed to prevent unchecked flow and to control the spacing of wells. More recently also, and chiefly, in the case of oil, with production quotas fixed and enforced by some administrative agency and operated in a large group of states in accordance with a significant interstate compact on the subject. Of particularly wide concern, too, is soil conservation, carried on in conjunction with the national government in soil conservation districts, established in the several states under supervision in each case of a state soil conservation committee and operated by district boards of supervisors or directors in part locally chosen.

REFERENCES

General

C. H. Chatters, *An Inventory of Government Activities in the United States* (Chicago, 1947).

Council of State Governments, *The Book of States, 1968–1969* (Chicago, 1968) pp. 303–546.

————, *State–Local Relations* (Chicago, 1946).

————, *State Government* (Chicago), published quarterly since 1958 and abounding in articles on topics dealt with in the foregoing chapter.

————, *State Government News* (Chicago), published monthly since 1959.

Particular Functions

F. F. Beach and A. H. Gibbs, *Functions of State Department of Education* (Washington, D.C., 1950).

————, *The Structure of State Departments of Education* (Washington, D.C., 1949).

F. F. Beach and R. F. Will, *The State and Education: The Structure and Control of Public Education at the State Level* (Washington, D. C., 1958).

Committee for Economic Development, *Modernizing the Nation's Highways* (New York, 1956).

Council of State Governments, *The Forty-eight State School Systems* (Chicago, 1949).

————, *Higher Education in the Forty-eight States* (Chicago, 1952).

————, *The Mental Health Programs of the Forty-eight States* (Chicago, 1950).

A. Deutsch, *The Shame of the States* (New York, 1949).

D. K. Freudenthal, *State Aid to Local School Systems* (Berkeley, Calif., 1949).

C. D. Hutchins and L. C. During, *Financing School Facilities* (Washington, D. C., 1958).

C. C. Killingsworth, *State Labor Relations Acts* (Chicago, 1948).

J. Labatut and W. J. Lane (eds.), *Highways* (Princeton, N. J., 1950).

L. Manning and N. Diamond, *State Child Labor Standards* (Washington, D. C., 1949).

N. A. Masters, R. H. Salisbury, and T. H. Elliot, *State Politics and the Public Schools* (New York, 1964).

A. P. Miles, *An Introduction to Public Welfare* (Boston, 1949).

R. L. Moran, *Intergovernmental Relations in Education* (Minneapolis, 1950).

Russell Sage Foundation, *Social Work Year Book* (New York), published biennially.

W. G. Smillie, *Public Health Administration in the United States* (3rd ed., New York, 1947).

H. M. and A. R. Somers, *Workmen's Compensation: Prevention, Insurance, and Rehabilitation of Occupational Disability* (New York, 1954).

L. M. Thurston and W. H. Roe, *State School Administration* (New York, 1957).

H. H. Trachsel, *Public Utility Regulation* (Chicago, 1947).

U.S. Department of Labor, *Growth of Labor Law in the United States* (Washington, D. C., 1962).

C. R. White, *Administration of Public Welfare* (2nd ed., New York, 1950).

5

FINANCING STATE GOVERNMENT

All of the services, regulatory programs, and administrative organizations described in the last chapter cost money. Each passing year, in fact, they seem to cost more than they did the year before. Rare indeed is the state legislature which is not bedeviled every session by financial problems of the most difficult kind. With the public demanding more and more services, the growing resistance to tax increases, the heavy exactions of the national government on the one hand and the urgent pleas for aid from the local governments on the other, to maintain the solvency of state government requires the highest caliber of statesmanship. Given these exigencies of modern life, the miracle is that many states are as well off as they are. It is not at all surprising that some are in desperate straits.

The states are not in as strong a position to cope with this situation as might be imagined. Constitutionally, it is true, the federal system permits them a great deal of leeway. Under their reserved powers, they can tax almost anything except national property and income from national securities, spend at least as freely as the national government, and borrow at will. Practically, however, there are limitations. From considerations of prudence, most states have tied their own hands with constitutional provisions severely restricting state borrowing, or even in some instances forbidding it altogether. Nearly everything of importance, except general property, which states undertake to tax—incomes, inheritances, gifts, motor fuel, liquor, tobacco, and what not—is already taxed heavily by the national government. At best the states can merely share in the overall proceeds. Urgently needing more tax revenue, all have watched the national government steadily moving in on them with tax programs and rates siphoning off most of what the people believe they can afford to pay for government's support. In the foreseeable future no more favorable situation can be envisaged. National activities and commitments are not likely to diminish; national pressures for tax money will hardly abate. In terms of expendable funds, the balance may be, and to considerable extent already is, redressed by

Limitations on state independence

Growth of State Expenditures
Selected Years, 1902–1966

FUNCTION	TOTAL EXPENDITURE (MILLIONS)					
	1902	1932	1942	1952	1960*	1966*
Payment to local governments	$ 52	$ 801	$1,780	$ 5,044	$ 7,521	$14,784
Education	17	278	391	1,494	3,557	7,553
Highways	4	843	790	2,556	6,070	8,624
Welfare	10	74	523	1,410	3,704	3,138
Health and hospitals	32	215	299	1,132	2,072	3,241
Police	—	15	40	106	251	390
Natural resources	9	119	159	539	862	1,567
General government	23	114	164	361	663	1,037
Interest on debt	10	114	122	144	536	1,894
Veterans' services	—	—	1	142	112	21
Employment security	—	—	59	177	313	500
Correction	14	87	80	223	433	691
Other	15	106	141	369	1,133	3,557
Liquor stores	2	—	288	723	907	1,081
Insurance trust (retirement and unemployment compensation)	—	63	505	1,413	3,461	3,952
TOTAL	$188	$2,829	$5,342	$15,833	$31,595	$52,030

SOURCE: Bureau of the Census, *Historical Statistics on State and Local Government Finances*, 1902–1953 (Washington, D.C., 1955); and Bureau of the Census, *Summary of State Government Finances in 1960* (Washington, D.C., 1961), and Council of State Governments, *Book of the States 1968–1969* (Chicago, 1968), pp. 174, 175.
*Includes Hawaii and Alaska.

Growth and pattern of state expenditures

multiplied and augmented national subsidies. But grants-in-aid are supported by tax money which the states otherwise might raise for themselves; they certainly do not contribute to state and local financial independence. More than one leading student of intergovernmental relations is urging that current trends be reversed by giving state and local governments exclusive access to more tax sources, for example, motor fuels; others recommend that the states share in national income tax proceeds, and by these methods discourage the habit of depending on the national treasury. The table indicates better than words what is happening to the costs of state government in this century. To be sure, post-World War II inflation caused a sharp upturn in expenditures without proportionate increases in the services rendered. It should be observed also that grants from the national treasury make up an increasing part of the income supporting the outlays listed. Many of the payments to local units, for example, are simply passed through the state treasuries on their way from Washington to city hall and county courthouse.

Earlier appropriation methods

METHODS OF APPROPRIATION—BUDGET SYSTEMS

One factor that has added immeasurably to the burden of state legislatures in dealing with their fiscal problems has been the pitiful inadequacies of state budget and appropriation methods. Prior to about 1913, it was impossible in virtually every state either to make comprehensive plans for the distribution of public revenues among the state's direct activities and state-aided local enterprises or to control, in any strict and effective way, the use of state money or property. With demands often pouring in from 100 or more state agencies and institutions, and with no method of balancing claims upon the treasury against one another, and of distributing appropriations on the basis of a full consideration of the state's requirements, unseemly scrambles for funds invariably took place whenever the legislature came into session. The departmental and institutional estimates were either merely "compiled" by some officer, such as the treasurer or auditor, and transmitted by him to the legislature, or presented directly and independently to the appropriations committees by heads of departments and institutions themselves. No administrative officer acquainted with the entire business of the state reviewed such estimates, compared them, cut them down to actual necessities, measured them against estimated revenues, and laid before the legislature a carefully prepared financial program. Furthermore, every member of the legislature was at liberty to introduce as many bills as he chose carrying charges upon the treasury. When the legislature adjourned, no one pretended to know, even approximately, how much money had been appropriated.

Meanwhile, without any knowledge of what the total of authorized expenditures for the next fiscal period would be when the governor had finished vetoing bills and items, the legislature would pass revenue bills prepared by separate committees with little or no relation to the work of the committees in charge of appropriations. Neither the governor nor the legislature could be held to a proper degree of accountability by the citizens of the state who had to foot the bills.

Relief from these conditions became imperative as the cost of government mounted. It has been found, in greater or lesser degree, in plans of budgetary procedure introduced by statute, or in a few instances by constitutional amendment, in all of the states after Wisconsin and California set the example in 1911—ten years before a budget system was adopted for the national government. *Adoption of budget systems*

The states have adopted a wide variety of budget systems differing in detail and in fundamentals. Most important among points of variation is the budget-making agency—in other words, the location of responsibility for formulating the budget or program of expenditures in relation to anticipated revenues. On this basis, the systems fall into three fairly distinct classes. (1) In Arkansas, the budget is legislative, prepared and submitted to the legislature by the Legislative Council. In recent years, however, the Council has been assisted by a budget division in a recently created Department of Finance and Administration. California and Texas have established legislative budget agencies in recent years which serve the legislature only. Formally, however, the budget in both states is prepared by the governor. *Various state budget systems*

(2) Five states have budgetary boards or commissions, consisting usually of the governor and one or two other executive officers and a few members of the legislature, or made up solely of the principal executive officers. (3) The remaining states have what is called the executive type of budget. In some of these, the governor is made directly responsible for formulating the program of state expenditures; in the others, budget-making is in the hands of a comptroller, a budget director, a budget bureau, or some other official or agency whose work is performed, at least nominally, under the governor's supervision. Concentrating responsibility in the executive officer best situated to be informed on the financial needs of all branches of the state government, the executive type is generally regarded as best.

Some states have budget systems which concentrate power in the executive to a greater degree even than that of the national government. In New York, Maryland, West Virginia, and Nevada, for example, the legislature may reduce or strike out any item in the budget, but may not (with slight exceptions) increase any amounts requested or insert new items. Elsewhere, however, amounts may be increased and new items inserted.

Essentials of a sound budget system

Some of the requisites of a sound budget system for a state—many of them still lacking in some states—are that (1) each department, office, or institution should be required to submit to a central budget-making agency, two or three months before the legislature meets, an estimate of its financial needs for the ensuing fiscal period, upon uniform sheets having items arranged in accordance with some uniform system of classification; (2) the central budget-making agency under the supervision of the governor should then make a careful review, revision, and compilation of the estimates submitted; and to aid in this work, it should be given a staff to conduct investigations and make reports; (3) at some time within the first few days of the legislative session, this budget-making agency should submit a complete budget, that is, a comprehensive program of recommended expenditures and estimated revenues, and accompanied by a balance sheet, a debt statement, and a statement of the financial condition of the state for each year covered by the budget; (4) all appropriations should be consolidated in a single appropriation bill; (5) as far as possible the budget should state the services or programs to be financed by the proposed expenditures; (6) the legislative committees should forthwith proceed to a consideration of the budget proposals, and should report their appropriation bills in ample time to allow full debate, criticism, and amendment, so that the bills may be passed well before the close of the session; (7) no supplementary or special appropriation measures should be enacted until after the final passage of the budget bills. Even if made effective on all of these lines, a state budget system would not serve all of its purposes unless accompanied by such ancillary reforms as (1) concentration of the handling of all appropriation measures in a joint committee of the two houses; and (2) a grant to the governor (where he does not already have it) of the power to veto items.

SOURCES OF STATE REVENUE

Over the years there has been a decided change in the tax and revenue program of the states. We have already noted how national grants-in-aid have multiplied in the twentieth century to the point where state expenditure programs are heavily dependent upon the national treasury. These subsidies today constitute the largest single source of state income. This fact alone is a compelling cause of the continuance of the grant-in-aid program at a high level. A second striking change in the state revenue picture has been the gradual abandonment by the states of the property tax as a source of income. As recently as 1902 the general property tax produced more than half of the tax revenues of the states and throughout most of the nineteenth century it was almost the sole revenue source. Virtually all of the states have, however, in this century relinquished this revenue source to their local units. It now yields less than 10 percent of the states' total income. There has been an increase in this century also in the receipts from state-operated enterprises, the most important of these being (1) the liquor stores operated by several states after repeal of the prohibition amendment; (2) the turn-

Composite Pattern of State Income
All States
1966

SOURCE	AMOUNT IN MILLIONS
Taxes	
General sales	$ 7,873
Motor fuels	4,627
Liquor and beer	985
Tobacco	1,542
Other sales and gross receipts	2,015
Motor vehicle licenses	2,236
Liquor licenses	135
Corporation—miscellaneous licenses	1,125
Individual income	4,303
Corporate income	2,038
Property	833
Death and gift	808
Severance	545
Miscellaneous taxes	323
Payments from other governments	
National	11,743
Local	503
Receipts from state services and enterprises	6,492
Payments for insurance and trust funds	7,128
Borrowing	3,724
	$58,978

SOURCE: Council of State Governments, *Book of the States, 1968–1969* (Chicago, 1968), pp. 174–175.

pike and toll road authorities; and (3) the sale of power in a few states. The automobile and the elaborate highway programs accompanying its introduction have drastically altered state tax practice. Since 1920, the gasoline tax and motor license fees have become one of the largest sources of state receipts. New Hampshire in 1963 inaugurated a new source of state income which may start a new trend in state financing: It established a state sweepstakes lottery with tickets sold through state liquor stores and at the two state-regulated racing tracks. New York followed suit in 1967 with a lottery system not related to racing and utilizing banks as sales agents.

THE GENERAL PROPERTY TAX

Nature and basis   Although the property tax is no longer an important source of state income, nevertheless many states continue to concern themselves in its administration and to seek methods of overcoming its limitations. It remains, furthermore, the very heart of local government financing. Looking at the tax program of the United States as a whole it is one of the two or three most important supports of our governmental system.

In its broadest meaning, the general property tax is a tax on the estimated exchange value of property, levied at a common rate for all property in the same taxing area. It is thus universal and uniform; it is imposed on the property where it is located; and it is paid by the owner. Taking, of course, a multitude of forms, property nevertheless falls broadly into two categories: (1) real estate, consisting of land, buildings, and permanent fixtures, and (2) personal property. The one is immovable, the other movable. Personal property, in turn, may be either tangible, for example, livestock, grain, merchandise, household furniture, machinery, and automobiles, or intangible, as stocks, bonds, promissory notes, mortgages, and bank deposits. Where the general property tax is really general, these distinctions are, at least in theory, of no great significance; all property of equal value is supposed to pay the same tax regardless of classification. In the majority of states, however, some categories of property are set apart for special (usually lower) rates of taxation, or indeed are exempted altogether; so that the term *general property tax* must often be taken in an approximate rather than a strictly literal sense.

The tax calendar   Although numerous, complicated, and varying somewhat from state to state, the stages or steps involved in administering the property tax—the *tax calendar* of which the experts speak—may be summarized as follows. (1) First comes the tax levy, the competent authority (usually the legislative body) of each unit of government, including the state itself where sharing in the proceeds, determines the amount of revenue that must be raised from this source and then imposes it as the year's tax burden, so to speak, on the property concerned. (2) The property is valued by local (county, township, or city) assessors in order to determine the valuation on which the owners' tax obligations shall be computed. Personal property is assessed annually, real estate also annually in about half of the states, but in other states at longer intervals ranging from two to four years; and all assessments are supposed to indicate value on a certain day. (3) Valuations determined by local assessors are far from uniform, and property-owners often raise objections. Hence a third step involves inspection of the assessments, with adjustment of inequalities and injustices, by a county, city, or township board of review.

(4) A fourth step is central assessment or equalization. Along with the locality, the county, and in many instances the state, makes a property-tax levy. Each taxing jurisdiction might, of course, set up its own separate assessment machinery. But this would involve expensive duplication, and what happens is that each takes the locally made assessments as a starting point and on the basis of them makes such equalizations and other adjustments as boards of equalization employed for the purpose may decide upon. Sometimes the work is performed on the state level by a board of equalization consisting of certain elective state officers serving ex officiis, but often it is in the hands of a specially appointed body known as the tax commission. This commission is likely to have the important functions of (*a*) issuing instructions to assessors and other tax officials regarding the proper performance of their duties, including methods of procedure, accounting, and recording, and (*b*) making the original assessments of certain kinds of property which are difficult to assess locally, especially railroads, telegraph and telephone systems, express and sleeping-car services, and other public utilities. Incidentally, it would, of course, be possible to let the state do *all* of the assessing; and this would make for considerably greater uniformity than even assiduous equalization authorities can hope to achieve. Local assessors, however, are supposed to have the advantage of familiarity with local property; and, although yielding grudgingly on many other forms of centralization, local jealousy of state authority has been at this point difficult to break down. (5) Once the results of assessment and equalization, the state over, are known, taxes can be apportioned and rates determined. In the city, township, or other local assessment district, the clerk or other proper official has only to figure out how many cents on the dollar, or dollars on the hundred, will be necessary to produce the revenue required locally. From the county will come similar information for purposes of county revenue, and finally also from the state for its purposes, except, of course, where the state no longer shares in the proceeds of the tax. Adding to the local rate the rates certified to him by the overlying units, the local official arrives at the total tax rate; and tax bills are made out and sent to property-owners accordingly.

Completing the tax calendar are three further stages which for present purposes require only to be mentioned: (6) collection of the taxes as levied, commonly by a local collector or treasurer, who forwards the county and state shares to the proper officials; (7) efforts to collect taxes that become delinquent; and (8) appeals from dissatisfied taxpayers or tax districts, first to the state tax commission, and afterwards, if desired, to the courts.

Advantages of the tax

For 150 years, the general property tax has been a cardinal feature of the American fiscal system and the rates and yields are now the highest in our history. Notwithstanding its many and serious faults, there are many points in its favor. Property receives protection from government, and may logically be asked to contribute to government's support. Lending itself particularly well to local use, the tax is in keeping with the persisting spirit of home rule. Its easy elasticity—the facility with which its yield can be moved up or down by simple manipulation of the tax rate—fits it to meet varying needs after other sources of income have been exhausted.

Disadvantages: 1. Concealment of personal property

Nevertheless, the tax has some serious defects. First may be mentioned the unfairness arising from frequent concealment of intangible personal property, resulting in complete escape from taxation. In early times, nearly all property was in the form of real estate or of tangibles such as livestock, furniture, merchandise, farm implements, and grain. Nearly everything could be located and its value determined by the tax assessor, and little, if any, taxable property failed to pay its just share. From this relatively simple situation, we have moved to one in which the value of stocks, bonds, mortgages, bank deposits, and other intangibles often exceeds that of real estate and tangibles. Furthermore, it has become virtually impossible for tax assessors actually to see and appraise all tangible personal property, to say nothing of intangibles. The common practice is to require taxpayers themselves to make out sworn statements of their personal property and simply hand them to the assessors—a method which amounts to self-assessment. Still further, while real estate and personal tangibles are usually immune from national taxation, intangibles (or at all events the income derived from them) are taxed so heavily from Washington that when national taxes and state taxes are added together, they amount to onerous exactions, at least in the eyes of many who pay them. Under these circumstances, vast amounts of property which the tax assessor has no chance to see are never reported to him—the portion actually reported depending almost entirely upon the personal honesty of the taxpayer in the given case. Responding to these and other difficulties, legislatures have exempted many kinds of personalty from taxation and have thus aggravated the inequities for those who still pay the tax.

2. Defective assessments

A second main defect of the general property tax arises from inequitable assessment of property actually reached. The reasons for such deficiency are numerous, but doubtless the chief one is that a substantial proportion of the thousands of assessors functioning particularly in the rural areas and small towns throughout the country are part-time elective officials, with little training qualifying them to weigh the many factors entering into the determination of property values; much of what they do is mere guesswork. Many of the full-time assessors of the counties of the South and Southwest are also elected. There are architects' tables, land-value maps, and other equipment which would be of assistance; but only rarely are they used. Directions from the state tax commission and readjustments made by equalization boards help considerably, but not enough to assure satisfactory results. In the outcome, what purports to be a uniform general property tax is in many states neither uniform nor general, and of course not equitable. Real property usually bears more than its fair share; and often there is glaring inequality in the valuations placed upon real estate located in different parts of the same state, and even within the same county. Personal property, on the one hand, either is shockingly undervalued or, being easily concealed, escapes taxation altogether.

Problems connected with these and other defects of the property tax have received much study, and in a good many states improvements, although certainly not full solutions, have resulted. Most important among changes undertaken has been the abandonment of constitutional or other requirements of uniformity, in order that property may be thrown into different classes for taxation at different rates. Approximately two-thirds of the states, in fact, have adopted classification at least in principle, and in half or more some classification has been carried out. Here and there, as in Minnesota, classification has been sufficiently extensive to admit of quite a number of rate levels. In most instances, however, it has not gone beyond differentiating intangibles from tangibles, on the theory that lower rates on the former will lessen the incentive for concealing them and draw them out of hiding. Gains undoubtedly have been realized; although concealment of intangibles is still common and yields sometimes have actually been smaller than before classification was undertaken. Because of the inequities referred to, several states are moving toward the abolition of personal property taxes.

Modes of improve-ment: 1. Classi-fication for tax purposes

Two or three other approaches to improvement have commanded attention. One relates to the quality of assessments. The need is to get away from untrained, part-time, popularly elected local assessors, and substitute a plan under which assessors would become state or local civil servants, appointed on a merit basis by the state tax commission or by the city mayor, manager, or county executive. A second improvement well might have to do with county and other boards of review or equalization, now composed commonly of members serving ex officiis and, for obvious reasons, hardly better equipped than the assessors themselves. If there is virtue in having assessors appointed by the state tax commission, the same arrangement well might be applied to members of equalization boards. Any plan tending to obviate the tug-of-war between members representing rural and urban taxing districts would be a clear gain.

2. Ap-pointive assessors and reviewers

Still another step in advance would be to place on the tax rolls a great deal of real estate now exempted—nearly one-sixth throughout the country as a whole. Real estate used for religious, educational, and philanthropic purposes long has been immune, on the ground that the institutions owning it are run, not for profit, but for performing essential community services. Presumably this is justifiable. But some states go farther—for example by

3. Re-duced ex-emptions

partly or entirely exempting property of veterans, manufacturing plants, farm implements, growing crops, and (in more than a dozen instances) homesteads, that is, urban or rural dwellings occupied by the owner, with the sites on which they stand. All such exemptions narrow the tax base and increase the tax rates on remaining taxable property. With heavy pressure for augmented public revenues promising to continue through the years, we are likely to see determined efforts to bring on the tax rolls much property now exempted, even though perhaps at reduced rates or valuations.

PRINCIPAL STATE TAXES TODAY

The general property tax has been crowded out of the state tax picture—and even on the local level is of diminished importance—partly as a result of distress of property-owners during the depression of the thirties, partly through taxpayer efforts to curb mounting public expenditures by influencing legislators and constitution-makers to surround property taxation with new restraints, but in large measure also because of the discovery of newer tax sources having the merits of liberal yield and easier and surer collection. If, for example, intangibles cannot be reached for taxation directly, they still may be made to contribute their share by taxing income derived from them, and also the transmission of them by inheritance. For local purposes, the general property tax still is indispensable; for state purposes, however, it no longer appears necessary. Several forms of taxation have, in most states, largely or wholly superseded it for state purposes. Each of six such taxes have of late yielded the states more revenue than the property tax: (1) general sales, gross receipts, and use taxes, (2) motor fuel taxes, (3) income taxes, (4) motor vehicle license taxes, (5) liquor taxes, and (6) tobacco taxes.

1.
General
sales and
use taxes

State as well as national taxes on sales of particular commodities, for example, liquor, tobacco, and motor fuel, long have been familiar. Desperate fiscal needs during the depression of the thirties led one state after another, however, to carry the principle farther by instituting *general* sales taxes. In terms of yield such taxes (along with related gross receipts and use taxes) have now taken top place in the overall state tax picture. Beginning with West Virginia in 1921—somewhat before the depression indeed—a total of 44 states introduced the general sales tax in one form or another, most of them between 1933 and 1936 and several more in the nineteen-fifties and nineteen-sixties. In some instances, the step was inspired, at least partly, by fear of inability, in the lack of such a tax, to meet the obligations imposed by the new social security system at a time when state revenues were sagging. In most cases, indeed, the tax was adopted as a supposedly temporary or emergency measure. The early unpopularity of the general sales tax because of its "regressive" character, bearing with greatest proportional weight upon consumers least able to pay, has largely given way before the compelling needs of the states for large and stable sources of income. Typically, the tax is imposed on retail sales only, but in some instances on sales by manufacturers and wholesalers as well. In most of the sales-tax states a compensating use tax is laid on the use, storage, or consumption of commodities that would have been subject to the sales tax if bought in the state instead of brought in from outside.

Wherever tried, the sales tax has been highly productive, and it is *Yield* difficult to see how some states could have avoided bankruptcy without it. The rate of the tax is now, typically, 3 percent and the yield exceeds $7.8 billion to the states that levy it. This is more than from *any* other source except grants-in-aid. Whether, as a matter of social policy, it is justifiable to deflect tax burdens in such degree from property and incomes to the mass of the people as consumers may be, and is, warmly debated. In some states the impact is alleviated by exempting food and other necessities; and in any event urgency for revenue seems likely to continue to overbear all scruples on the point in many states.

The first significant chapter in the history of income taxation in this *2. Income* country was written on the national level (starting in 1861), and cul- *taxes* minated in the Sixteenth Amendment and the income tax law of 1913. In the states, there were a few earlier unsatisfactory experiments, but the first permanent and effective law was passed in Wisconsin in 1911. Two years later, Massachusetts, Delaware, Missouri, and Mississippi enacted similar legislation; in 1915, New York and North Dakota joined the growing list. Thereafter the movement spread until at present (1968), 38 states have income taxes applicable to either individuals or corporations, and usually to both. In aggregate yield the income is the third most important source of state tax income. But in a few states, notably Wisconsin, it is the main support of the state government. Though differing in details from state to state, the principal features of the tax are (1) taxation of net income only; (2) exemption of specified amounts (usually from $500 to $1,000) for single persons and of larger amounts (commonly $2,000 or $2,500) for a married couple, with allowances ranging from $200 to $400 for dependents; (3) a scale of rates rising from commonly 1 percent on the first $1,000 of taxable personal income to usually 5, 6, or 7—but in a few instances as high as 10 percent in the highest bracket; (4) a "normal" rate sometimes supplemented by surtaxes (general or for specific purposes such as educa- tion) after a certain point is reached; (5) usually a flat, but sometimes a progressive, rate on incomes of corporations; and frequently (6) review and collection, not by local officials, but—as started in Wisconsin in 1911— through the state tax commission and a force of civil service employes. In the state as in the national field, the graduated, or progressive, income tax is widely regarded as the most equitable tax form. However, the pos- sibility of realizing more from it is sharply restricted by the extremely heavy (and increasing) taxation of both personal and corporate incomes by the national government.

3. Motor fuel and vehicle taxes

Until comparatively recent times, highways and streets were financed almost entirely from the general property tax. The advent of the motor vehicle to almost universal use led, however, to demand for more and better roads, and prompted the idea that the highways, rural and urban, used by the insatiable motorist should be paid for and kept up by him. The result has been the development of the country's present remarkable network of hard-surfaced thoroughfares and the rise to great prominence of a newer group of tax levies, essentially in the nature of privilege or service charges, and often referred to as the "motor vehicle tax family." Chief among the members of this family are (1) the motor vehicle license, which in essence is an annual charge for the privilege of operating a motor vehicle on the highways, and whose yield exceeds the yield of state income taxes paid by corporations; and (2) the motor fuel tax, starting as simply a gasoline tax in Oregon in 1919, and now employed in every state. Currently the rates range from three to eight cents a gallon and the average is about seven cents. Over the protest of rural and road-building interests, not to mention automobile associations, varying portions of motor vehicle and motor fuel proceeds were, in depression years of financial stress, diverted, in two-thirds of the states, to education, welfare, and other state purposes. Efforts to halt such diversions have been successful in a large number of states. At the same time, even with no such diversion, proceeds throughout the country as a whole have never sufficed (except during wartime suspension of construction) to meet the full outlay on roads and streets. The property tax still supplies a good share of the costs of local streets. Both motor vehicle and motor fuel taxes have the great merits of being highly productive and easy to administer.

4. Liquor and tobacco taxes

Prior to the prohibition era, the states, while making license charges in connection with the liquor traffic, left excise taxation of liquor to the national government. Subsequently, however, they, too, entered the excise field. Combined with license fees on dealers when there is no state monopoly and on bars and taverns almost everywhere, the taxes on liquor yield about half as much as do state income taxes. In the more than a dozen states where the traffic is a state monopoly, income from licenses is replaced by profits from the operation of dispensaries. Like excises on liquor, taxes on tobacco and tobacco products represent a more recently developed source of state revenue; as in the case of liquor, also, dealers usually are licensed and the commodity itself taxed. Nearly all states tax cigarettes (most commonly at about eight cents a package), and several tax tobacco also in other forms. Like liquor, tobacco is subject also to heavy national taxation. Few taxes are as popular as those on liquor and tobacco for by them the state can encourage virtuous living and raise revenue at the same time. The only limits to these taxes would appear to be those fixed by rising enforcement costs.

TAX ADMINISTRATION—
THE COLLECTION AND CUSTODY OF FUNDS

In times when nearly all state revenue was derived from the general *Tax* property tax, the state financial authorities had little to do except receive the *collection* money passed along after being locally collected. Nowadays, the situation is different, because the taxes on which the state depends have become highly diversified, and many are collected by officers or other representatives of the state itself. The general property tax is still gathered by local collectors or treasurers, county or city, with the proceeds apportioned among the various taxing units (including the state where it shares) according to the different rates that have been imposed. A difficulty often presented is that of tax delinquency, which became serious indeed during the depression of three decades ago, with often as high as 30, 40, or even 50 to 60, percent of the amounts due in individual taxing districts going unpaid. With considerable uniformity, the states provide for (1) a regular payment period (on the basis of payment either at a single time or, in about half of the states, in instalments), and (2) an additional period during which, if payment is not made, accrued interest must be included, with often the amount of the tax somewhat increased also by way of further penalty. Procedures in cases of persistent delinquency vary, but in most states there are "tax sales" enabling the taxing authorities to get their money, and giving private purchasers ownership of, or at least an interest in, the properties involved.

Local collection of virtually all other forms of state revenue is not *Local vs.* economical, the expense entailed often consuming a large share of the sums *central* gathered. Centralized collection has therefore grown in favor, especially in *collection* connection with income, estate, inheritance, motor vehicle, sales, and business taxes. In Wisconsin, the founder of the modern income tax, taxes on incomes are collected by income-tax assessors, selected according to merit principles and each functioning in one of four districts, where their duties are performed under direction of the state tax commissioner. This is an exact reversal of procedure in the case of the property tax, in that 60 percent of the proceeds of the income tax in that state is turned over to counties and other local areas. All other states employing income taxes have substantially similar arrangements, at least for collection, and 12 of them also share the proceeds with local governments. Revenues gathered by state agencies and retained for the state do not always, however, go into the state general fund. Fees collected by the secretary of state or the insurance commissioner, for example, frequently are used to pay the expenses of the office collecting them, only the surplus, if any, being returned for general state use. Much of the money paid directly into the treasury is earmarked for particular purposes, for example, education, highways, and conservation, making it necessary for the fiscal officers to maintain an accounting system permitting of separate accounts for various funds. Among experienced persons, sentiment is growing in favor of concentrating all state tax administration in the state tax commission or some other single department and all state revenues in a single, general, all-purpose fund.

The care of funds

In some states, all state funds are kept in the state's vaults, with no interest received. Elsewhere the practice is to deposit such money in banks located in different parts of the state and designated as depositories. Of course the latter plan opens a way for favoritism and collusion in selecting the banks, and for losses arising from bank failures. After unhappy experiences at these points, most states, however, have protected themselves, at least against loss, by requiring depository banks to furnish adequate guarantees of security; and some profit to the state usually accrues from interest at a modest rate on deposits made.

STATE CONTROL OVER LOCAL FINANCES

It must be apparent at this point that the finances of a state and of its political subdivisions are so intermingled that neither can be understood in isolation from the other. For the ordinary taxpayer, the finances of his local governments (there almost always are more than one) are, in fact, more important than those of his state. Such governments, in the aggregate, spend more than do the 50 state governments combined. These local governments, however, raise by no means all of this money by their own efforts; and this leads, first of all, to a word about the sources from which local revenues are derived.

Sources of local revenue: 1. Local taxes

(1) First among these (mentioning only the most important) is locally imposed taxes, supplemented by many kinds of license and other fees. On this matter, little need be said. The one universally employed and chiefly important local tax is the general property tax already described. The great bulk of the proceeds of this tax (in many states all of them) goes for local needs; and it is difficult to see how the tax, with all its faults, could be replaced by any other. (2) Next may be mentioned the proceeds of shared taxes. These are taxes (like several we have mentioned) which, although imposed, and usually collected, by the state, are by law so administered that some agreed proportion of the yield is automatically turned over to counties and other local units. Technically, the general property tax is not such a tax, because although the taxpayer gets a single tax bill, he is really paying, by a single transaction, two or more property taxes—county, city, state—included in one bill for purposes of convenience. A taxing unit on any taxing level can put into the composite bill whatever proportion it desires. The truly shared tax is *one* tax, state levied, and with the locality having no part in it except to receive such percentage of the yield as has been allocated to it by law. Good examples in different states

2. Shared taxes

are motor vehicle license taxes, motor fuel taxes, and in varying numbers of states, income taxes, liquor taxes, and general sales taxes.

(3) Finally, there are grants-in-aid—extended almost as generously by state governments to localities as by the national government to the states. For the year 1966 the states extended $11.7 billion (including shared taxes) to their local subdivisions. However, a share of this originated in the national treasury and the state acted only as intermediary in the transaction. Aids may be distinguished from shared taxes in that, whereas under the shared tax the state automatically hands over to the localities from year to year such proportion of the proceeds of a given tax as has been fixed by law, under the grant-in-aid system the state bestows on the localities such amounts, for such purposes, and on such conditions, as it may choose. In the one case, the amount distributed is dependent on the yield of a particular tax; and usually the distribution is such as to return the money to the communities where it was collected. In the other case, a fixed amount for a given year, from general funds, is distributed by appropriation and commonly on some basis of demonstrated need. Funds received by localities from shared taxes may usually be expended for any purposes whatsoever, but those from grants-in-aid only for purposes expressly indicated in the grant. Both shared taxes and grants-in-aid have attained their present proportions fundamentally because of (1) the greatly superior taxing means and powers (as well as borrowing facilities) of the state governments as compared with local governments, and (2) the general trend in later times toward centralization, expressing itself in fiscal relationships as well as in other ways.

Even in imposing their own taxes, local units are likely to be subject to constitutional or state statutory restrictions, for example, as to the maximum tax rate they may employ. In any case, local assessments are likely to come under the scrutiny of the state tax commission or other equalization agency, which may readjust them or even (usually on appeal from taxpayers) cause reassessments to be made. In spending their funds, too, local governments are under some state controls. (1) Grants-in-aid are received on condition that the services for which they are earmarked are kept on a satisfactory level of efficiency. The states have a good deal to do with establishing such levels and, through inspection and direction, seeing that they are maintained. (2) Local budgets often are subject to review by state authorities, who may protest items which they consider excessive or otherwise unjustified. Deficiency appropriations and transfers from one fund to another also may come under the critical eye of a state auditor, board of accounts, or other agency. (3) Local finance officers often are required to use uniform systems of records and accounting; and in any event, in nearly all states, representatives of a state finance officer or department pay annual (usually unannounced) visits to spending officers of local governments, look over their accounts, require carelessness to be corrected, and cause embezzlers to be brought to justice. (4) Debt limits

3. Grants-in-aid

Forms of state control

commonly are imposed. While borrowing within these limits usually may proceed without intervention from the outside, a county board or city council proposing to issue bonds to build a highway, develop a park, or construct a court house or city hall may find a group of taxpayers arguing before a competent state authority that the outlay is unnecessary, extravagant, or ill-advised at the particular time, and may be obliged to convince state examiners that the proposal is sound, on penalty of seeing it vetoed at the state capital. In protest against all of these forms of state intervention, many people cry out that the sacred principle of home rule is being violated, and that the officials who impose and enforce the restraints are too far away to know the needs and conditions involved. In some states, however, large sums have been saved by protection given in these ways against the looseness and waste too often characterizing the local administration of affairs by inexperienced, careless, partisan, or even corrupt, public officials.

STATE AND LOCAL DEBTS

State debt   A final phase of state and local finance requiring a word of comment is borrowing and indebtedness. Unlike the national government, which can borrow without constitutional restraint, the governments of all but three states (New Hampshire, Vermont, and Connecticut) are restricted by constitutional provisions designed to prevent a recurrence of the reckless piling up of debts which marred the work of many state legislatures before the Civil War and during the Reconstruction period. Despite these limitations, state borrowing has increased many fold in this century. Today every state carries some debt, even though in some states (Wisconsin, for example) the debt is not a charge on the general resources and in several others this debt is quite small. As of 1967, the total long-term debt of the 50 states was $28.5 billion. Some of this was covered by accumulated sinking funds.

Local debt   Debt burdens incurred by counties, cities, and other local units weighed heavily on taxpayers during the Great Depression, and Congress came to the relief of embarrassed local governments through a Municipal Bankruptcy Act under which any of them unable to service their debts could voluntarily go into a bankruptcy court and get plans approved for readjusting their obligations. After 1940, the wartime economic upsurge enabled local governments of all kinds to reduce indebtedness, but in the postwar years the trend has reversed and local debts are again increasing. The main pressure on local income nowadays is in the field of education. In order to house the flood tide of new children, school building is pushing on the debt limits of local units almost everywhere in the country. As of 1967 the outstanding debt of local governments in the United States exceeded $72.5 billion.

State and local governments borrow money ordinarily by issuing interest-bearing bonds running for periods of from ten to perhaps 20 years, and taking the form of either sinking-fund issues or serial issues. Under the sinking-fund plan, all bonds of a given issue mature at one time, and a definite sum is set aside each year from current revenues to meet principal and interest in full when the date arrives. Serial bonds, on the other hand, mature in installments or series, thus enabling a definite proportion of a given debt to be extinguished every year, or at other stated intervals, by payments from current revenues which, under the other system, would go into the sinking fund. Serial bond issues have grown rapidly in popular favor in the past three decades and are fast supplanting the earlier sinking-fund system.

Methods of bor- rowing

REFERENCES

Advisory Commission on Intergovernmental Relations, *Measuring State and Local Fiscal Capacity and Tax Effort* (Washington, D. C., 1962).

————, *State and Local Taxes: Significant Features* (Washington, D. C., 1968).

Council of State Governments, *The Book of the States* (Chicago, 1968).

————, *Federal Grants-in-Aid* (Chicago, 1949).

————, *Grants-in-Aid and Other Federal Expenditures Within the States* (rev. ed., Chicago, 1947).

————, *Postwar State Taxation and Finance* (Chicago, 1947).

————, *Sources of State Tax Revenue, 1940–49* (Chicago, 1960).

————, *State–Local Relations* (Chicago, 1947).

J. F. Due, *Sales Taxation* (Urbana, Illinois, 1960).

II. M. Groves, *Financing Government* (5th ed., New York, 1964).

W. Kilpatrick, *State Supervision of Local Budgeting* (New York, 1940).

————, *State Supervision of Local Finance* (Chicago, 1941).

L. H. Kimmel, *Taxes and Economic Incentives* (Washington, D. C., 1950).

J. A. Maxwell, *Financing State and Local Governments* (Washington, D. C., 1965).

U.S. Bureau of the Census, *Historical Statistics on State and Local Government Finances, 1902–1953* (Washington, D. C., 1955).

————, *Summary of State Government Finances* (Washington, D. C., published annually.

6

THE STATE JUDICIARY

Functions Rounding out the government of every state is a system of courts providing means for (1) adjusting disputes between private parties, and between such parties and state or local governments; (2) determining the guilt or innocence of persons accused of violating the state's criminal laws; (3) protecting the constitutional rights of individuals and corporations; (4) keeping the executive and legislative branches of government within the bounds fixed for them by the state constitution; and (5) promoting adjustments of sundry kinds, including the settlement of estates of deceased persons.

Some general features: 1. Scope Three cardinal features of these state courts require emphasis at the outset. First, the state judicial system embraces not only tribunals operating on a statewide basis (of such, in fact, there are few), but those functioning in counties, cities, and other local areas as well. From justice of the peace and police court to supreme court—and regardless of whether created by the state constitution or established and regulated only by legislative act— all of the courts on all levels form parts of a single system, even though not

2. Status completely integrated. Second, and contrary to a common popular impression, the state judicial system is in no way subordinate to the national system. The two sets of courts are separately rooted and mount through their successive grades on parallel lines, each with its own field of jurisdiction and operating independently within it. Any case, it is true, originating in a state court, but involving determination of a right claimed under the national constitution, laws, or treaties may be removed or carried on appeal to a proper national court. The great majority of cases coming before the state courts do not, however, raise any such federal question, but involve simply the adjudication of rights claimed under the state constitution, the state statutes, or the common law when not modified by state legislation. Nearly all judicial actions started in a state court are completed there with just as

3. Jurisdiction much finality as if there were no national courts at all. A third fact is that, while many suits may be instituted in either a state or a national court, and while the dockets of national courts are nearly always crowded, the great bulk of judicial business the country over—probably nine-tenths of it—is transacted in the courts of the states. Under the principle of delegated powers, the national courts have only such jurisdiction as the national Constitution expressly gives them, and in general are confined to administering national law. Under the principle of reserved powers, the state courts have everything else, the state law which they administer covering not only a wider and more indeterminate range of matters, but matters often peculiarly provocative of legislation, and consequently of litigation. Much of the time, state courts and their decisions do not attract as much attention as those in the national sphere. Nevertheless, here it is, rather than in the national courts, that most people, as plaintiffs, defendants, jurors, or witnesses, have their contacts (if any) with the judicial process.

THE SYSTEM OF COURTS

Regulated partly by the constitution and partly by statute, the court structure in almost every state has some individual features. In general, however, differences are minor and the court systems of the states tend to follow a standard pattern as follows: (1) justices of the peace and other courts of petty jurisdiction, (2) intermediate courts, (3) courts of general trial jurisdiction, (4) appellate courts, and (5) supreme court.

At the bottom of the scale stand tribunals of purely local character, *1. The lowest courts: a. Justices of the peace* consisting of justices of the peace, municipal magistrates, or other officers of similar grade. Originally, justices of the peace functioned in rural and urban areas alike, and some still are found in cities of considerable size. The tendency, however, has been to displace them in urban centers by other magistrates, and today they are largely confined to rural communities. As a rule, justices are chosen by popular vote in townships or other subdivisions of the county, and for short terms (usually two years); although in a few states they are appointed by the governor. In any case, their jurisdiction commonly extends throughout an entire county, and includes both petty civil suits (involving up to perhaps $100) and breaches of the peace and other minor infractions of law. They may also issue warrants for the arrest of persons charged with more serious offenses, may hold preliminary hearings, and if the evidence warrants may bind over a suspect to await action by a grand jury or prosecutor. In contrast with other state and local courts, the justice courts have no official seal, no clerk, and keep no permanent official record of their proceedings. Accordingly, they are not courts of record, as are most of the others. Furthermore, they may render final decisions in only the most petty misdemeanor and civil cases. In all others, appeal lies to the next higher court, which, however, ordinarily will consider an appealed case *de novo,* without reference to what has taken place in the justice's court.

b. Munici-
pal or
police
courts

In most incorporated places of appreciable size, the functions else-where performed by justices of the peace are assigned to one or more minor tribunals variously known as municipal courts, police courts, or magistrates' courts, with jurisdiction confined to the given municipality. Sometimes the judges of these courts are elected by the people, sometimes they are ap-pointed by the mayor or even by the governor. In any event, their handling of the multitude of petty cases coming before them too often is inept if not actually corrupt. Unhappy experience with such tribunals, especially where two or more were found operating in the same jurisdiction, has led most large cities, for example, New York, Chicago, Philadelphia, Detroit, Boston, and Baltimore, to coordinate and integrate all work of the kind in a single municipal court. Of necessity such a tribunal must parcel out its tasks among sections or branches dealing with cases in particular fields such as traffic, juvenile offenses, domestic relations, small claims, and the like. The jurisdiction of courts of this nature usually transcends that of justices of the peace.

2. Inter-
mediate
courts

In many states, the next level above the justice and municipal courts is occupied by courts of general trial jurisdiction in which most important litigation originates and most persons accused of crime are tried. In others, however, there are courts intermediate between these tribunals and the justices, organized frequently on a county basis and with jurisdiction so defined that a plaintiff may choose whether to sue before a justice or in an intermediate court.

3. Gen-
eral trial
(county,
district, or
circuit)
courts:
a. Organi-
zation

Even where such intermediate courts exist, however, greater impor-tance attaches to the courts of general trial jurisdiction on a somewhat higher level. In many states, a tribunal of this grade is called the county or superior court, and there is a single judge in each county. More often, how-ever, two or three counties are grouped for the purpose, with a district or circuit court serving each group, and with usually a single judge except in urban or other areas where the volume of work requires more. In any case, a trial court session is held at least once a year in virtually every county, either by the county court judge or by a district or circuit judge making his rounds in accordance with a regular schedule. It is in these court sittings that trial juries are most extensively employed. In 34 states, all county, district, or circuit judges are chosen by popular vote, and for terms most commonly of four years. On this level and above, too, all judges may be assumed to be men of legal training.

b. Juris-
diction

Whether held by a local county or superior judge or by a district or circuit judge making periodic visitations, county courts regularly have both criminal and civil, and also both original and appellate, jurisdiction. On the criminal side, they handle all cases except those of a petty nature taken care of by the justices of the peace or magistrates, or by an intermediate court. Ordinarily their decisions are final insofar as questions of fact are concerned, although if disputed matters of law are involved, a case may usually be carried on appeal to a higher tribunal. Jurisdiction in civil cases is commonly unlimited, although in a few states restricted to actions involving less than $1,000 or some other stated amount. Here again most cases have their first hearing, although some are brought up on appeal from decisions of justices of the peace or magistrates. In populous counties, the settlement of the estates of deceased persons and the discharge of functions relating to the property, custody, and welfare of minor children and other persons under guardianship are in the hands of a separate probate, surrogate, or orphans' court. Elsewhere, however, these duties commonly devolve upon the regular judges, who also, in several states, have important administrative duties in connection with the enforcement of certain state laws and with specified phases of county government, for example, poor relief.

4. Appellate courts

Above their general trial courts, and with a view to relieving congestion in the supreme court, about one-fourth of the more populous states have placed one or more appellate courts. The judges are sometimes appointed but usually elected from a few large judicial districts into which the state is divided for the purpose and sit in "benches" of three or more, with decisions reached by the majority. Limited original jurisdiction is occasionally conferred by the legislature, but most of the time of these courts is devoted to hearing appeals from the general trial courts and rendering decisions which in many classes of cases are final. As a rule, only questions of law are involved, with juries therefore not employed.

5. Supreme courts: a. Structure

The highest state court is usually called the supreme court and consists of either five or seven judges (including a chief justice) sitting together when hearing cases. In at least one-third of the states it is permissible to sit in sections. In any event, a majority of the whole number of members of the court or section must concur in any decision rendered. The judges are nearly always elective, most often on a statewide nonpartisan ticket, although in a few states by districts. There are instances in which nominations are made in districts, but with election by the voters of the state at large. Ranging all the way from two years in Vermont to 15 and 21 years in Maryland and Pennsylvania, respectively, and "good behavior" in Massachusetts, New Hampshire, and Rhode Island, the term of office is most often six years (in 18 states). Salaries vary from $16,500 in Oklahoma to $39,500 in New York.

b. Functions

The work of the supreme court consists almost entirely in hearing and deciding appeals on questions of law coming up from the lower trial courts or appellate courts where they exist. In most states the court may also issue certain writs, and in a few others it may give first hearing to cases of one or two types, for example, those in which the state is a party. In performing its appellate functions, the court not only adjudicates cases, but becomes—like the Supreme Court of the United States within its sphere —the highest interpreter of the constitution and laws. Its decisions and interpretations, too, are final, except for those which may be carried to the national Supreme Court.

STRUCTURAL DEFECTS AND REMEDIES

The system of courts outlined is far from uniform in detail from state to state and undergoes frequent minor changes in any particular state. Viewed in the large, however, it is deeply rooted in American practice. This being the case, a general overhauling such as virtually all experts agree to be needed has proved difficult to bring about.

Principal faults: 1. The outmoded justice of the peace

Of structural faults challenging attention, the first centers in the layer of courts closest to the people and for many years handling more cases than all other tribunals combined: the courts of the justices of the peace. Usually these leave a good deal to be desired. To begin with, the justices themselves are invariably devoid of legal education, with the justice which they administer likely to be of a more or less rough and ready sort. Of course there are handbooks of law for them to consult. On the elementary level on which they operate, lack of formal training may be offset by a good stock of common sense. Nevertheless, if they are to be continued, some surer guarantee of competence is highly desirable. Equally serious is the circumstance that, with rarely any salary attached to the office, the justice normally must look for his compensation to such fees as he can collect. In the great majority of instances, he derives but little from this source—perhaps a few hundred dollars a year, perhaps less. There have been instances, however, in which favorably located justices pocketed thousands of dollars a year. A system of justice which puts a premium on drumming up business and squeezing the utmost out of every offender is hardly to be commended. Too often, it has been marred by fee-splitting with conniving constables, "speed-trap" abuses on public highways, and other forms of chicanery and extortion. In the early history of the country, when travel to the county seat (where the higher courts dispensed justice at infrequent intervals) was difficult and time-consuming, rural justices of the peace performed useful, if not indispensable, functions as tribunals near at hand for adjusting minor differences between members of the same community. With the greatly improved means of travel and communication existing today, such usefulness has largely disappeared.

2. Lack of judicial articulation

A few years ago a thoughtful writer ventured the observation that the most serious weaknesses growing out of existing state judicial organization are (1) lack of specialization, (2) inequalities in the distribution of work, and (3) lack of uniformity in interpretation and administration of the law. And he went on to comment as follows: [1]

> By and large, the organization of our courts on a geographical rather than a functional basis prevents any substantial degree of specialization. Each court usually serves a city, county, district, circuit, or some other geographic area, and handles all types of cases therein. Hence it is practically impossible for a

[1] C. F. Snider, *American State and Local Government* (New York, 1950), p. 281.

judge to become a specialist in any particular kind of cases, such as criminal, equity, or domestic relations. Moreover, under the geographic basis of organization the dockets of some courts are crowded while those of others are light, and no adequate provision is made for transferring judges temporarily from courts having little to do to those that are overworked. Finally, in the absence of central supervision, judicial administration is far from uniform, especially in the field of criminal law. Considerable discretion is commonly vested in the courts with respect to criminal penalties to be imposed, with the result that a given offense is likely to draw widely different penalties at different places in the same state, depending upon the attitude of the particular judge before whom the case is tried.

In our study of state administration, we saw how disadvantageous is the usual lack of unified supervision and control over the many separate administrative officers and agencies. Unhappily, the same lack too often interferes with the most effective functioning of the state's judicial machinery. It seems self-evident that all of the courts belonging to the so-called judicial system should be closely articulated with one another, and that there should be some chief justice or other authority in a position to coordinate the work of the several courts, devise plans for a useful division of labor among them, transfer cases, assign judges, and do other things needed to promote speed and efficiency. Instead of this, however, we find in the majority of states "a jumble of disconnected and disjointed courts, each pursuing its own way, with little regard to any other"—a "heterogeneous assortment of miscellaneous courts of miscellaneous and often overlapping jurisdiction." In earlier and simpler days, there was some unity and coherence; but so much new machinery has been tacked on without regard to system that any former articulation has almost disappeared.

Likewise, in the case of any particular court, it seems manifest that efficiency calls for a chief justice or effective head clothed with authority to supervise the work of all judges belonging to that court, to require them to make periodic reports showing the state of business on their dockets, to admonish the careless and indolent, to relieve the overworked, and to keep all reasonably busy. As matters stand, however, in nearly every part of the country the judges in the same court are elected independently of one another and seldom are made subject to any actual directing or supervisory control. Each judge can hold court when he pleases, for as few hours a day as he pleases, and hear cases on such calendars as he pleases. Whatever cooperation, teamwork, or division of labor exists depends almost entirely upon voluntary cooperation of the judges constituting the court.

With so loose organization, or lack thereof, it is not surprising that there are few reliable statistics showing what our different state courts are doing or how much they are costing the taxpayers. Of most of our states it may truly be said that "the judiciary is the one department which publishes no data bearing upon the efficiency of its work"—though without

3. Inadequate reporting

such data there is no adequate basis for judging how well it is performing its duties or what changes are needed to increase its efficiency.

Some limited improvements:

For many years, crime commissions and other analysts of judicial administration have urged abolition, state by state, of the entire justice-of-the-peace system. The obstacles are great—and not merely tradition and inertia, but the necessity (in most states) of constitutional amendment,

1. Justices of the peace abolished or partly superseded

and also the influence of existing justices with local electorates. In only a few states—Missouri (1945), New Jersey (1947), Connecticut (1959), North Carolina (1962), Colorado (1962), New Mexico and Wisconsin (1966)— has the system been suppressed outright. In some half-dozen others, however, the essential purpose has been wholly or partially attained by constitutional or legislative action stripping justices of their power to try cases, even though leaving them authority, for example, to issue warrants and subpoenas and perform marriages. Thus Virginia, in 1934, supplanted former justices for purely judicial purposes by salaried trial justices appointed for each county by the circuit court, and supervised by it; Tennessee has replaced justices in most counties by salaried general sessions courts; North Carolina in 1937, and Indiana in 1939, empowered counties (only more populous ones in Indiana under an amendment of 1941) to create courts with appointive and salaried judges handling most cases formerly tried by justices; Maryland in 1939 made such courts statewide. Missouri in 1945 replaced justices altogether by magistrates' courts, at least one in each county; and New Jersey in 1947 replaced them by district and municipal courts under appointive magistrates. California in 1951 replaced them with district courts in the most populous areas of the state. Hawaii and Alaska entered the union without justice courts. Justices have been dispensed with also in a number of cities, for example, Chicago in 1905 and Milwaukee in 1945. The justice of the peace is clearly on the way to oblivion.

2. Coordination through state departments of justice

An important aid to the efficient functioning of our state courts would be a state department of justice, charged with exercising general supervision over the administration of both criminal and civil justice, and also with collecting and publishing judicial statistics covering the entire state—an agency performing for the state courts functions analogous to those now performed for the national courts by the Department of Justice and the Administrative Office of the United States Courts at Washington. A few have provided themselves with such a department but in no one of the number does the establishment appear to be working effectively as an agency for imparting vigor and uniformity to the administration of criminal justice. In addition, about one-fourth of the states have conferred upon the attorney general limited power to supervise the work of county or other local prosecuting attorneys. Here again results have not proved impressive. Undoubtedly the attorney general's office might be made a nucleus around which to develop an effective state department of justice, as envisaged in California under a constitutional amendment adopted in 1934.

In about a dozen states, including Wisconsin, Missouri, and Louisiana,

NEW JERSEY'S COURT SYSTEM
UNDER NEW CONSTITUTION

SUPREME COURT

Chief Justice and 6 associates. Jurisdiction—final appeals in selected cases as defined by the Constitution.

SUPERIOR COURT

Court has state wide jurisdiction and is divided into 3 divisions.

| APPELLATE DIVISION | LAW DIVISION |
| | CHANCERY DIVISION |

Decides appeals from Law and Chancery Divisions and County Courts.

COUNTY COURT

Minimum of 1 Judge in each county. Jurisdiction includes that of 5 former county courts. Equity powers when required for complete determination of case. Jurisdiction subject to change of law.

INFERIOR COURTS

Either created prior to and not abolished by the Constitution or created by law subsequent to the Constitution. All subject to abolition or change by law.

| DISTRICT COURTS | MUNICIPAL COURTS |
| JUVENILE & DOMESTIC RELATIONS COURTS | SURROGATE'S ACTIONS ARE PARTIALLY JUDICIAL |

All judges appointed by Governor with approval of Senate except Municipal Judges, who are appointed by governing body excepting where serving in two or more municipalities and then appointed by the Governor. Surrogates are elected.

3. Judicial councils the constitution vests in the supreme court "a general superintending control" over all inferior courts. As yet, however, the contemplated authority has rarely been employed to bring about any notable measure of unification and coordination. More significant has been the establishment, in approximately three-quarters of the states, of investigative and advisory judicial councils charged with collecting and studying judicial statistics, formulating rules for the equalization and more efficient handling of court business (with power in California and a few other states to put them into operation), and recommending to the legislature desirable changes in the laws governing court organization and procedure. In these states, as elsewhere, however, many desirable improvements remain to be made, with often the adoption of a constitutional amendment a necessary first step.

4. Unified state courts Impressed by the efficiency of a highly integrated judicial system in Great Britain, the authors of the National Municipal League's Model State Constitution provide in their plan for a general court of justice, or unified state court; and many bar associations and other interested groups have endorsed it. The proposal is (1) that in each state all courts of the various grades (at least those having civil jurisdiction) be merged into a single statewide tribunal, organized in branches or divisions (with probably subdivisions) permitting judicial business to be distributed more logically and judges to develop more specialized experience and talent than now; (2) that all judges be members of this unified court and subject to service at any point in the state where needed; (3) that the court be headed by an elective chief justice, perhaps with power to appoint all other judges from panels presented by the judicial council; and (4) that the chief justice, acting singly or in conjunction with the judicial council under his chairmanship, be vested with broad supervisory powers, including assigning judges to the various branches, transferring them from courts with light dockets to others with heavy ones, requiring systematic reports, and imposing rules designed to speed up business and promote uniformity of action. Plans of court organization based on similar principles have yielded good results within the narrower limits of several of our larger cities. With adoption on the state level manifestly promising large gains, it is significant that Missouri, in her new constitution of 1945, went a considerable distance by empowering her supreme court to make rules for all courts and to transfer judges from court to court; and that New Jersey in 1947 went farther (also in a new constitution) by boldly adopting the unified state court system in all of its essentials. Both Hawaii and Alaska provide for a completely unified system of state courts in their new constitutions. Wisconsin in 1959 began an extensive court reorganization. Virtually complete unification has also been achieved in Arizona (1960), Colorado (1962), Illinois (1964), and North Carolina (1962). Michigan (1963) and New York, Idaho, North Carolina, New Hampshire and Connecticut (1962–1963) have all carried out extensive reorganizations. Judicial reformers hope and expect that as other constitutions are rewritten or amended, similar advances will be made.

JUDICIAL PERSONNEL—SELECTION AND REMOVAL

In most foreign countries (except the U.S.S.R.), and in our own na- *Prevalence* tional government, judges are appointive rather than elective. And so they *of popular* were in all of our earlier states, with appointments made either by the *election* governor and council or by the legislature. In 1812 Georgia, and in 1832 Mississippi, made judges of certain courts popularly elective. In this, they stood alone until near the middle of the century. Then, however, general change set in, reflecting somewhat belatedly the democratic impulses associated with the rise of the West and with the equalitarian philosophy of the Jacksonian era. Curiously, it was an eastern state that led off—New York in 1847. But New York was strongly infected with the democratic spirit; and most of the middle states were borne along on a current of judicial popularization which by 1860 engulfed everything west of the Alleghenies. After that time every new state admitted came in with the elective plan until Hawaii came in with an appointive system and Alaska with a combination of an appointive and elective system. Today in 34 states judges are elected by popular vote, usually in partisan elections.

Long experience has disclosed two inherent weaknesses in the elective *Defects* system. The first is that it is no more likely to result in the choice of persons qualified to perform the highly technical work required of the judiciary than it is to secure the selection of experts in other branches of state government or in the field of municipal administration.

A second defect of popular election, too, is that what passes under that name often is only a fiction, being in reality nothing more than a method of appointment by partisans who succeed in putting their judicial "slates" through so-called nonpartisan primaries, or through party primaries, or through nominating conventions. All that is generally left for the voter on election day is to endorse one or the other of two judicial tickets thus submitted by persons not interested primarily in the efficient administration of justice, and therefore quite unlikely to pick candidates having the qualities most needed in a judge, namely, unquestioned integrity, dignity, independence, judicial temperament, and adequate legal training for highly technical duties.

It is not to be inferred that results under popular election are invari- *Some* ably bad. Our state judiciary, the country over, contains plenty of judges *partial* deficient both in learning and in ability, but also many who measure up ex- *remedies* ceedingly well both in learning and in other qualifications. In a good many states (notably New York, Pennsylvania, Maryland, Michigan, Wisconsin, Minnesota, and Iowa) the elective system has proved at least moderately satisfactory partly because of a strong local tradition in favor of reelecting incumbents. All in all, nevertheless, the plan's shortcomings usually outweigh its advantages—in some states very heavily. A great many people are now prepared to concede that a different one well might prove superior.

So firmly entrenched, however, is the system where it prevails, and so warmly would state and local political leaders resist abandoning it, that most proposals for reform do not go beyond devices aimed at securing better choices with popular election still operating. One such device— subject to discount of the manner in which politicians frequently manipulate it—is the choice of judges on nonpartisan ballots; and this method is employed in 16 states. Another, aimed also at minimizing partisanship, is the holding of judicial elections separately from others. And a third, utilized to advantage in a few states, takes the form of nomination of candidates for higher judicial posts, not in the usual primaries or conventions, but by the state bar association, as a body presumed to have special knowledge of the qualifications to be sought and of the fitness of persons aspiring to judicial preferment.

Three notable plans:
1. California

Three plans of judicial selection, however, which are attracting increasingly favorable attention are those operating in California, Alaska, and Missouri. They combine the better features of appointment and popular election and at the same time provide safeguards not offered by either of those methods alone. In 1934, the voters of California approved a constitutional amendment under which (1) a judge of the supreme court or of a district court of appeals may, as the end of his term approaches, declare his candidacy to succeed himself, and the people at the ensuing election simply vote for or against him; (2) if an incumbent chooses not to seek another term, the governor nominates someone for the post, and he similarly is voted on without any opposing candidate; (3) if in either case the popular vote is unfavorable, or if a judicial vacancy occurs otherwise, the governor makes a temporary appointment until the next general election, when the voters approve or disapprove of the person appointed, with a defeated candidate, however, ineligible for appointment to another judicial vacancy; and (4) as a further check upon the governor, all judicial appointments must be approved by a majority of a commission consisting of the chief justice of the supreme court, the presiding justice of the appellate court of the district involved, and the attorney general. The plan is not expressly made applicable to superior (county) court judges; instead, each county is left free to employ it or not as the voters choose. The system has several significant advantages. In the first place, judges are nominated by intelligent and responsible agents, while the ultimate selection nevertheless remains in the hands of the people. Secondly, a nominee is not running against somebody, but on his own record as a judge or as a lawyer, thus greatly diminishing the likelihood that irrelevant considerations will influence the voters. Finally, sitting judges are relieved of the necessity of devoting a large amount of their time to political activity in order to retain their positions; all they need do is fortify the judicial record on which they will appeal to the electorate.

2. Missouri

The Missouri plan, adopted by popularly initiated constitutional amendment in 1940 and continued with little change by the constitution of 1945, is so similar that only two differences (neither fundamental) need be mentioned. (1) When temporarily filling a higher judicial vacancy, the governor must appoint one of three persons nominated by a nonpartisan commission consisting of the chief justice of the supreme court as chairman, three lawyers named by the organized bar, and three laymen named by the governor. (2) On lower levels, the plan is applied to circuit and probate judges in the city of St. Louis and Jackson County (Kansas City) and to judges of such judicial circuits elsewhere as may adopt it by popular vote. In these cases, nominations to the governor are made by a local five-member commission in the judicial circuit concerned. Under the new arrangements, we are told by the chief justice of Missouri's supreme court, the state judiciary is being gradually improved, with partisanship completely eliminated and judges, freed from primary and election campaigning, able at last to bring their dockets up to date—to "keep their minds on the next case and not the next election." Alaska's new constitution provides still a **3. Alaska** third plan. Under it the governor appoints to vacancies on the supreme or superior court benches from nominations made by the judicial council. Three or more years (ultimately every ten years for supreme court justices and every six years for a superior court justice) thereafter the justice must run for election on a nonpartisan ballot and on his record.

Some form of the plans outlined above appears to be gaining increased support and Illinois, Iowa, and Nebraska have recently changed their procedures for judicial selection in the direction indicated.

In the national judicial system, judges retain their posts during good **Removal** behavior, and the only method of removing them is impeachment. Even in **of judges** times when state judges were largely or wholly appointive, there was a **a difficult** tendency to give them only limited terms. With the spread of the elective **problem** system, the practice became general, so that today "life" tenure survives only in Massachusetts, New Hampshire (until the age of seventy), and Rhode Island. As a rule, however, terms, in the higher courts, are relatively lengthy (four, six, eight, ten, 15, in Pennsylvania even 21, years). How to retire incumbents proving incompetent or otherwise unworthy of public confidence presents a problem as yet not solved satisfactorily. A fully acceptable method must be one which can be put into operation without undue delay, and one which at the same time insures for the judge whose removal is sought a fair hearing before a tribunal free from partisan bias and not subject to the influence of waves of popular passion. Three or four principal methods now in use in the different states fail, in varying degrees, to meet these standards.

A judge sitting by popular election may, of course, be retired by **Methods** failure to secure renomination, either because his character or work is **in use:** considered unsatisfactory or because party leaders want his position for **1. Failure** someone else. Even though he wins renomination, the people may retire **to renom-** him by failing to vote for him in sufficient numbers at the election. Popular **inate or** choice, however, is almost as likely to bring wrong results as right ones, **reelect** for often it happens that a judge whose work has been beyond reproach is defeated for renomination or reelection by circumstances wholly unrelated to his record as judge, perhaps because some overshadowing issue in state or national politics, wholly unconnected with the judicial election, has swept down to defeat the entire party ticket on which his name appeared. Furthermore (apart from the recall), a popular election furnishes a means of retiring an unworthy judge only at a given time, at the expiration of his term of office. The public has also shown a very strong disposition everywhere to reelect incumbent judges, even those who have become superannuated.

2. Impeachment or legislative removal or address

In most states, judges may be removed before the close of their term only by impeachment proceedings begun in the lower house of the legislature and tried before the senate, a two-thirds vote of the latter usually being required for conviction and removal. The constitutions of about half of the states, however, provide also for removal (without trial) by the legislature (or by the governor in pursuance of legislative action) upon "address," that is, concurrent resolution, of the legislature, after the English manner. Neither impeachment nor legislative removal is without serious defects. Under either method, there is much delay; and partisan considerations are likely to exert undue influence. Furthermore, evidence sufficient to convince two-thirds of the senate may be difficult to obtain; and the dereliction may not be grave enough to seem to merit extreme measures, yet sufficiently serious to warrant public condemnation and impair the judge's usefulness. In practice, it has been found that impeachment and legislative removal do not really work, and that unfit judges sometimes remain on the bench because no other modes of removal are available.

3. Recall election

This experience has led eight states to adopt the seemingly drastic policy of authorizing special elections at which the voters may recall judges whose removal is desired. Thus far, however, the plan has proved drastic only on paper. In no instance has the recall been invoked against a judge of a superior or supreme court, and instances of its use against judges on lower levels have been negligible. At one time it was predicted that fear of recall would place judges under unfair pressure and even impair judicial independence; but no ground for such apprehension has thus far appeared.

THE JUDICIAL PROCESS

Nature and regulation

In handling a case of any kind, a court of any grade has three essential things to do. First, it must inform itself as fully as possible on the facts involved. At the lower levels, for example, in a justice's or magistrate's court, this may entail little more than hearing a police officer's charges against the defendant and giving the latter a chance to reply and explain. Farther up the scale, it is likely to entail, in civil cases, hearing the different versions of the two parties, with evidence introduced through witnesses or in other ways, and perhaps with final determination by a jury. In criminal actions there is, typically, a hearing of the case as presented by the prosecution, the defense as offered by the defendant and his counsel, with almost certainly witnesses heard on both sides and other evidence weighed, and with nearly always a jury striking the balance and declaring whether the facts as brought out establish the defendant's guilt and in what degree. In the absence of a jury, whether the case be civil or criminal, facts are determined by the judge. In any event, the remaining two steps necessary to complete the process fall to that official. Of these, the first is to decide what provisions of law are applicable in the particular situation; and the second, to apply these provisions in terms of a specific judgment or verdict. All of these stages, furthermore, are governed by elaborate and often highly technical rules of procedure covering such matters as the rights of the accused, the admissibility of evidence, the selection of jurors, the privileges and limitations of counsel, the role of the judge, and many others. The promptness and quality of justice are greatly affected by the spirit and terms of such regulations.

Except insofar as predetermined by occasional constitutional provision, procedural rules were in earlier days made almost entirely by the courts themselves. At present, however, not only do constitution-framers write them more freely into their documents, but legislatures often enact them in such detail in statutes that residuary powers of the courts to supply whatever is needed but not otherwise furnished amount to little. Students of judicial administration, including many judges and lawyers, regard this development as unfortunate, not only because legislatures have neither the time nor the technical competence to perform the task satisfactorily, but because they sometimes are not above amending given rules at the behest of influential litigants hoping to gain some advantage in a particular case.

The heart of the judicial process consists in applying the law in each particular case after the facts have been established. This, of course, involves determining what law is applicable. In our American situation any one or more of several different bodies of law may be relevant. First of all is national law—the Constitution, acts of Congress, treaties, and regulations of executive or administrative authorities having the force of law. Although most litigation in state courts turns on state law, national law is the "supreme law of the land," and the judges in every state are bound by it, "anything in the constitution or laws of any state to the contrary notwithstanding." Second comes state law, also constitutional statutory, or regulatory. Even local law in the form of city and county charters, ordinances, and regulations sometimes must be taken into account, especially in lower courts. And supplementary to all else is the common law operating in the state. Classified differently, the law that may be applicable in a given case is (1) constitutional, (2) statutory, (3) regulatory or administrative, and (4) common. In descending order of priority, the judge must be guided by (1) the national "supreme" law, (2) state constitutional and statutory law, which, however, he can declare to be no law at all if found in conflict with national law, (3) state and local ordinances and regulations, which also he

Kinds of law applied

can hold invalid under either national or state constitutions or statutes, and finally (4) the common law.

Role of the common law

With national law always latent in the background, the law invoked in the great majority of cases tried in state courts is state law—constitutional, statutory, or common, with the third resorted to only when, and insofar as, the others do not cover a given situation. Constitutions and statutes are, of course, *enacted law*—written, and in the case of statutes often gathered into systematic codes kept up to date by periodic revisions. Common law, on the other hand, is law originally built up by the decisions and procedures of judges in medieval England, brought to America by the colonists, carried over and gradually modified to fit the American scene (to some extent even the localized needs of particular states) after the country became independent, and operating today in all of the states except Louisiana. There, as a result of early French influence, Continental "civil law" is followed instead. In the sense that judges developed it by selecting among earlier decisions those to be followed as precedents, and by incorporating principles and rules deduced from general custom where precedents failed, common law is essentially *judge-made* law. In their use of it, as well as in their interpretation of constitutions and statutes, judges still add to and otherwise "make" law. A frequent popular conception of common law as *unwritten* law is, however, inaccurate—first, because every element of it will be found set forth, here or there, in written decisions and opinions published in court reports, and second, because in many states important portions of it have been reduced to formal codes. Suggestions for complete codification, however, have been generally opposed by jurists on the ground that this would destroy the flexibility and capacity for adaptation which always have been among the common law's principal virtues. Important as is the common law in our legal system, it applies only insofar as not modified or superseded by constitutional provision or statute.

Types of cases tried:
1. Civil

In general, cases tried in state courts fall into two broad categories— civil and criminal. The essential aspect of a civil case is that it turns on a dispute between private parties—a plaintiff and a defendant—over possession of use of property, payment of a claim or debt, execution of a contract, a wrong (or tort) for which damages are sought, the validity of a will, an action for divorce, or any one of many other possible things. The method is that of a suit in a proper court by one party against the other. Except when (usually only with its own consent) a state or one of its subdivisions is one of the parties, no government is involved, save in the sense of having made or authorized the law under which the action is brought and of having provided the judicial machinery through which a settlement may be reached.

2. Criminal

Criminal cases are quite different. From petty misdemeanors up the scale to felonies, offenses coming under the criminal laws, although they usually involve personal or property damage, are regarded as injuries done to society; and their perpetrators are prosecuted by *public* officers, not in the name of individuals who may have suffered, but in that of "the people of the state of" New York, Ohio, or Texas, as the case may be. The object of the court action which follows is to determine whether the accused is guilty; if so, of what, and in what degree; and what penalty should be assessed. And when the verdict is in, if guilt is found, the state, which started the proceeding in the first place, finishes it by seeing that the penalty is enforced.

Long before the American colonies were founded, the right of an accused person to be tried by a jury of his peers was a bulwark of English liberty. On this side of the Atlantic it has been equally treasured. In the national sphere, all persons accused of crime are guaranteed the right to "a speedy and public trial by an impartial jury," and (with certain exceptions) no one may be proceeded against on a capital charge unless "on a presentment or an indictment of a grand jury." State constitutions and statutes everywhere abound in provisions of similar nature. Coming straight out of English common law, the jury in this country thus presents itself in two characteristic forms—the grand jury, which brings indictments against suspected persons, and the trial or petit jury, which (in addition to functioning in civil cases) determines their guilt or innocence. Both are important, and both are sharply criticized. They are important adjuncts of the judicial machinery of courts and prosecutors described above.

The jury system:

With the county, typically, as its area of operation, and with criminal, rather than civil, proceedings as its field, a grand jury is a body normally from 13 to 23 persons, chosen by lot or by some other prescribed procedure, convening at regular intervals, and charged with bringing indictments on its own initiative against persons who in its opinion have transgressed state laws and should be held for trial. More commonly it considers such indictments after examining the evidence against persons brought to its attention as suspected transgressors by a justice of the peace or by the county or district prosecuting attorney. If, in the latter situation, the jury considers the evidence sufficiently incriminating, it endorses on the draft indictment prepared by the prosecutor the words, "A true bill"; the foreman attaches his signature; and the accused person is held for trial. If, on the other hand, the jury is not satisfied that a prima facie case has been made out, it instructs its foreman to inscribe on the draft indictment, "This bill not found," and the accused is discharged. Indictments found are duly reported to the county court, and the county or district attorney proceeds to prosecute.

1. The grand jury

Indictment by grand jury is cumbersome and expensive, and the tendency nowadays is to get away from it. In England, the land of its origin, it has been almost completely abandoned. While in the United States it cannot be dispensed with in national practice as long as the Constitution's clause on the subject stands unchanged, in the states the device is gradually breaking down. In about half of the number, grand-jury procedures still are required when felonies are involved, but optional in the case of lesser charges. In several states, the legislature is constitutionally empowered to do away

The alternative device of information

with grand juries altogether. The procedure everywhere substituted is a simpler and more direct one known as *information,* under which the prosecuting attorney, on his own initiative, merely files with the appropriate court a formal charge in which, upon his oath of office, he "gives said court to understand and be *informed"* that the offense described therein has been committed by the person named.

2. The trial or petit jury

At common law, the trial or petit jury consisted of 12 impartial men chosen from the community. Its function was to judge of the facts in a case, the court itself passing upon all questions of law. Verdicts could be rendered only by unanimous vote. All criminal, and substantially all civil, cases called for jury procedure. Fundamentally, this is still the situation. Many states, however, have introduced significant modifications. (1) Whereas through long centuries it would have been inconceivable that jurors be other than men, 45 states now (1968) permit women to serve, and others probably will be added to the list. (2) In a few states, for example, Maryland and Illinois, juries serve as judges of both law and facts. (3) The constitutions of 22 states now authorize civil trials by juries of less than 12 persons (most commonly six), and eight states have similarly relaxed the old rule for criminal trials except in capital cases (involving a death penalty). (4) More than half of the states, including New York, now authorize verdicts by something less than unanimous vote (usually three-fourths) in civil cases, and eight have similarly modified the old rule for criminal (but not including capital) cases. (5) Nearly all states allow jury trial to be waived altogether in civil cases if both parties are willing; and a large majority permit similar waiver in criminal cases as well if the offense is a minor one and the accused person agrees—about a third, indeed, extending the option also to cases of a more serious nature, although in no instance to capital cases.

Short-comings

The grand jury has proved so defective, or at any rate superfluous, that it is being widely discarded. No such fate would appear in store for the trial jury, even though, as indicated, it too is not so uniformly employed as formerly. But one has only to read newspapers and law journals, or even hear lawyers and judges talk, to realize that all is not entirely well with the trial-jury system. To start with, the caliber of jurors could be improved. Jury service is supposed to be one of the primary obligations of the citizen, with the jury itself representing a cross section of the community. Many occupational groups, however, including persons in public employment, are usually exempted by statute; business and professional people rarely are called upon to serve; and the elements from which jurymen are actually drawn are neither entirely representative nor usually of the experience and capacity that might be desired. Legal exemptions ought to be cut down and the practice of letting useful people off merely because they are otherwise occupied should be tightened up. Another criticism, often heard from judicial experts, is that whereas in national practice judges are expected, and indeed required, to assist juries in understanding and evaluating evidence, state judges usually are without such authority; and that, in the absence of such help, juries often flounder and waste time, occasionally bringing in verdicts influenced by serious misconceptions. Finally may be mentioned the problem of making the lot of the juror more tolerable also by greater courtesy from court officials than sometimes is shown, and by curbing the verbosity and dilatoriness with which lawyers often draw out proceedings to inordinate length.

Lower state courts confine themselves to the function for which all *Judicial* courts exist primarily, that is, deciding cases. Like higher national courts, *review* however, state supreme courts, in addition, look into the constitutionality of laws and executive actions, refusing to enforce any found contrary to a national or state constitutional provision. In ten states, *advisory opinions* on constitutional questions will be given in advance to the governor if requested, and in seven of these to the legislature also. But elsewhere, judgment on such questions will be rendered only in deciding actual cases. The power of judicial review has been exercised almost from the beginning of the nation's history, but with increasing frequency in later decades (especially since about 1890), and for reasons closely associated with the overloading of state constitutions in this last half century with subject matter, and with detailed specifications, which ought to have been left to legislative discretion. A great deal of criticism has been stirred, particularly by the frequency with which statutes, or portions thereof, are invalidated (sometimes by narrow margins of four to three or three to two) on the ground of taking property or denying liberty without due process of law. Dislike of such control over public policy in virtual defiance of the people's elected representatives in the legislative branch has encouraged (*a*) a dozen states to adopt the popular initiative for constitutional amendments as a means of circumventing obstructive courts; (*b*) three states (Ohio, North Dakota, and Nebraska) to change their constitutions so as to require something more than a bare majority for declaring a law null and void; and (*c*) some people even to propose that due-process clauses be deleted from state constitutions, leaving all protection of private rights, when involving due process, to the national courts. Unless expunged by the legislature, a measure judicially invalidated remains, of course, on the statute books; it simply can no longer be invoked against anyone violating it.

PREVENTIVE JUSTICE

For a long time our state judicial establishments largely confined *Declara-* their activities to the redress of wrongs already committed, and agencies *tory* of "preventive justice" remained almost entirely undeveloped. Only within *judgments* very narrow limits was it possible to clear up in advance of hostile litigation any doubt as to the legal status of persons, the title to property, or the meaning of a contract. In the last three or four decades, however, the view has gained favor that "a system of law that will not prevent the doing of a wrong, but only affords redress after the wrong is committed, is not a complete system, and is inadequate to the present needs of society; that whenever a person's legal rights are so uncertain as to cause him potential loss or disturbance, the state ought to provide instrumentalities of preventive relief to remove the uncertainty before a loss or injury has been sustained." And in pursuance of these considerations, more than 40 states, beginning with New Jersey in 1915, have authorized their courts, on proper application, to define or declare disputed rights and duties before any suit involving them has been fought through the courts. In 1934, too, the national courts were authorized to render similar "declaratory judgments."

Concilia-
tion and
arbitration

The courts always have favored the settlement of legal disputes by arbitration, or compromise, after a trial has commenced; and almost contemporaneously with the adoption of declaratory-judgment laws, legislation appeared authorizing less formal, time-consuming, and expensive methods of adjusting legal disputes than prevail in ordinary judicial proceedings. Small-claims courts have become common, especially in cities; and special courts of conciliation and arbitration have been set up, or existing courts have been empowered to adopt rules providing for such procedures. Conciliation takes place when parties to a dispute reach a settlement through the mediation of a third party called a conciliator. An agreement of the kind, however, is not legally enforceable in the courts if either party fails to abide by it. In arbitration proceedings, on the other hand, the parties submit their controversy to a third party, called the arbitrator, and agree in advance to be bound by his decision; and his award is enforceable by either side like the judgment of a regular court. Not the least among merits of these newer judicial agencies and practices is the way in which they tend to encourage a spirit of good will between parties to a dispute, thereby lessening or averting the animosity and rancor usually attending hostile litigation.

REFERENCES

F. R. Aumann, *The Changing American Legal System* (Columbus, O., 1940).
Council of State Governments, *The Book of the States* (Chicago), section on "Judicial Systems and Legal Procedures" in successive issues.
——, *Courts of Last Resort in the Forty-eight States* (Chicago, 1950).
——, *State Court Systems* (Chicago, 1962).
——, *Trial Courts of General Jurisdiction in the Forty-eight States* (Chicago, 1951).
S. D. Elliott, *Improving Our Courts: Collected Essays on Judicial Administration* (New York, 1960).
J. Frank, *Courts on Trial: Myth and Reality in American Justice* (Princeton, N. J., 1949).

W. E. Hannan and M. B. Csontos, *State Court Systems* (Chicago, 1940).

E. Haynes, *The Selection and Tenure of Judges* (Nat. Conf. of Judic. Councils, 1944).

J. W. Hurst, *The Growth of American Law; The Law Makers* (Boston, 1950).

H. Jacob, *Justice in America* (Boston, 1965).

L. Mayers, *The American Legal System* (New York, 1955).

L. B. Orfield, *Criminal Procedure from Arrest to Appeal* (New York, 1947).

R. Pound, *Criminal Justice in America* (Cambridge, Mass., 1945).

————, *Organization of Courts* (Boston, 1940).

A. T. Vanderbilt, *Judges and Jurors: Their Functions, Qualifications and Selection* (Boston, 1956).

————, *Minimum Standards of Judicial Administration* (New York, 1949).

II Local Government and Administration

7

LOCAL GOVERNMENT PATTERN AND LEGAL BASIS

From seventeenth-century England early Americans inherited a strong liking for managing their own affairs. With the ideas of limited government and popular sovereignty and the practice of representative government, the English tradition of local self-government was transplanted to America. The institutions and offices that embodied this tradition—the county, the town, the borough, the coroner, the sheriff, and others—remain with us to this day. Though adapted somewhat to the needs of the new environment and later to the growth and industrialization of the country, they have shown remarkable resistance to change. More so than any other part of our governmental system. There are many reasons for this endurance. Foremost among these is the importance of the functions they perform. Next our theories of local government have strengthened them. Lastly is the importance to the political parties of their organizations in the local units.

By tradition local governments have responsibility for many of the basic functions of government. They have the primary responsibility for protecting buildings from fire and persons and property from robbery, theft, and criminal violence. In urban areas, the necessity for maintaining a pure water supply and a sanitary environment puts a large burden for public health protection on the local units. In a democratic society, education is ranked with protection as a government duty; and here again, the local units have the basic responsibility. *Importance of local government*

Granted that the functions of local government are important, why are they administered locally? Tradition has always been an important element in the creation of local units. The English colonists brought with them a devotion to local autonomy which has continued throughout our history. The image of the New England town meetings as the archetype of "true" democracy is firmly fixed in American political philosophy. It *Theories of local self-government* is commonly called "grass roots" democracy. It means both that the existence of many small units of government gives people a chance to practice democracy at the "grass roots" or home level where the issues are easily understood and the necessary knowledge upon which to base judgments is available and that the closer a political unit can approximate the conditions of the New England town with its town meeting, the purer the democracy will be that is practiced. Essentially, government in small units is personal government. The individual can identify himself more easily with this kind of government, even when it no longer represents a social community whose members have common interests. "Grass roots" democracy holds a special attractiveness for the suburbanite, partly because it provides a rationale for his "separateness" from the city, but partly also because the suburban environment recalls the simpler patterns of life that were the base of the theory.

Local political organization

Our local governments are training grounds for party leaders. The roots of party organization are here. In the county government, especially, is usually found the base of the state organization. In these units are the strongholds of Jackson's legacy—the spoils system, the amateur in public office, many elected officials, and short terms of office. Local governments, therefore, are of paramount importance to the political parties.

TYPES AND NUMBERS OF LOCAL GOVERNMENTS

Rural forms

The general picture of local government in rural America is towns in New England; counties in every state except Rhode Island, Connnecticut, and Alaska; and, townships in sixteen states in a broad northern belt from New York westward to the great plains. In colonial New England the town was dominant and the county played a minor role. This is true today. In the old South, the county was dominant and no towns or townships existed. Because westward migration was largely along parallels of latitude, we find today that the county system is used throughout the South and West. There are very few towns or townships south of the Mason–Dixon line or west of the Rockies. In Illinois, Nebraska, and Missouri, where two lines of migration met, there are townships in some counties but not in all. In the Middle Atlantic states a mixed system prevailed and this was carried westward also. Local government in these states in general follows the New England pattern of township importance; however, the county tends to be dominant in border states such as Ohio, Indiana, Kansas, and Missouri. As a rule, civil townships are created and their boundaries may be changed by the board of supervisors or commissioners of the county in which they are situated.

Urban forms

Urban centers, both large and relatively small, are set apart and incorporated as cities with their own governments. Less populous places, desiring some of the powers and services of cities, may be similarly incorporated as villages or boroughs. Some boroughs and villages are larger than some cities, but in general the opposite is the case. These units are termed *municipalities* because they are incorporated. Any unit as it increases in population may progress from a town or township to a village or city by using procedures prescribed by the state in which it lies.

Other units

Numerous artificially constructed areas, mostly small, and seldom coinciding geographically with any of the subdivisions thus far mentioned, have been erected into school, fire protection, sanitary, and other units called *special districts*.

Numbers of local government units

The variety of local government units so far described has been the result of historical development. The same can be said for the large numbers of them. The number of units in any given region does not often correspond to population. Until lately, no one—not even the Bureau of the Census—could have indicated the number for the country as a whole. Even now, all that one can say is that the figure is in the neighborhood of

NUMBER OF LOCAL GOVERNMENTS IN THE UNITED STATES, BY TYPE

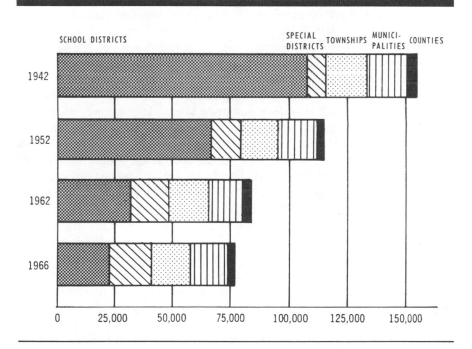

SOURCE: Bureau of the Census, *Census of Governments, 1962* (Washington, D. C., 1963) and Council of State Governments, *Book of the States 1968–1969* (Chicago, 1968) p. 278.

80,000. The most highly saturated portion of the country is the west north central section containing the states of Illinois, Michigan, Missouri, Kansas, Nebraska, Minnesota, and Wisconsin. These states have over one-third of the total number of local governments but less than one-fifth of the total population (1960 census). The most populous state, New York, ranks ninth in the number of local governments.

LOCAL GOVERNMENT REFORM

General need

Fixed in a rural environment and before the development of rapid transportation, the local government pattern is one of too many and too small units for the management of local affairs. Our two newest states have entered the union with a distinct advantage over the older ones in this regard. Determined to profit from the experience in the older states, Alaska expressed its philosophy of local government in its constitution—namely, "to provide for maximum local government with a minimum of local government units, and to prevent duplication of tax levying jurisdictions" (Art. X, Sec. 1). In Hawaii, the legislature may create subdivisions in addition to the county but has not done so. Elsewhere, however, people live under several layers of government, overlapping in intricate patterns.

The first effect of this is that the average voter is confused and the result is all too often a lessening of democratic control of the political process rather than the better control the advocates of "grass roots" democracy hope for. In addition, many citizens reside and work under different jurisdictions. When this is the case, they are disfranchised from having a voice in decisions that are taken by the municipality where they work. Only indirectly can they influence these. The second effect is an inefficient duplication of activities. The American people have shown a willingness to pay for this inefficiency, considering other less mundane goals more worthy. However, the recent spectacular population growth has aggravated the situation so acutely in urban areas that many concerned citizens have joined students of the subject in urging disentanglement and simplification. The most important aspect of this phenomenon is the shift of the urban population from the more crowded central cities to the less crowded suburbs and beyond to rural areas. This has brought problems to areas ill-equipped governmentally to handle them. Paradoxically, the first response of the people affected has been to *increase* the numbers of local units. Special districts have been created to provide urban services and townships or parts of them have incorporated for the same reason.

Suburbani-zation in detail

Cities in the United States have been growing at their peripheries for a century, but before 1920, the central cities grew more rapidly than the outlying parts. The reverse did not become a widespread pattern until after World War I though it was evident earlier in the older and more densely populated cities. Since World War II, this trend has accelerated. The following figures show the trend:

| | PERCENT OF INCREASE | |
	1940–1950	1950–1960
U. S. total	14.5	19.
Metropolitan areas—total	22.	26.4
Central cities	13.9	10.6
Outlying parts	35.6	49.

From 1940 to 1950 the oldest and largest central cities increased but slightly in population and from 1950 to 1960 many of them actually declined. The bald fact seems to be that given the means and the opportunity people no longer find the central city attractive as a place in which to live. The increased use of the private automobile, postwar prosperity, and national government inducements to home ownership have combined with other factors to produce a suburban spread over the landscape.

In 1962 (the latest census of local governments) there were 18,442 local governments in the 212 Standard Metropolitan Statistical Areas of that year. Most of them were incorporated municipalities, special districts, and school districts. The surprising number of townships (2,573) reflects the suburban spread. The leaders of most metropolitan areas are conscious of the disparity between modern urban living and this inherited governmental pattern that is expected to facilitate it. In almost every recent year a study of local problems has been started in some metropolitan area. The recommendations proposed in these studies are many and various but the difficulties and problems uncovered are markedly alike. The common problems reported are that the multiplicity of governments is a serious impediment to the administration of governmental services; many units are so small and financial resources vary so widely that there is an inadequacy or even absence of certain services. The main problem fields are

Problems posed by the multiplicity of units in metropolitan areas

(1) *Transportation.* Traffic congestion and frustration is ubiquitous. An integrated system of local streets, major arterials, and mass transit is necessary for the efficient movement of people and goods. Perhaps this is an ideal impossible to achieve in the larger urban areas, but it is clear that the problem can not even be attacked without an areawide approach.

(2) *Disposal of sanitary and industrial wastes, storm water drainage, and provision for a water supply.* Adequate and equitable provision for these is virtually impossible or excessively costly on an individual basis. The result of individual effort in too many cases is water pollution, flooding of streets and basements, and mutual recrimination.

(3) *Land use planning.* Competition among units for industrial, business, and "desirable" residential development in order to bolster local

finances widens the gap between units in their relative ability to provide services. Typically, too, a unit that secures a new industry does not consider the effect of this on the rest of the area—the changed traffic pattern and the new residents who find homes in other places with their needs for schools and other governmental services. In addition, it is difficult for small governments to obtain or set aside the large areas needed for parks and playing fields by an urban population.

GOVERNMENTAL COMPLEXITY

Taxing and Charging Jurisdictions in a Typical Metropolitan Area

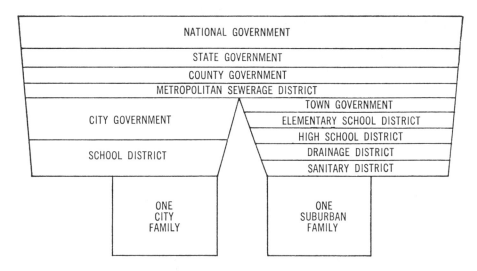

A composite from units existing in the Madison Metropolitan Statistical Area, Dane County, Wis.

Total local units in the urbanized area—129   Total local units in the county—212

County population in 1960—222,095

All of these problems are particularly troublesome in rural areas that are in the process of becoming urbanized. In some instances, the needed services and controls are not provided to the detriment of other areas. Since the solutions proposed hinge on the powers and finances of the individual governments, discussion of them will be postponed until a later chapter.

Local units as public corporations

LEGAL BASIS OF COUNTIES AND MUNICIPALITIES

All units of local government are public corporations, created by, or under authority of, state law to provide services more appropriately furnished in this way than through private effort. As such, they have continuous existence, regardless of population changes, as long as the state does not revoke them; as such, also, they enjoy all customary corporate rights, such as those of suing and being sued, making contracts, acquiring, holding, and disposing of property, and exercising every power conferred. All, however, are not of quite the same nature and function. One category, known as municipal corporations proper, includes those at least presumed to have been created primarily in response to local initiative based on desire for local management of affairs. Cities, villages, boroughs, and incorporated towns are of this sort. A second category, termed quasi-municipal corporations, consists rather of units created by the state (or the county as agent of the state) on its own initiative, regardless of local opinion, and for locally carrying on statewide activities such as enforcement of law, assessment and collection of taxes, and educational and public health services. Counties, towns, townships, school districts, and numerous other kinds of special districts are here included. Legally, the distinction is significant; practically, it is not. Units of both types serve at the same time as organs of self-government and as areas for state administration. Many townships, counties, and special districts have also been created because the people in the area wished or asked for them. The distinction is thus one of *primary* purpose only, but it assumes some importance when broad grants of power are contemplated for counties and special districts to enable them to provide more urban-type services.

From the fact that all local-government units are created by, or on authority of, the state in which they are situated, and by it are endowed, expressly or by fair implication, with whatever functions and powers they possess, it follows that the relation between the state and its subdivisions is totally different from that existing, in the reverse direction, between the state and the United States. In the latter case, the state is not a division existing for the use and convenience of the national government; on the contrary, it is, within limits, a separate and independent area of government, in some respects on a footing of equality with the nation itself. Whether counties, towns, townships, or districts, created primarily for state purposes, or cities, villages, or boroughs, organized primarily to meet the demand for local control of local affairs, local units exist by no original or inherent right and have no reserved or residual powers. On the contrary, all (at least broadly) are instrumentalities of the state, employed by it in the enforcement of its laws, the collection of its revenues, and the performance of others of its functions. In short, the United States is organized on a federal basis, but the governmental system of each state is strictly unitary. *Local units as state instrumentalities*

Every city has as its fundamental law a charter (its own separately, or one shared with other cities through the medium of a code) establishing its boundaries, defining its powers, outlining its system of government, prescribing the method of electing its council and choosing its mayor and other officials, assigning to some or all such officials their respective *Legal position of the city— the charter* duties, and fixing with varying degrees of precision the relations of officials with one another. City charters (or at any rate the right to frame them) come from the legislature; and since charters or charter laws differ in no essential respect from other acts of the legislature, that body has authority to grant, withhold, suspend, alter, or revoke them at will, even against the expressed wishes of the people of any city concerned. In practice, such legal autocracy is tempered by considerations of political expediency, by moral inhibitions where charters have been made locally under express legislative grant of authority, and of course by such restrictions upon state legislative power as may be found in the national or the state constitution.

Legal position of the county
Counties are created and their boundaries fixed by act of the legislature, with, however, constitutional provisions protecting them in most states against extinction or loss of territory unless assented to by the voters concerned. Once established, they become quasi-corporations. As such, they generally have less broad powers to deal with matters of local concern and have more duties to fulfill in matters of statewide concern. Their forms of organization, the officers they shall have, and the powers they may exercise are prescribed by state laws and constitutions. Whereas, most provisions for the organization and powers of municipalities are found in the statutes, constitutional provisions relating to county government are more numerous. For this reason, the framework of county government is more rigid than that under which municipalities operate.

State methods of prescribing for local governments:
1. Special laws
Some state legislatures grant charters and pass laws governing counties and municipalities by special act (as well as by general law). This is the practice in New England (except Massachusetts) and in parts of the South. Under this system, there may be as many varieties of city and of county government as there are cities and counties. Varying local conditions can be taken into account and change is sometimes more easily accomplished when only one unit is involved; but, since the system also lends itself to flagrant abuse, it came into disrepute during the latter 19th century—a time when local and state governments were notably corrupt. The constitutions of the rest of the states were changed to prohibit such special legislation. General laws only can be enacted in these states.

2. General laws and classification systems
General laws limit factious and arbitrary interference in local affairs on the part of the state legislature but the local governmental framework suffers from a surfeit of uniformity. The difficulty of prescribing for all cities or all counties the same powers, duties, and forms of organization, regardless of differences in size, character, or need is obvious. The result is a compromise—the classification system. The most popular and the most practicable method is to classify by population. Thus we find that cities of over 25,000 people and less than 50,000 will have a different set of rights and duties or a different form of government than cities of more than 50,000. The usual number of classes is four or five. Classification systems are more commonly created for cities than for counties. Though

several states have set up four or five classes of county government, two is more common—one for the largest county, if it contains a metropolis, and one for the rest of the state's counties. Like most compromises, the plan has not been very satisfactory for cities. As they grow in population, they may be forced to change their form of government or assume burdens against their will. Two other and newer methods of prescribing for local governments are receiving more attention today—the home rule and the optional charter plans.

All the above methods of providing the legal framework within which local governments operate are vulnerable from the standpoint of local initiative and local desires for self-determination and control of their own governmental destinies. The fundamental idea of home rule is that the people directly affected by their local government should have the right to draft their own charter and embody therein whatever plan of government they prefer, as well as to exercise under it all powers not inconsistent with the constitution and laws of the state and nation. The home rule method of charter drafting has been constitutionally authorized for cities in half the states and in eight additional ones the legislature has granted broad authority to some or all cities to amend their charters or adopt new ones. More than 600 cities and villages in 25 states are now operating under home rule charters including most of the 30 largest ones. County home rule is currently widely discussed for urban counties. Though the number of counties with home rule is small, the movement is spreading. The chief difficulty with framing county home rule charters is the frequent provision that separate majorities be obtained—one in the city and one in the rest of the county—to ratify them. More proposals have thus been defeated than have been adopted.

3. Home rule charters

The home rule plan has a number of manifest merits. First, it enables the people of a city or county to have whatever form of government they consider best adapted to their needs and to formulate it locally rather than have it handed down to them by the legislature. In determining, too, what is best adapted, they are free to experiment and thus to assist local governments everywhere. Secondly, home rule stimulates greater interest of citizens in their own local government. When the charter is being framed and adopted local citizen interest and participation in governmental affairs reaches a peak. Finally, the plan would seem to benefit the state legislature by relieving it of the necessity for considering a multitude of local questions that it is poorly prepared to answer intelligently, even if it had unlimited time which it doesn't. Actually, this has not happened to anything like the degree anticipated by its sponsors. No system, however, completely frees the municipality or county from state domination. Locally made charters are subject to the general state laws and state laws take precedence over local ordinances in most states. This is as it should be. A city or county is part of the state and is inextricably interlocked with the state in its interests and responsibilities. Even if the

Home rule appraised

legislature is disposed to leave a city entirely free to deal with purely local matters as it desires, there is no clear line of demarcation today between things that are wholly local and those that, while perhaps primarily local, transcend city boundaries and concern the people of other portions of the state. As a method, therefore, for carving out a sphere of local autonomy for cities into which no higher level of government ought to intrude, home rule has lost much of its early attractiveness. Our society has grown too interdependent. However, as a method for reforming county government and equipping it to meet the needs of an urban population where this is necessary and for distinguishing these urban counties from the vast majority of rural ones, home rule is extremely useful.

4. Optional charters and permissive legislation

In recent years, an alternative method for providing local charters has been growing in popularity. This is the optional charter system. Over half the states now employ it for cities, including 15 home rule states, and several states provide alternative forms of county government. Noteworthy among the latter are New York, Virginia, and North Dakota. The optional charter system was designed to avoid both the disadvantages of uniform local government codes and the special law system. Like classification it permits variety within a standard framework but unlike the classification system it is not used to define local powers and responsibilities. Optional charters prescribe alternative *forms* of local government only. In effect, this system introduces a sort of *à la carte* charter service by incorporating into the general law of the state several standard types of charter providing for different forms of government—for cities the commission form, the council–manager plan, and sundry varieties of the mayor–council type; for counties alternative forms that may be used to replace the existing one. The county options all have features of reform; for instance, they usually include provisions that would consolidate offices or provide for a county executive, manager, or administrator. Each local unit can select for itself a form of government from the menu thus provided.

Permissive legislation is the same sort of menu service. Grants of authority to local units or to classes of them to perform certain functions if and when they so desire are given by the state. The desires of the local units for self-determination are more or less satisfied and questions of what is and what is not solely a matter of local concern are avoided. For these reasons, among others, permissive legislation combined with the optional charter system has worked as well as, if not better than, formal home rule.

5. State administrative supervision

The main object of all of these different plans of charter-framing, except the special-charter system, is to reduce state interference with local autonomy. While this effort has been pursued energetically and with some success, a contrary trend of almost irresistible force has been taking place: the development of administrative supervision over certain local activities by state officers or boards. Thus in New York, Massachusetts, and

Ohio, the state civil service board is authorized to exercise direct supervision over the work of local civil service commissions. In order to check local abuses, several states have placed supervision of the enforcement of their election laws in the hands of a state official or board. Similarly, state boards of health or education, state finance departments or commissions, and state public utilities or public service commissions have, in a number of states, taken over in recent years many of the functions previously performed by the state legislature. A number of states go so far as to provide for state auditing of local accounts, and require the adoption of a uniform system of bookkeeping and submission of regular financial reports in a specified form to the state auditor or some other state authority. Whenever, also, a public service problem transcends the boundaries of several adjacent municipalities, there is a tendency to invoke state administrative control. Under circumstances of this kind one is likely to find a state-established park, sewerage, or police board such as now exercise authority throughout the metropolitan district of Boston. As a rule, state administrative supervision has proved more beneficial to local units directly affected than has legislative supervision. With a view, indeed, to unifying and harmonizing such supervision it has been advocated that every state create an agency concerned only with local affairs—as did Pennsylvania in 1919, when a state bureau of municipalities was set up. New York, New Jersey, Connecticut, Vermont, Ohio, Minnesota, Missouri, Alaska, Rhode Island, and Wisconsin have all recently followed Pennsylvania and created state agencies to provide financial and technical assistance to local governments. Small cities in particular, might be helped by such an agency.

REFERENCES

For details on points discussed in this and in the following chapters, the student is referred to the following texts:

C. R. Adrian, *Governing Urban America* (2nd ed., New York, 1961).

Advisory Committee on Intergovernmental Relations, *Reports and Special Studies* (Washington, D. C.).

H. F. Alderfer, *American Local Government and Administration* (New York, 1956).

B. Baker, *Urban Government* (Princeton, N. J., 1957).

A. W. Bromage, *Introduction to Municipal Government and Administration* (2nd ed., New York, 1957).

M. J. Fisher and D. G. Bishop, *Municipal Government and Politics* (New York, 1950).

D. R. Grant and H. C. Nixon, *State and Local Government in America* (Boston, 1963).

C. M. Kneier, *City Government in the United States* (3rd ed., New York, 1957).

C. M. Kneier and G. Fox, *Readings in Municipal Government* (New York, 1953).
L. W. Lancaster, *Government in Rural America* (rev. ed., New York, 1952).
D. Lockard, *The Politics of State and Local Government* (New York, 1963).
A. F. Macdonald, *American City Government and Administration* (6th ed., New York, 1956).
E. F. Nolting and D. S. Arnold (eds.), *The Municipal Year Book* (Chicago), published annually by the International City Managers' Association.
J. E. Pate, *Local Government and Administration* (New York, 1954).
J. C. Phillips, *Municipal Government and Administration in America* (New York, 1961).
C. F. Snider, *American State and Local Government* (New York, 1950).
———, *Local Government in Rural America* (New York, 1957).
P. W. Wager (ed.), *County Government Across the Nation* (Chapel Hill, N. C., 1950).
H. Zink, *Government of Cities in the United States* (rev. ed., New York, 1948).

8

RURAL LOCAL GOVERNMENT

THE COUNTY

From previous comment on the nature and position of the county, one would infer that the role played by that local unit in our governmental system is difficult to evaluate; and so indeed it is. In the first place, it is not the same in all parts of the country. In New England, the county has no great importance except as a judicial unit; in the South and Far West, it controls justice, education, public health, public works, welfare, highways, and many other things; in the middle and midwestern states, it holds an intermediate position, frequently sharing many local functions with the township. In the second place, the county is at the same time an area for purposes of its own locally controlled government and an area for carrying on state administrative and judicial activities. In fact, it is an area for the performance of a few functions promoted by the national government as well. In many instances the powers and duties entailed overlap and can be disentangled only by one willing to spend patient hours grubbing in the laws, records, and accounts stored up in the courthouse. Observing the steady transfer of functions from county to state in later years—to say nothing of the ever-advancing hand of the national government—some people have been puzzled about what the role of the county really is, and even have predicted that, whatever it is, it is doomed to extinction. Such observers fail to perceive that if the county as a self-governing unit is losing it also is gaining—that, indeed, the number of functions passing under state or national control is counterbalanced by the number of new ones acquired as activities on all government levels continue to multiply. Judged, in fact, by the variety of functions performed (for the county itself or by it for state or nation), the number of employes on its payroll, and the amounts of money expended, the county is today, on the whole, a more vital part of our governmental system than at any time past.

The county's complicated role

Confusing variety

To the governmental organization of counties, very little thought appears to have been given by constitutional conventions, state legislatures, or the general public—at any rate in comparison with the amount of attention bestowed on the government of states and cities. On this account and on account of their position as creatures of the state the governments of counties not only differ from state to state, but sometimes even from county to county within the same state. City governments are of different types, for example, mayor–council, commission, council–manager; but, speaking broadly, all city governments of the same type are much alike, allowing only for differences of population and physical environment. County governments, however, classify in no such convenient fashion. There are officers, boards, and commissions, but no standardized nomenclature; some are elected by the people, others are appointed, still others are ex officio; each often occupies a little island of separate power, with hardly a trace of supervision or coordination; there are deputies, assistants, and employes—sometimes small armies of them. The overall impression gained by any one seeking to penetrate the labyrinth is that of jumble. Amid the disorder, however, arises one agency—the county board—which comes closest to being a central governing body.

The county board:

Although under different names, a county board is found in all states except Rhode Island and Connecticut where there is no county government at all. With a few exceptions (mainly in the South), it is everywhere elective, with the term two years in one-fourth, and four years in nearly half, of

1. Structure

the counties. Structurally, there are two main types. One is a board made large by allotting one or more representatives (locally elected as supervisors) to every town or township and to every city ward within the county; and such a "board of supervisors" (found chiefly in New York, New Jersey, Virginia, Michigan, and Wisconsin, and in parts of Kentucky, Tennessee, and Louisiana) often has 40 or 50 members—in Wayne County (Detroit), Michigan, 97. The other type is a board consisting rather of a few—commonly three, but sometimes, five, seven, or more— "commissioners" elected (usually) by the voters of the county at large, and known as a "board of commissioners." At least 70 percent of all counties have a board of this nature. In so far as the board is a legislative body, the broader representation provided by a large membership seems appropriate; and in many localities the constituent areas of the county cling resolutely to it. In practice, however, the board's functions are far more administrative than legislative; and for purposes of administration the small board is clearly preferable. Large boards do most of their work through more or less autonomous committees, are often scenes of petty log-rolling among members owing primary allegiance to their townships, and are more expensive. In the large representative board system it should be noted, the system of apportioning seats among the county units is reviewable by the national and state courts under the equal-protection clause. Several have been declared inequitable. If counties were adequately organized, with an integrated administrative branch and the board simply a policy-deter-mining agency, a board of intermediate size probably would be desirable. Given the typical administrative organization, the large board is rarely advantageous.

In some states, the county judge or some other designated official serves as ex officio chairman of the board. In a few instances, for ex-ample, Cook County, Illinois, a chairman is elected by the people. In the great majority of cases, the position is filled by the board members them-selves. In any event, with occasional exceptions, the incumbent has little if any more power (except for appointing committees) than his associates. As indicated, large boards work chiefly through committees, with general meetings occurring about once a month. With committees unnecessary, small boards commonly meet more frequently. *2. Organi-zation*

In powers and functions, as in other respects, the county board is purely a creature of the state. All powers conferred upon the county and not delegated by law to any other authority are regarded as belonging to the board. One important field of authority is finance. The board levies taxes for county purposes; equalizes the assessment of taxes among the different townships and cities in the county; borrows money; fixes the salaries or other compensation of minor county officials and employes; and appropriates money for various county purposes. Highways are also a major area of board concern and in recent years regulatory activities such as zoning have been undertaken. The county board also supervises elec-tions and administers state, national, *and* county programs in welfare and public assistance. In populous counties, the board is likely to have power to fill a very large number of positions on the county payroll, and ap-pointments frequently show the spoils system at its worst. Fourteen states, however, have merit laws applying either to all counties or to more populous ones, and in more than 300 counties some effort has been made to supplant spoils by competitive civil service examinations. *3. Powers and functions*

Besides the county board, counties, typically, have six or more elective officers, all largely independent of one another, of the county board, and usually of the officers of the state as well. Titles and duties vary widely, but the officers of chief importance are always the sheriff and the prosecuting attorney. *Other county officers*

Historically descended from the old Saxon *shire-reeve,* the sheriff is found in nearly every state. Usually, he is elected. In Rhode Island he is appointed by the governor, and in New York City a single sheriff for the five counties is appointed by the mayor. His term is usually two years, although three-year and four-year terms are not uncommon. In a number of states the constitution unwisely makes him ineligible for immediate reelection. Included among his prerogatives is that of appointing almost any number of deputies, whose powers become the same as his own, but with himself responsible for any official acts performed by them. In most states he is a salaried official; but sometimes both he and his deputies *1. Sheriff:*

receive much (if not all) of their compensation in the form of fees, which, in very populous counties, sometimes amount to tens of thousands of dollars a year.

a. Police duties

The duties most commonly assigned to the sheriff fall into two main groups: those relating to the preservation of the public peace, sometimes called police duties, and those connected with the operation of the courts. On paper, the sheriff's police duties are impressive, including as they do management of the county jail, arrest and safe-keeping of persons charged with crimes or misdemeanors, and enforcement of status against gambling, vice, and liquor-selling. Except, however, in some of the more sparsely settled portions of the country, they actually are quite limited. No county police, corresponding to a city police force, is at the sheriff's command, and as a rule neither town and village constables nor city police units are in any way subject to his control. In time of public disorder, therefore, the sheriff is likely to be obliged to summon to his aid the *posse comitatus* (such able-bodied men of the county as he may select), or even to call upon the governor for assistance from the state militia (National Guard) or—where such a force exists—the state police.

b. Court duties

The greater portion of the sheriff's time is consumed in the performance of his duties as executive agent of the courts. He attends court sessions; he serves the various writs and other processes in connection with civil suits, and also warrants for the arrest of persons accused of crime and subpoenas for the attendance of witnesses; he carries out the judgments of the courts in civil cases (for example, seizing and selling property to satisfy judgments), and executes court sentences upon persons convicted of crimes or misdemeanors. These activities are more lucrative than tracking down criminals, and thus they often are the ones to which the sheriff devotes himself most assiduously.

Although sheriffs are elected locally, they are, in law, agents of the state; and many, if not most, of their functions have to do with the enforcement of state laws. In very few states, however, do the higher state officials exercise effective control over them. In New York, Michigan, and Wisconsin, the governor may remove a sheriff for cause; and in Illinois, he must remove a sheriff who allows a prisoner to be taken from his custody by a mob.

2. Prosecuting attorney:

Of considerably greater importance is the prosecuting attorney—known in different states as state's attorney, district attorney, or county solicitor. Generally such an official is elected in each county; but in some states he is (or may be) chosen in a district containing more than one county, in which case his jurisdiction extends throughout his district. In a very few states, the attorney is appointed by the governor, as in Florida, or by the judges of some court. Selected in most instances county by county, and by popular election, such attorneys inevitably vary greatly in character and ability. They are likely to reflect the dominant sentiment of their communities toward law enforcement, a fact which partly explains the unfortunate lack of uniformity sometimes found in different parts of the same state in the enforcement of laws against gambling, vice, illicit liquor-selling, and other offenses. However chosen and supervised, the prosecuting attorney is paid a salary in a number of states, and in others is recompensed with fees. The tendency is to substitute salaries for the fee system.

In most states, the prosecuting attorney has important civil duties: he is the legal adviser to most, if not all, of the county officials; he draws up and passes upon the validity of county contracts; he institutes and conducts suits brought by the county and defends those brought against the county, or against any officer thereof in his official capacity; he prosecutes all cases of forfeited official or bail bonds; and he cooperates with the attorney general of the state in the handling of important cases affecting the county. *a. Civil duties*

But the prosecuting attorney's most conspicuous duties, as his title implies, relate to the enforcement of criminal statutes; and the extent to which crime is repressed depends largely on his ability, judgment, honesty, and energy. He investigates crimes which come to his attention through the public press, the police, or on complaint of private citizens; he institutes proceedings for the arrest and detention of persons accused or suspected of crime and the detention of important witnesses who otherwise might leave the state; he commences criminal actions where in his judgment the facts warrant doing so, either by filing an "information" with the proper court or by drawing up indictments and submitting evidence in support of them to a grand jury; and, either in person or by deputy, he conducts the trial of criminal cases. Recommendations which he makes concerning the fixing of bail, the discontinuance or nol-prossing of criminal actions, and the severity of sentences are usually given serious consideration by the courts. It is often his duty, also, to bring to trial public officers accused of official misconduct. *b. Law enforcement*

The office is truly one of great responsibility and invested with ample possibilities for good or evil. Control of it in counties containing large cities is a political prize of the first magnitude for both the law-abiding classes and the criminal and vicious elements interested in lax law-enforcement and a "wide-open town." It should invariably go to a lawyer of unquestioned ability, a citizen of the highest character, a man forceful and fearless in the discharge of duty, and one who is above suspicion of being controlled by, or under obligations to, any corrupt organization. Courageous and efficient prosecuting attorneys often have won distinction and political advancement. The governnor's chair has been attained by many. *c. Demands of the office*

The office of coroner is of nearly the same antiquity as that of sheriff, although considerably less important. Almost everywhere the incumbent is popularly elected, for two or four years, although in six or seven states he is appointed by the county board or by the judges of one of the higher courts; in Rhode Island, he is appointed by the town council, *3. Coroner* and therefore is not a county official at all. As set forth in a New York statute, the coroner's main function is to investigate the circumstances under which any person has died "from criminal violence or by casualty, or suddenly when in apparent health, or when unattended by a physician, or in prison, or in any suspicious or unusual manner." When holding an inquest to determine the cause of a death, a coroner acts both as a medical examiner and as a magistrate, with authority in the latter role to conduct a hearing and examine witnesses; and he may act singly or may (in some states must) enlist the assistance of a jury, usually of six, selected from bystanders or other people of the neighborhood. A verdict of natural death, accidental death, or suicide usually ends the matter. If, however, reason appears for believing some person or persons to have been criminally responsible, the district attorney or police are supposed to start work on the case, with the coroner himself empowered to issue a warrant for the arrest of any suspected person whose identity is known. In many counties the coroner's office is little more than a booby prize awarded to some insignificant adherent of the dominant political machine, with most incumbents having neither the medical nor legal qualifications presumed. A far better situation exists in five New England, two southern, several other eastern and midwestern states, where the coroner has been supplanted by an appointive medical examiner (full-time in larger cities) required to have competence as a physician or pathologist, and with all legal aspects of the work left to the prosecuting attorney. The coroner well may be on his way out along with the justice of the peace.

4. Clerk   In about half of the states, there is a county clerk, nearly always popularly elected, and for two or four years. Duties vary widely, but as a rule they include (1) serving as secretary to the county board; (2) making formal records of ordinances, resolutions, and other board actions; (3) performing the duties of an auditor or comptroller where no such officer exists; and (4) issuing marriage licenses, hunting and fishing licenses, and other licenses and permits. Not infrequently, too, the clerk has electoral duties, such as registering voters, receiving nomination petitions, and supervising the preparation of ballots. In other words, he is a sort of clearing house for county business. In one or two states, for example, Wisconsin, he somewhat approaches the character of a county chief executive.

5. Other offices and boards   This outline of county offices might be continued at wearisome length. For the rest, it must, however, serve merely to enumerate the most important ever found in some counties. The general nature of the duties attached will be apparent from the name: (1) one or more court clerks; (2) a treasurer; (3) an auditor or comptroller; (4) a recorder or register of deeds; (5) a superintendent of schools; (6) a surveyor; (7) a highway superintendent; (8) an assessor; (9) a county agricultural agent; (10) a female home-demonstration agent; (11) a health officer; (12) a welfare superintendent; (13) a purchasing officer; and (14) a veterinarian; and of boards, (1) a board of (tax assessment) review; (2) a board of education; (3) a library board; (4) an election board; and (5) a planning commission. In total officers and employes, about 700,000 persons serve county governments in this country.

THE PROBLEM OF COUNTY REFORM

Fifty years ago, a challenging book was published under the title of *The County; The Dark Continent of American Politics* (New York, 1917). What the author (H. S. Gilbertson) had in mind was that county government was a labyrinth whose intricate windings were known to very few people except practical politicians, and that even professional students of government had paid scant attention to it in comparison with the governments of nation, state, and city. To a considerable extent, this unfortunate situation still exists. In the interval, however, an increasing number of disinterested explorers have penetrated the jungle in different states (notably New York, New Jersey, Illinois, Minnesota, North Carolina, Oklahoma, and Virginia), afterwards reporting significantly on what they found. And all accounts agree that in general the county has been largely untouched by reform movements which have yielded remarkable improvements in states and especially in cities; that, almost everywhere, cumbersome machinery and antiquated methods persist, along with divided authority and responsibility—defects which, until the depression of three decades ago, went almost unchallenged.

Belated recognition of a bad situation

Troubles associated with that hard experience did what scattered reformers never had succeeded in doing, they convinced public officials and taxpayers alike that there was more ground for criticism than they had been wont to admit. Even yet, changes for the better have been only sporadic and most have occurred in urban counties, which comprise only one-tenth of the total number. The first need is the recognition that there are two main kinds of counties, urban and rural and subtypes within these. Appropriate state laws should be designed for each type. In urban counties, in particular, the powers should be enlarged and the boards made more representative. The main shortcoming of the rural counties is that there are too many of them. Common to both types is the need for internal reorganization.

Governmental shortcomings and suggested remedies:

With rare exceptions, county governments are not departmentalized and correlated but are aggregations of scattered and almost independent offices and boards. In particular, too many county officers are elected. This results in (1) lengthening the ballot and confusing the voter on election day; (2) preventing overall direction of these officials by a responsible superior; and (3) preventing the making and administering of a comprehensive county budget.

1. Internal reorganization— the need for central control of county functions:

As most counties now are organized, the most serious shortcoming, however, is the lack of any chief executive. Any administrative reorganiza-

a. Too many elective offices

b. Need for a chief executive — tion would fall short unless some such apex, as in city, state, and nation, were provided. In a few scattered counties, something approaching such a unifying authority has been supplied. Since 1900 Hudson and Essex Counties in New Jersey have had an elective executive somewhat like a weak mayor. Since the mid-thirties, Nassau and Westchester Counties in New York have had an elective executive with powers of appointment, removal, supervision and veto. An elective chief executive with powers generally similar to those of a mayor in a strong-mayor city also serves in Cook County (Chicago), Ill. and in Milwaukee County, Wis. The home-rule charters adopted in St. Louis County, Missouri, and Baltimore County, Maryland (in 1950 and 1956, respectively), provide for a similar head.

The county managership — Another type of executive which is finding favor is the county manager, patterned after the city manager now found in so many municipalities. Some counties (for example, in Georgia, North Carolina, and Wisconsin) have taken hesitant steps in the direction of a managership under authority to vest limited duties of a managerial character in some one of the older county officials—the chairman of the county board, the county clerk, or the auditor. In some counties in other states, an appointive executive will have varying degrees of administrative responsibility but without having the duties associated with true managership. Noteworthy among these are California's chief administrative officers and those in two counties in Oregon. Other counties with modified manager plans are Cuyahoga County (Cleveland), Ohio; Hamilton County (Chattanooga), Tenn.; Clark County (Las Vegas), Nev.; Wayne County, Ga.; and Charleston County, So. Car. Where true managership exists, a full-time salaried manager is appointed by the county board, for no fixed term, and presumably without reference to politics or local residence. To him is assigned, under responsibility to the board and through it to the electorate, the entire task of coordinating and directing county administration. The board continues to levy taxes, borrow and appropriate money, enact ordinances, and determine the nature and extent of county services. It is supposed to leave the conduct of administration entirely to the manager and the higher officials appointed by and responsible to him. He should be operating through the integrated departments that almost of necessity go along with the system. If the board does not approve the way in which things are done, its proper course is to change managers rather than to interfere with and embarrass the existing one.

Its outlook — Authorization, constitutional or statutory, for the manager system in a few states, followed by actual adoption in 39 scattered counties by 1967, undoubtedly may be regarded as the most significant advance recently recorded in the field of county government. Many obstacles are encountered: tradition, which perhaps is nowhere stronger than in local government; popular fear of one-man rule; and constitutional impediments, as, for example, in Nebraska, where an optional county-manager act of 1933 was overthrown as incompatible with a constitutional requirement that all county officers be elected. In any state authorizing county home rule, however, the plan may be adopted by any county to which the privilege applies; in other states, it usually is constitutionally possible for the legislature to approve the system for a particular county. With testimony almost universal, where the scheme has been tried, that it yields good results, further progress may be confidently predicted. The one qualification to be added is that experience thus far has been almost entirely in populous, urbanized counties, and that it is there, rather than in sparsely inhabited counties with comparatively few activities, that one would expect the system's benefits to be greatest. In strictly rural counties of small population, the advantages might be less demonstrable, although from the one such county in the present list (Petroleum County, Montana, with a population in 1960 of less than one per square mile) come no less impressive reports of successful operation.

In early days, when travel was mainly by horse, a large number of counties in a state was required if the county seat was to be within a day's roundtrip from all parts of the county. Today, despite the railroad, the automobile, and the telephone, the number of counties (3,043) remains about what it formerly was, eight states having 100 or more. With the country's population shifting from section to section, and even within the same section, in response to changing economic conditions, many counties have come to be sparsely inhabited. All, however, are required by rigid constitutional or statutory provisions to maintain the same forms of government as more favored ones. All must also meet the costs of improved highways and of the multiplied social services now so conspicuously added to the older county functions—with the result that numerous small and poor counties are unable to finance themselves out of local resources. In most states the number of counties could be reduced by two-thirds, without harm to the principle of local self-government. This could be done by (1) consolidations, (2) deorganization by local action, or (3) abolition by the state. Consolidations have been authorized in several states, but only two have been accomplished. Authorizations for counties to deorganize (go out of existence) exist in many states. This requires local voter approval. The best statutes on this subject are in the Dakotas. The record in this type of reform is virtually *nil*. Connecticut and Rhode Island have abolished their counties as we have seen, but they are our most densely populated states. Rural local government has been largely untouched by this movement to reduce the number of counties as it has been largely untouched by the other reforms. Local pride, opposition of county officeholders and county-seat tradesmen, and reluctance of legislatures to force the matter, joined to constitutional obstacles, have combined to keep the number of counties constant.

An aroused public opinion might compel a county board to adopt a sort of self-denying ordinance and introduce the managership into the

2. Excessive number of counties

Ultimate need for constitutional amendment

existing government, without waiting for special authorization from the legislature. A progressive county board might also, within limits, consolidate offices, or at least introduce more businesslike methods in them. Probably no legislature is without power to provide for a thorough survey of county government, to authorize the employment of county managers, to abolish the fee system as some states have done, or to remedy loose financial methods by state supervision, audit, or inspection of accounts and the requirement of uniform systems of accounting and budgeting. A legislature might also enact county civil service laws, such as California did in 1939 and New York in 1941, abolish any unnecessary county offices created by statute and reassign their functions, or convert statutory elective offices into appointive ones.

In most states, however, "The roots of county government are imbedded in the legal granite of the state constitution and can be removed only by blasting them out with a constitutional amendment." Even the most intelligent and sympathetic legislature is limited, under existing powers, in what it may do to promote better county government and county boards are even more limited in what they can do on their own. There are constitutional provisions making all offices elective, frequent provisions imposing a uniform type of government upon all counties, and others. Nothing less, therefore, than a series of constitutional amendments in most states, will clear the way for the simplification and unification of county organization essential to effective local government. Reform proposals on such drastic lines, however, are likely to encounter sturdy opposition. The county commonly is the most important unit of "grass-roots" party organization, and county government the chief reservoir of party resources in local political contests.

THE NEW ENGLAND TOWN

The New England town is usually a rural trade center. There are towns with populations running into the thousands, but the majority of the 1,400 or more are not urban.

The town
meeting
The principal organ of government is a primary assembly composed of the town's qualified voters, and known as the town meeting. Substantially all of the town's powers are exercised by this body directly or through committees or officers acting as its agents. The town meeting is convoked in the town hall once every year (in October in Connecticut, but elsewhere during the spring months), with special meetings called if needed. For every meeting an itemized list of matters to be taken up is prepared and circulated by the selectmen, with ordinarily no topic permitted to be considered unless it appears on the list. Among items enumerated will certainly be appropriations for all of the town's supported activities (including schools), a tax rate designed to produce the necessary funds,

and provisions for borrowing if any are required. Among them, too, are likely to be proposed by-laws relating to public buildings, water supply, gas or electric lighting, highways, upkeep of cemeteries, and indeed anything else within the town's range of authority, including, of course, local police. Any voter present at a meeting is entitled not only to vote but also to speak; indeed even nonvoters usually may attend and sometimes may participate. Many times the proceedings, as carried on under the guidance of an elected moderator, are stereotyped and dull. But occasionally issues arise which provoke wide differences of opinion, and even divide the towns-folk into hostile camps; and when this happens, meetings may become lively, with much of the wire-pulling, speechmaking, and excitement ordinarily associated with political conventions. In smaller towns, where town-meeting day takes on the aspect of a neighborhood holiday, there still is, as a rule, good attendance and plenty of action, even though to an outsider many of the matters discussed might seem ridiculously trivial. In larger places, attendance is likely to be more scant and business to be pretty much of the cut-and-dried variety. Sometimes, in fact, the moderator simply appoints a committee which brings in recommendations on the various items and the voters approve them with little or no discussion.

As towns grow in population, a mass meeting is likely to be found ill-adapted to satisfactory handling of business, and one of two remedies may be adopted: (1) A standing advisory budget committee of from 10 to 40 members may be set up to expedite the work of the general meeting; or (2) a limited town meeting may be substituted with all voters still privileged to attend, but only 50 to 300 chosen representatives entitled to vote. The latter course has been taken thus far largely in Massachusetts. The effect is to convert the meeting, somewhat clumsily, from a primary assembly according to the original design into a rather crude *ad hoc* representative body. Sooner or later, however, an overgrown town may take the logical course of giving up the town-meeting idea altogether and applying for incorporation as a city or borough. A good many larger towns have done this. Usually there is reluctance to abandon the old usages, and many towns hold off from doing so until long after they have outgrown the homogeneity of population and the neighborliness of spirit that make government-by-meeting feasible. *Representative town meeting*

No mayor or other chief executive exists. Instead there is the board of selectmen (called town council in Rhode Island) already mentioned—a group of three, five, or sometimes as many as nine, persons chosen to serve as an executive committee of the town meeting and as such to act for that body during the long intervals between its sessions. Usually the term is one year, but in many Massachusetts towns it is three years; and in any event reelections frequently assure fairly extended periods of service. As an executive committee, the selectmen have authority only to enforce the orders of the meeting and carry on such of the town's affairs as do not fall in the province of some different agency. They do not act as executives by wielding centralized control over other town officials because they do not appoint them. *Selectmen*

In smaller towns, purely minor officials are likely to be appointed by the selectmen, but aside from this, officials and boards are chosen by the voters—not on the floor of the town meeting as such, but by balloting carried on while a meeting is in progress, and sometimes prolonged for a day or two after it adjourns or, in a few towns, on a different date. The town selectmen may, however, grant licenses, lay out highways, care for town property, award contracts, and arrange for town meetings and elections.

TOWNSHIPS

The township meeting

From a reading of the laws, one might deduce that the township meeting required by statute in the civil townships of eight states (confined to the northernmost tier across the central portions of the country) would look and act very much like the New England town meeting on which it is modeled. All qualified voters are entitled to participate; the body has an annual spring meeting in the town hall, with special meetings as required; an elected moderator presides; and functions include electing township officers, levying taxes, making appropriations, and enacting by-laws. Almost everywhere, however, the township meeting, if kept up at all, is only a pale image of the usually well attended and reasonably vigorous New

DISTRIBUTION OF TOWNSHIPS BY STATE*

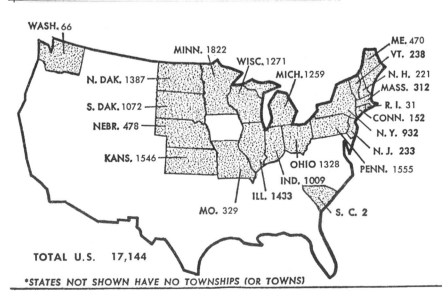

WASH. 66

ME. 470
VT. 238
MINN. 1822
WISC. 1271
MICH. 1259
N. H. 221
MASS. 312
N. DAK. 1387
S. DAK. 1072
R. I. 31
CONN. 152
NEBR. 478
N. Y. 932
N. J. 233
KANS. 1546
OHIO 1328
PENN. 1555
IND. 1009
ILL. 1433
MO. 329
S. C. 2

TOTAL U.S.   17,144

*STATES NOT SHOWN HAVE NO TOWNSHIPS (OR TOWNS)

SOURCE: Bureau of the Census, *Census of Governments, 1962* (Washington, D. C., 1963).

England gathering. Interest is lax and attendance scant; often there are not enough persons present to prevent the officers from completely dominating the perfunctory proceedings. In New York, experience has been so unhappy that the meeting has been abolished; and altogether, as a recent writer has observed, "the spirit of town-meeting government has failed to take root in most . . . townships in which the meeting system has been established by law." [1]

The township board

Whatever the township meeting may amount to in states employing it, every township state provides by law for a governing board in each township, variously termed board of supervisors or trustees, advisory board, or board of auditors, but usually consisting of three members, all elective, all ex officio, or partly both. Functions, both of the board as such and of individual members, vary widely. They are more important where there is no township meeting; for in that situation the board may become the nearest approach to a general governing authority, with usually the elective, financial, and regulatory powers that the meeting would exercise if there were one. In any case, the board frequently is charged with responsibility for any township affairs not expressly assigned to some other agency.

The supervisor or trustee

In about half of the township states (whether with or without town meetings), management of affairs, however, centers rather in a single elective officer known in New York, Michigan, and Illinois as supervisor, in Indiana, Kansas, and Missouri as trustee, and in Wisconsin as town chairman. Where such an officer exists, the function of the township board becomes mainly that of advising and checking him. In Indiana, where this chief officer's functions attain their peak, the trustee serves the township— not only in its general civil capacity but as a school township as well—as ex officio clerk and treasurer, with responsibility for the care of property, the administration of poor relief, the preparation of civil and school budgets, and even the selection of teachers for rural schools, though not for taxing, appropriating, or borrowing, which remain functions of the township board.

Other officers

Where the chief township officer does not serve as ex officio clerk and treasurer, there are likely to be separate officers bearing those names; and where tax assessment and collection have not been transferred to the county, an assessor also and perhaps a separate collector. An overseer of the poor and a highway commissioner will likely exist in addition unless the duties are otherwise provided for. Almost invariably there will be two or more elective justices of the peace, with an equal number of elective constables charged with tasks, within the smaller area, similar to those of the county sheriff.

Township abolition

Most authorities agree that, under modern conditions of travel and communication, the township, where and as it exists, is an institution which well might be discarded. In several states, upwards of a fourth of all townships contain fewer than 400 people living outside any village or city, and

[1] C. F. Snider, *American State and Local Government* (New York, 1950), p. 357.

in any case the area is bound to be very small—commonly only 36 square miles. In more than half of the states the township as a unit of government has never existed at all. Principal township activities usually relate to law enforcement, poor relief, and highway maintenance. All of these are at the same time functions of the county. Ordinarily, much would be gained, in both economy and efficiency, if the township were simply eliminated, with everything left to the county, or in some cases to county and city. Some progress in this direction is being made. Under a statute giving county boards the necessary power, some 96 townships in northern Minnesota have been dissolved since 1933; all those of Oklahoma (about 900) were, for all practical purposes, abolished in the same year by withdrawal of their power to levy taxes, followed by transfer of their tax-supported functions to counties. Iowa townships have also ceased to exist for all practical purposes since 1952. In Maine and Vermont in areas classed as "wild lands," townships have been deorganized by the state legislatures and their functions assumed by the states. Approximately three-fourths of the states have laws under which local units can be deorganized by local action and in North Dakota more than a score of townships have disappeared in this way, when their corporate existence proved too expensive to maintain. The functions of a deorganized unit are performed by a neighboring unit of the same level.

REFERENCES

Counties

G. S. Blair, *American Local Government* (New York, 1964).

J. C. Bollens, P. W. Langdell, and R. W. Binkley, Jr., *County Government Organization in California* (Mimeo., Berkeley, Calif., 1947).

W. S. Carpenter, *Problems in Service Levels* (Princeton, N. J., 1940).

National Association of County Officials, *The County Officer* (Washington, D. C.), edited by B. F. Hillenbrand.

National Municipal League, *The County Manager Plan* (new ed., New York, 1950).

———, *Model County Charter* (New York, 1956).

Nebraska Legislative Council, *Report of the Committee on Reorganization of County Government* (Lincoln, Neb., 1950).

M. Rohrer, *County Manager Government in California* (Mimeo., Berkeley, Calif., 1950).

C. F. Snider and I. Howards, "American County Government: A Mid-Century Review," *Am. Pol. Sci. Rev.* Vol. XLVI (March, 1952).

———, *County Government in Illinois* (Carbondale, Ill., 1960).

G. W. Spicer, *Fifteen Years of County Manager Government in Virginia* (Univ. of Va. Extension, 1951).

E. W. Weidner, *The American County—Patchwork of Boards* (New York, 1946).

Towns and Townships

R. P. Bolan, *Handbook for Massachusetts Selectmen* (Amherst, Univ. of Mass., Bur. of Govt. Res., 1956).

C. L. Fry, *American Villagers* (New York, 1926).

J. Gould, *New England Town Meetings; Safeguard of Democracy* (Brattleboro, Vt., 1940).

W. B. Guitteau, *Ohio's Townships; The Grassroots of Democracy* (Toledo, O., 1949).

G. E. McLaughlin, "Town Manager," *Vermont Life*, Vol. VIII, No. 3, 19–24 (Spring, 1954).

A. E. Nuquist, *Town Government in Vermont* (Burlington, Vt., 1964).

C. J. Rohr *et al.*, *Local Government in Massachusetts* (Amherst, Mass., 1941).

C. F. Snider, "The Twilight of the Township," *Nat. Mun. Rev.*, Vol. XLI, 390–396 (Sept., 1952).

M. R. White and S. Raissi, *Forms of Town Government in Connecticut* (Storrs, Univ. of Conn. Inst. of Public Service, 1952).

9

URBAN GOVERNMENT AND POLITICS

CITY GOVERNMENT

The form of government for American cities has been much less static than that for counties and, in many instances, a city government has a more progressive form than the state in which it lies. The impact of the industrial revolution has fallen directly on the cities. By necessity, they have had to adapt their governmental forms and methods to a more rapid tempo of life and a more complex society. Two basic forms have been invented in this century and new ones are being experimented with to meet the challenges that are constantly appearing. Urban government, therefore, is characterized by change and diversity. Amidst this diversity, however, three patterns stand out: mayor–council, commission, and council–manager.

The mayor-council form
  The mayor–council form, once monopolizing the field, is still found in about one-half of all municipalities of over 5,000 population and in all but six of the nation's large cities (over 500,000 population). Something resembling it is found also in villages, boroughs, and a few incorporated towns. Based on the historic principle of separation of powers, its most distinguishing characteristic is a division of authority between an elective council and an elective chief executive, or mayor.

1. The council: a. Structure
  Municipal councils of earlier days, especially in larger cities, consisted almost invariably of two branches or houses. A pattern borrowed from the state and nation served no useful purpose, however, and many practical disadvantages developed, with the result that municipal bicameralism has now been very widely abandoned. Only one of our 25 largest cities and two places of over 5,000 retain it. No municipality that has once discarded it has ever gone back to it. Except in Illinois and a few other states, where the number of council members is by law graduated according to population, there usually is little correspondence between population and the council's size. New York City has a council of 25 members (to be increased to 35

under the new charter); Cleveland one of 33, and Chicago one of 50; elsewhere the number runs from 20 to 30 downwards all the way to nine, even in cities as large as Detroit, Denver, Seattle, Boston and Pittsburgh.

At one time, council members were chosen almost invariably by dis- *b. Method* tricts, or wards, each returning one or two representatives. This still is a *of election* common method. Generally speaking it results in a larger council and often one larger than is needed. Many places (including virtually all with manager governments) have discarded it, substituting election on a general citywide ticket giving every voter a voice in the selection of the entire membership. This latter plan, too, has disadvantages, especially in cities of considerable size; and in not a few instances some combination of the two systems is found: A small proportion of the councilmen are elected by the city at large; the majority are chosen by wards. Six municipalities elect not only by general ticket, but under a system of proportional representation. The term of members has been commonly two years, but the trend everywhere is to four years and about half the cities have moved to longer terms. Formerly on a partisan basis, elections now are at least nominally nonpartisan in more than 60 percent of the cities of over 5,000 population—commonly places with commission or council–manager rather than with mayor–council government.

To the council it falls chiefly (1) to adopt the yearly municipal budget, *c.* levy taxes, borrow money, and allocate funds to the spending offices and *Functions* services; (2) to grant franchises to lighting, telephone, street railway, and other public service corporations; and (3) to serve as the municipal legis- lature for enacting, amending, and repealing local laws, known as ordi- nances, on a great variety of subjects and commonly implementing one phase or another of the police power. In the state municipal code, or in individual charters, the scope of the ordinance power is always set forth in more or less detail, and no council enactment is valid and enforceable unless clearly authorized in, or properly inferred from, some code or charter provision—and, of course, unless consistent with all statutes and all pro- visions of the state and national constitutions. More and more, however, American city government has become a matter of administration rather than legislation—with corresponding decline of lawmaking importance.

In earlier days, when popular suspicion of strong executives still lin- *2. The* gered, municipalities endowed the mayor with comparatively little authority. *mayor—* He could make few appointments, and only with council approval; if he had *"weak"* a veto at all, it could be overridden rather easily; and management of the *and* municipal services was largely in the hands of departments, boards, or *"strong":* commissions subject to little mayoral control. Under this "weak"-mayor plan, the city's chief executive was in very much the position in which the governor still is found in many states—and with the same bad effects upon unity, economy, and efficiency. In more than half of all mayor–council cities (mostly smaller ones, but including such large ones as Chicago and Los Angeles), this "weak"-mayor arrangement persists. In others, however,

FORMS OF CITY GOVERNMENT

"WEAK" MAYOR

Voters

Council — Mayor — Auditor — City Assessor — Treasurer

Board of Public Safety — Board of Health — Department of Public Works

Chief — Health Officer — City Engineer

"STRONG" MAYOR

Voters

Council — Mayor — Personnel Director — Planning Director

Director of Health — Director of Public Works — Director of Finance — Director of Recreation — Director of Public Safety the mayor has been given considerably more authority; and some, for example, Boston and Cleveland have gone over unreservedly to a "strong"-mayor type, in which the power of appointment and removal is substantially increased, the veto power strengthened, and control over administration expanded and integrated. Although numerous other municipalities still present only varying compromises between "weak"-mayor and "strong"-mayor types, the office has been distinctly on the upgrade. In cities retaining the mayor–council form, reform movements have been aimed principally at making the mayor actual as well as nominal head of the city government, and responsible for unified management of affairs.

a. Election and term

American mayors are normally chosen by direct popular vote—although in many cities where the mayor is not really an executive he is chosen by the council—sometimes on a partisan ballot and sometimes otherwise. Terms vary from one year in some smaller cities, especially in New England, to six years; in larger places, it is typically four years; elsewhere it most commonly is two. Salaries vary also from mere nominal sums in smaller places to $50,000 in New York. The mayors of our largest cities get as much as or more than the governors of the states in which the cities are located.

b. Powers and duties

From what has been said about the varying and transitional position of the mayor in our mayor–council governments, it is obvious that no single generalized statement of powers and duties is possible. A few broad facts, however, may be indicated. Everywhere it falls to the mayor to represent the city in its dealings with other municipalities and on ceremonial occasions. Everywhere he is expected to enforce the council's ordinances, to maintain order, and in general to cooperate with the law-enforcing authorities of county, state, and nation. Everywhere, too, as chief executive, he is supposed to exercise some supervision over the work of the various city departments. How effectively he can do this, however, depends on the actual authority with which he has been endowed, and especially on his power of appointment and removal. The tendency has been to confer more independent power at these latter points. Nevertheless, in a great many cities appointments (and often removals also) still are contingent on approval by the council; and where removals cannot be made independently, the effect is to lessen responsibility for efficient conduct of administration.

Considerable growth of mayoral authority has come also in connection with budget-making. In earlier times, this function commonly belonged to the council exclusively, and in some cities it still does. In Boston and an increasing number of other cities, however, it has been vested in the mayor alone. Finally, may be mentioned the mayor's relation to municipal legislation, that is, ordinance-making. In most cities he presides over council meetings and convokes special sessions. Everywhere he transmits recommendations (by formal message or otherwise), along with reports of department heads or of other officials. In approximately two-thirds of all mayor–council cities he has power of veto (sometimes extending to veto of items).

A veto usually may be over-ridden in the council by a two-thirds vote—in some strong-mayor cities by three-fourths, or even five-sixths.

3. Advantages of the mayor–council system

The mayor–council system has been criticized because legislative and administrative authority is often clumsily diffused and responsibility scattered. This criticism—in so far as the troubles come from a separation of powers—is less valid, the larger the electorate concerned. The larger cities cling to the traditional mayor–council form while many smaller places have successfully instituted forms in which legislative and administrative authority is either combined or even more sharply separated. The advantages of executive control of the administration can be realized to the degree in which the mayor is made "strong." The political advantages of the mayor–council system are, however, sometimes paramount. The commission and the council–manager forms seem to work best in a nonpolitical atmosphere and in a homogeneous community with more rather than less agreement on fundamental goals. The larger a city, the more complex the social groupings within it and the more diverse the social and economic goals of these groups. There is a need in these places to represent these groups, even if a large council results, and to mediate among them. (The council–manager and commission forms typically have small councils.) There is also a need, especially in the larger cities, for political leadership and for arousing the voter to action and organizing sentiment for the public good. This the mayor—an elected executive—can do, and he can be held politically responsible for his program. Therefore, especially in the larger cities and where the office of mayor has been strengthened, the mayor–council form is still widely preferred.

4. The public administrator

An increasingly popular practice aimed at more coordinated direction of municipal administration is the appointment of a professional administrator to serve under and at the direction of the mayor. The usual title for this post is chief administrative officer. This official differs from a city manager. He is appointed by the mayor and is responsible to him, not to the council. The mayor is still ultimately responsible for the conduct of the city's affairs. The creation of this post with adequate staff frees the mayor for policy-making and leadership. Though this arrangement was designed for large cities, smaller places find it useful to provide the mayor with an administrative assistant, which is a version of the same idea.

The commission plan

A number of cities have instituted forms in which executive and legislative powers arc combined in one body. The first experiment in this line was the commission form of city government instituted first in Galveston, Texas, in 1900. This reform captured the imagination of many municipal reformers in the period 1900 to 1920. About 500 cities of all sizes, though mostly small or of intermediate size, adopted it in this period. Since that time, the commission system has lost favor and in 1967 only 243 cities of 5,000 or more population still clung to it. The best known are Tulsa, Memphis, Portland, and St. Paul.

The commission plan is remarkably simple. Instead of a large and unwieldy council, one finds a small commission, consisting usually of five full-time salaried members elected on a general ticket. All other elective municipal offices are eliminated. In this commission are concentrated all of the legislative, and most of the administrative, authority of the city government. Each commissioner serves as a legislator, fixing the tax rate and passing ordinances, and as the head of one of the five departments—such as public safety—into which the administrative work is divided.

1. Essential features

The foregoing constitute the essential features of the system. In addition, certain incidental features almost invariably appear. The ward system has almost everywhere been abolished. The commissioners are elected from the entire city. Moreover, candidates are generally nominated either by petition or by nonpartisan primary, and are voted for on election day on a nonpartisan ballot. With such extensive powers vested in a small group, it has seemed wise for the public to retain means of direct and prompt control; and to this end, provision is made in most commission-governed cities (outside of Pennsylvania) for the recall of an unsatisfactory commissioner in a special election held before expiration of his term of office. Another common safeguard is the initiative and referendum in connection with ordinances. In varying degrees, all of these devices have contributed to the improved civic conditions which usually have followed adoption of the commission plan. None is either essential or peculiar to commission government, and any mayor–council city can make use of any or all, as some do, without adopting the commission plan.

2. Incidental features

In almost all cases, a mayor is still provided for, and as a rule elected directly to the office by popular vote, although in a few cities the commissioner who receives the highest popular vote automatically becomes mayor. In New Jersey and Nebraska, the commissioners select a mayor from their own number. In any event, the commission-government mayor is traditionally little more than first among equals. Commonly he wields no veto power; usually he has no appointing power as mayor; and almost never does he have any general power of removal. To be sure, he is the nominal head of the city government, and on ceremonial occasions he acts as such. But of real authority he usually has little or none beyond that of his colleagues.

3. The mayor under the commission form

There is no doubt that at first it revitalized city government. How much of the improvement came from the commission system's inherent virtues and how much rather from the awakened civic consciousness that accompanied the plan's adoption was never easy to say. Certain advantages of the plan are obvious. It is simple. Theoretically it provides unified governmental policies. However, in practice, administration may be divided, each commissioner going his own way. Neither is anyone responsible for the city as a whole. In addition, the elected commissioner is (at least at first) an amateur in the department assigned to him. If the city can hire professional technical staffs, things may go not too badly, but the essentials of good administration so necessary in a city are largely unprovided. There is no apex to the administration to insure unity, teamwork, and the proper

4. Decline of the plan

gradation of authority. Reversions to the mayor–council form have occurred in Buffalo, Oakland, Newark, New Orleans, and Omaha. Changes from the commission form to the newer council–manager system are more numerous but have usually been by smaller cities.

A more enduring pattern of municipal government designed to meet the defects in the mayor–council system and also invented in this century is the council–manager system. Introduced first in any sizable city in Dayton, Ohio, in 1914, this plan has won converts steadily in the years that have followed. In fact there have been more adoptions of it in the last two decades than at any other period in its history. Its popularity has never waned. In 1967, more than 40 percent (1245) of all cities with more than 5,000 population as well as a large number of smaller places were governed under the manager system. The plan has been especially popular in cities of 25,000 to 500,000 population.

Under the council–manager form, there continues to be an elective council, but always a small one. In about three-fourths of the manager cities, its members number five, and where the number is larger, it rarely exceeds seven, eight or nine. Furthermore, the council has, in general, the functions of the council in the mayor–council system except in the domain of administration—and except also for the very important function of choosing the manager. It enacts ordinances and regulations, levies taxes, votes appropriations, authorizes borrowing, grants franchises, creates and abolishes departments, investigates the financial transactions or official acts of any officer or department—in short, serves as the supreme policy-determining and general supervisory authority of the city. Restricted, however, to these functions, it devotes only limited time to the city's affairs (rarely meeting more than once a week, and frequently not oftener than once in two or three weeks). Its members are paid only nominal sums for their services. Councilors usually are elected on nonpartisan tickets, and their work may be subjected to checks imposed by the initiative, referendum, and recall. They are also, typically, elected at-large rather than by wards.

The really distinctive feature of the system arises in connection with administration. Under the mayor–council plan, administration is carried on in departments subordinate to the mayor, but with control considerably diffused between that official and the council and in the "weak"-mayor system among numerous elected administrators. Under the commission plan, it is vested in the commission and exercised through departments distributed among the commissioners. Under the council–manager plan, on the other hand, the entire job of administrative management is concentrated in the hands of a single well-paid official—and manager—chosen by the council and fully responsible to it, but picked as a professional administrator and presumed to be divorced from all political connections and motivations. The council has only to determine larger matters of policy, find the necessary money, and keep a watchful eye on what goes on. Day-to-day operations of the police, fire, public works, and other departments, are not its

FORMS OF CITY GOVERNMENT

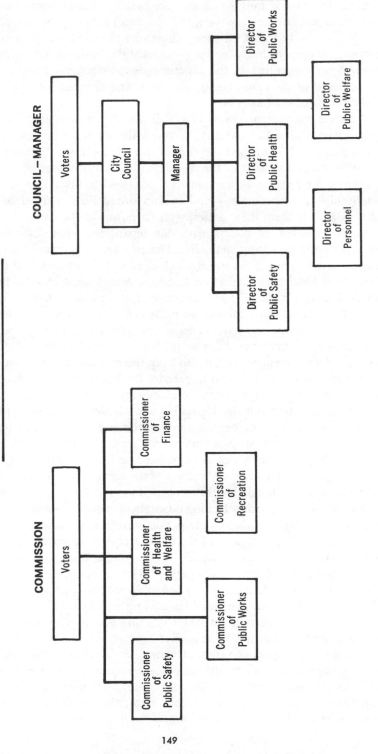

concern. The plan is thus essentially like that of a big business corporation, with the electorate corresponding to the stockholders, the council corresponding to the board of directors, chosen by the stockholders and charged with general responsibility for the conduct of the business, and with the city manager corresponding to the superintendent or general manager, chosen by the board of directors, responsible to it, and charged with looking after all the details of the business.

The manager's functions
As the most conspicuous official in the city government and the one around whom all administration revolves, the manager has many and exacting duties. (1) With the exception of the city auditor or comptroller, the city attorney, and sometimes the city clerk (all usually chosen by the council, or even by the people), he appoints city officials—heads of departments and usually higher subordinates—and (within broad lines marked out by the council) assigns them their duties, with no power in the council to confirm or reject, although of course with due regard for whatever civil service regulations the city may maintain. The manager also can independently suspend or remove. (2) As the city's chief executive, he sees to the enforcement of all local ordinances and likewise of such state laws as the city is expected to administer. (3) He supervises and, insofar as necessary, directs all administrative work carried on in the various departments, issuing instructions, receiving reports, advising and guiding. (4) Only the council, representing the taxpayers, can adopt the municipal budget. But it is the business of the manager not only to keep the council informed on financial conditions and needs, but also to prepare the budget for council consideration and to explain the significance of its various items. Finally, (5) as the connecting link between the legislative and administrative branches of the city government, and the person knowing the city's affairs most intimately, the manager not only must attend council meetings (taking part in discussions, although of course not voting), but stand at all times ready to assist with information and advice. Members of the council are expected to refrain from meddling with administrative activities and from attempting to influence the manager in selecting department heads, awarding contracts, and the like. This they do not always do, and in many places sound traditions as to the proper sphere of the council under the system remain to be established. Properly the council's functions are exhausted when it has picked a good man for the manager's job, set up adequate machinery with which he may work, laid down any broad lines of policy that it wants to see followed, provided the necessary funds, and placed itself in a position to keep informed on what the manager is doing and to avail itself of the information and advice that he can give.

Qualifications and selection of managers
The foregoing enumeration of managerial functions and duties carries obvious implications as to the qualifications that a city manager should have. In all cities employing the plan, the council makes the selection. Appointment usually is for no definite term, the understanding being that an incumbent will be retained as long as he gives satisfaction. The salary is

fixed by the council, usually at whatever figure it becomes necessary to pay
in order to obtain the person desired. Manifestly, the manager must be a
man of energy and of demonstrated executive ability; he must be skillful in
dealing with people, yet interested in administration rather than in politics.
It is desirable that he shall have had previous experience as a manager,
presumably in some smaller city, or at all events as a mayor, council member, or other municipal official. He need not be an expert in any one branch
of municipal activity, for example, public works or public health, but he
must have at least some acquaintance with all branches and an intelligent
appreciation of the importance and interrelations of all. City managership
is now a profession followed by many hundreds of experienced people.

*Results
achieved*

The steadily lengthening list of council–manager cities suggests that
the manager plan has come to stay. Eighty cities that have tried it have,
it is true, given it up (sixteen of them later went back to it). The most conspicuous abandonment was that of Cleveland. Sometimes partisan politics
has been allowed to scuttle the system, or it has been abandoned for other
reasons not reflecting on the plan's intrinsic merits. In scores of cities, administrative personnel has been improved, better business methods have
been introduced (especially with respect to purchasing, accounting, and
awarding of contracts), budget-making has been placed on a more scientific
basis, debts have been reduced and expenditures held within the limits of
revenues, partisan politics has been eliminated from administrative planning
and operation, and general administrative efficiency has been promoted.
Not all of the credit should go to the plan as such; some of it is due the
awakened civic interest which led to adoption of the plan in the first place.
Unquestionably the managership has in plenty of places demonstrated its
very great merits.

*Impedi-
ments and
problems*

There is, however, no golden road to efficient, economical, and completely satisfactory municipal government, and the council–manager plan
has its obstacles and problems as does any other. The initial high hurdle
is the selection of the manager himself. The manager is the key figure in
the system, and unless he is the right man, things will not go well. A second
problem is that of the proper functioning of the council under the system,
often aggravated by the almost incurable inclination of legislative bodies
to dabble in administrative matters about which they know little. If, as is
true, the average tenure of city managers is brief (perhaps four or five years)
a main reason—apart from resignations to accept better positions—is the
tendency of councils to interfere with their work and make good relations
impossible. Some councils go to the opposite extreme, taking the road of
least resistance, thinking *all* of their responsibilities are discharged when the
manager is selected, abdicating even their role of policy formulation.

*The man-
ager as
civic
leader*

There is also the question of the extent to which the manager shall assume an active leadership in municipal life and affairs. The earlier idea was
that he should be a strictly professional and almost impersonal administrator, leaving it entirely to the council not only to shape policy but to set

the pace and fix the tone of municipal public life. Indeed, the professional organization of the craft—the International City Managers' Association —once expressly advised its members not to try to assume leadership in their city's general affairs. Leadership by a council or any other collective agency is likely, however, to be rather colorless; people like to see leadership dramatized in some conspicuous personality. Reports from many council–manager cities indicate a present tendency of the manager to emerge in the role of community leader, in the sense at least of giving primary public expression to municipal aims, aspirations, and objectives. Such a role involves hazards. The council may take offense, and there is danger of being drawn into politics. More and more managers are finding, however, that the risks must be taken. For leadership of a more or less personalized character there must be. If not supplied from within the city's government, it will arise outside, where it is likely to become a source of embarrassment. Leadership, however, is not dictatorship; a manager obviously will be well advised to respect public opinion and keep within the limits of what it will support.

VILLAGES

Status
When a portion of a New England town, or of a western township, or of a county that does not have township government, becomes more thickly settled than the rest and begins to take on a semiurban aspect, its inhabitants are quite certain to demand more public services, such as fire protection, street paving and lighting, water supply, and sewerage facilities, than the town, township, or county authorities will be willing to provide. Sooner or later such communities are likely to be incorporated as villages or boroughs. State law often requires that a community seeking incorporation as a village shall meet certain standards of area and population, and that the question of incorporation be submitted to a popular vote. In Illinois, for example, any area of not more than two square miles, with at least 100 inhabitants, if not already within a village or city, may become a village by a vote of the people at a special election. It then remains a village until it has 1,000 inhabitants, when it may (but is not obliged to) change to a city government. Incorporation gives a village power to undertake community services of the kinds referred to above, to levy taxes and borrow money to support them, and to have its own village government, distinct from the governments of township and county. There are more than 10,000 such incorporated villages in the United States, and they are found in all parts of the country, including New England and the southern and western states— although by far the greater number are in the north–central section, where Illinois alone has some 800.

The government of villages is a comparatively simple affair. In some states, notably New York, there is a village meeting, much like the town or township meeting. In most states, however, there is no meeting, and control of most matters is left to certain elected officials. In such cases, the main governing authority is likely to be a village board of from three to nine members, called by various names: trustees (New York), assessors (Maine), commissioners (New Hampshire), burgesses (Connecticut), or the village council. Other village officers include a mayor or president or chief burgess, who is the village chief executive, with sometimes a veto upon the acts of the village board; also a clerk, a treasurer, a marshall or police officer, and a police magistrate with functions similar to those of a justice of the peace. Thus, in structure and functions, the government of villages resembles that of cities, except that it is on a smaller scale. However, as a village increases in size and urbanization, it need not become a city in order to operate on a larger scale. State legislatures have heeded the desires of village residents to keep their village governments by passing permissive legislation and providing alternative forms of government. By taking advantage of these laws villages can provide essentially "city" services and modernize their governmental machinery in line with the best management practices in the same way cities can.

*Govern-
ment*

Though the distinction in law between cities and villages (or boroughs) is disappearing, real differences in character exist when the latter are suburbs, especially dormitory ones. The first difference is psychological. The term, *village,* is appealing to some suburbanites. It connotes a cohesive community with the old-fashioned rural virtue of neighborliness. They are, therefore, apt to cling to a village form of government even though the city form might be more advantageous. As it is, for instance, in Wisconsin where cities have more representatives on county boards than villages do. The second type of difference is social and economic. The residents in dormitory suburbs tend on the whole to have higher income levels than central city residents and to be employed in white collar, professional, and executive occupations rather than in the labor force. Lastly, these differences exhibit themselves in political behavior of a distinctly suburban flavor. In the dormitory suburb (and most suburbs are of this variety), there is a high regard for nonpartisanship in local elections, independent political thinking, and citizen participation in government. There is a corresponding reliance on amateurs. The volunteer fire company performs not only a governmental function but a social one as well. Their politics, too, are apt to be run by political amateurs who need neither office nor patronage and are usually free from the pressures of the tightly organized groups that play so prominent a part in the politics of the city. In national elections, the suburbs often return a Republican vote (i.e., in the north) while the city returns a Democratic one.

*Villages as
suburbs*

Altogether, these characteristics result in a bifurcation of patterns of thought and behavior and of political aims that makes a meeting of minds between a central metropolis and its suburbs difficult. When any metropolitan area tries to achieve solutions to problems that cover the entire area, a *modus operandi* that brings these diverging elements together is essential.

REFERENCES

E. C. Banfield, *Big City Politics, A Comparative Guide to the Political Systems of Atlanta, Boston, Detroit, El Paso, Los Angeles, Miami, Philadelphia, St. Louis, Seattle* (New York, 1965).

E. C. Banfield and J. Q. Wilson, *City Politics* (Cambridge, Mass., 1963).

A. W. Bromage, *On the City Council* (Ann Arbor, Mich., 1950).

Bureau of the Census, *Local Government Structure* (Washington, D. C., 1957).

R. S. Childs, *The First Fifty Years of the Council–Manager Plan of Municipal Government* (New York, 1965).

W. C. Hallenbeck, *American Urban Communities* (New York, 1951).

International City Managers' Association, *City Management—A Growing Profession* (Pamphlet, Chicago, 1957).

E. C. Lee, *The Politics of Nonpartisanship* (Berkeley, Calif., 1961).

National Municipal League, *The Municipal Year Book* (Chicago), published annually.

J. Reichley, *The Art of Government: Reform and Organization Politics in Philadelphia* (The Fund for the Republic, New York, 1959).

C. E. Ridley, *The Role of the City Manager in Policy Formulation* (Chicago, 1958).

W. S. Sayre, *Governing New York City* (Russell Sage Foundation, New York, 1960).

F. M. Stewart, *A Half Century of Municipal Reform* (Berkeley and Los Angeles, Calif., 1950), a history of the National Municipal League.

R. C. Wood, *Suburbia; Its People and Their Politics* (Boston, 1959).

10

MUNICIPAL SERVICES AND FUNCTIONS

A city is fundamentally a physical place that is the work, indeed the achievement, and perhaps nowadays the disgrace of man. Characterized by its built-up nature, this environment is very difficult to make and keep livable. Most of the activities of our city governments have as their prime objective the mitigation of the effects of congestion on people. Their greatest contributions to human welfare, for instance, in public health, have been made with this goal in mind. The outstanding city problems today can be traced back to shortcomings in this environment that have not yet been adequately resolved. Hardly an activity of our city governments is uninfluenced by the physical form of the city. The density pattern influences the kind and amount of police and fire protection that is needed and the kinds of streets and highways that are laid. The size of a city affects the kind of sewage disposal system that will be adequate and virtually determines what water supply sources will be required. The fact that city land is used for different purposes in different areas of the city, such as residential, industrial, and commercial areas and subclasses within these, makes simple movement a prime concern and the city government is called upon to *add to* the city's physical plant in order to facilitate it. In fact, many city governmental activities revolve around providing physical facilities that in rural areas are privately provided or virtually nonexistent—from playgrounds to garbage incinerators—because "built-up-ness" devours the open land. Lastly, like all physical things, cities decay and we find our city governments today assuming new functions like urban renewal.

Influence of the physical environment

The services of city government that are closely related to its physical form are often called by the generic term, *urban services,* for as the built-up area expands, the same service needs are brought to other local governments outside the city proper. The prior experiences of our cities and older boroughs and other municipalities in providing these services should be invaluable to the people in these areas that are newly becoming urbanized.

PUBLIC SAFETY

The police depart- ment

In a municipality of any size a police chief is the head of a department organized on quasi-military lines into specialized divisions: patrol, detective, traffic control, vice, juvenile and women's, and housekeeping (records, etc.). The backbone of the force is the patrol division, upon whose efficiency largely depends the quality of the whole establishment. The patrolmen are the most numerous of the department's personnel and perform its most important function—patrolling the streets, day and night, on foot, on motorcycles, and in one-man or two-man "prowl cars," for the detection and prevention of crime. They also arrest offenders, gather and preserve evidence, and are usually called upon to handle street traffic and exceptional throngs of people. The detection and apprehension of criminals whose identity, or at least whereabouts, are unknown is the responsibility of detectives and plainclothes men who in the larger cities are organized in a highly specialized bureau or division of criminal investigation. Crime prevention is also a function of the department. Since juvenile delinquency is a major urban problem, women are often used since they are peculiarly qualified to work with children, advise parents, watch dance halls and other places where youth congregate, and maintain helpful contacts with social-service and recreational agencies.

Police effective- ness

The increase in criminality that has continued since the end of World War II has been blamed on the war's aftermath, the restlessness of the young in a time of cold war and an uncertain future, and on police inability to keep pace with changing conditions. The last is our present concern and is as difficult to document as the first two. Some facts and figures do, however, emerge. Our police are the best equipped in the world but our crime rate is consistently higher than Europe's. Our police are most successful against crimes of violence and least successful in enforcing those laws not supported by public sentiment. However, the recent wave of rioting, looting, and arson associated with the increasing militancy of Negro and other ethnic minorities in the slums of our large cities has severely taxed police capabilities and diverted much of their energies from the "normal" business of crime and traffic control. The American public is curiously apathetic about loss by theft, for instance, probably thinking that the "insurance will pay for it." The public is less tolerant when crimes against the person (violence) are involved. Public apathy, however, is not the only reason for the generally acknowledged poor record of our police departments. Public distrust and false economies instituted to "save the taxpayers' money" are also factors. Cries of police brutality against racial minorities have attracted much criticism to the police and their methods and have cost them heavily in public support. The number of police employes has increased gradually over the last ten years and has approximated the increase in total population but has not nearly kept pace with the rise in crime. Meanwhile, more of the force has been employed in traffic duties.

Across the nation the work of the police is complicated by the large number of units of government. The tradition of localism means many local police forces and uncoordinated activity that favors the extremely mobile criminal. Also the spread of urbanism has tended to bring urban crime into more areas. The inherent weaknesses of small police establishments and amateur forces in these areas have led to the establishment of state and county professional forces, that, however, where they exist, usually supplement rather than replace the traditional sheriffs, deputies, and town constables. There are vast interstate networks for radio and teletype communication. The states and the federal government have also established laboratories for the scientific examination of evidence, helped train recruits, and in other ways improved police administration and coordinated local activities without abandoning the tradition of local responsibility. In fact, spurred by the spread of rioting and the mounting criticism of police methods, the national government has since 1966 provided a substantial grant-in-aid program for police training and technical assistance to state, county, and city police forces. *Police protection outside the city limits*

No branch of municipal administration offers more opportunities for corrupt influences to make themselves felt than does the police force of a large city. In virtually every startling revelation of corruption connected with city government the police have been more or less implicated. It may be stated categorically that organized vice on any scale is impossible in an American city without the connivance of the police department. Temptation to favoritism, collusion, and graft besets the department's personnel on all levels; every lawless element deriving profit from its activities is prepared to share its ill-gotten gains with the police in return for immunity from prosecution. The possibilities of misconduct become especially grave when the police are expected to enforce laws not supported by the moral standards in the community, as frequently happens in the case of laws against the sale of liquor, gambling, and prostitution. However, even in cities where the citizenry and the police both have the will to stamp out the "rackets," they do not always have the means. A "gang" driven from a central city merely moves to a sympathetic suburb or county area. *The problem of police integrity*

The objective in traffic control is safety coupled with the expeditious movement of vehicles into and out of the central city. Automobiles cause approximately 40 percent of the total number of accidents. The duties of the police (in the largest cities a special force) are regulating traffic flow, enforcing traffic laws and ordinances, and educating the public on traffic safety and changes in the regulations. An increasing number of cities is separating from departments of public works and streets, duties relevant to traffic engineering and putting them under a professional traffic engineer. He needs to work closely with the police but he is usually not part of their establishment. Typically, the traffic engineer designates the locations for *Traffic regulation and control* stop and caution signs, the intersections for signals, and the locations for curb loading zones. He also often engages in planning for off-street parking, conducts mass transit surveys, and reviews plans for street layouts in new subdivisions. These specialized city activities, plus the work of highway engineers in designing safer highways, are gradually reducing the number of motor vehicle deaths in relation to the number of miles travelled on the nation's roads, streets, and highways in spite of the growing number of vehicles engaged. The annual death toll, however, remains scandalously high.

Fire de-
partments
and forces

A few decades ago, paid professional fire departments existed in only the largest cities, with fire-fighting left elsewhere to unpaid volunteer bands of citizens armed only with leather hose, buckets, and hand pumps. Now all is changed; any city, large or small, without a professional, paid, adequately equipped fire department is regarded as decidedly backward. Except in places of 25,000 or less, the basic pattern is a system of fire districts or precincts covering the city, each with a fire company operating, with full equipment, from a fire station serving as headquarters, and in large places with company commanders usually grouped under subchiefs. Like police protection, fire protection must be available around the clock, and consequently the force operates in platoons, or shifts, most commonly two, each with one day on duty and one day off, but sometimes three, each serving eight hours a day.

Fire
department
functions:
1. Fire-
fighting

The primary function of a fire department is, of course, to fight, check and extinguish fires when they break out. For doing this American firemen have at their command equipment and facilities far surpassing any ordinarily to be found in European cities. Huge pumpers (a pumper company is the basic fire-fighting unit), ladders extensible to great heights by mechanical power, water-tower trucks, turret pipes, "fog trucks" carrying equipment for smothering fire with fine spray, asbestos clothing, two-way radio communication, special high-pressure water mains serving areas containing tall buildings are only parts of the apparatus available in large cities. Even in small ones there has been great advance since the old horse-drawn "fire engine" used to go clanging down the street.

2. Fire
prevention

Despite all this, the annual fire loss in the United States is shockingly heavy—an estimated 12,000 deaths, twice as many serious injuries, and in terms of money, more than $1.8 billion. With inferior facilities for fighting conflagrations, Europe suffers far less from them (in peacetime), partly because less inflammable building materials are used, but partly also because of other precautionary measures. American cities in the past two or three decades have been waking up to the need for fire prevention. Through their National Board of Fire Underwriters, insurance companies look anxiously into the facilities of cities for fire fighting and into programs of prevention and advise with the proper authorities. City councils now fix areas within which inflammable buildings may not be erected and prohibit structural arrangements favorable to the spread of fire. Since more fires occur in private dwellings and the main causes are children playing with matches and careless smoking, fire departments are increasing their educational activities, especially in the public schools. Faulty electric equipment and wiring and other substandard building practices also contribute greatly to the nation's fire losses. These can be uncovered only by inspection and fire department personnel are engaging in this more and more. When private dwellings are inspected by firemen with the homeowner present and cooperating, public education in fire prevention can be furthered at the same time. In spite of all this, the number of building fires increased more than 33 percent from 1948 to 1968. Since the increase in manufacturing and mercantile building fires has been much lower than that for dwelling fires, monetary loss has not increased proportionately. The results of fire prevention activities are, therefore, mixed, but a good deal more attention and concern is required, for the last decade showed more loss of life than the previous one.

PUBLIC HEALTH AND SANITATION

Where, as in the modern city, large numbers of people are massed within relatively small areas, much is required not only to promote safety but also to safeguard health. To do this cities own and operate water supply and distribution systems to provide pure drinking water. They own and operate facilities to dispose of waste. And direct health services are provided by a department that may regulate personal conduct in the interests of the public health and in other ways provide a healthy environment for the people of the city.

Health departments The head of a municipal health department is usually a professionally trained public health administrator. In large places, he typically heads a more or less elaborate and specialized administration with medical officers, sanitarians, nurses, inspectors, and other employes. Smaller places, considering that they cannot afford such a set-up, frequently leave public health matters to be attended to by a designated physician devoting most of his time to private practice. In such situations what is done may leave a good deal to be desired.

Health department activities and current problems In times past, municipal health departments concerned themselves almost wholly with discovering and abating nuisances, fighting epidemics, and controlling communicable diseases. Nowadays, effort is focused far more upon preventive measures made possible by advancing medical and sanitary science. Vital statistics are gathered and compiled to afford a continuous picture of the state of the community's health; inspections of water and milk supply, and of every establishment and operation (often in both production and distribution) through which articles of food reach the consumer are carried on; campaigns of health education are carried into homes, schools, and factories; and, of course, the battle against contagion still goes

on with health departments enforcing quarantines, supervising immuniza-
tion, and administering isolation centers. Tuberculosis is still a threat,
especially in some metropolitan areas where the mortality rate is comparable to what it was in the general population 20 years ago. Nor does the
infant mortality rate seem to be declining as it should in some metropolitan
areas. Whether or not the influx of migrants from cultures that usually
experience a higher infant mortality rate is the cause, population movements do not make public health work any easier. Port cities usually have
to be particularly careful. This is pointed up in the annual surveys of the
American Public Health Association which reveal that suburban expansion
is one of the major current problems of public health leaders. The others
ironically reflect public health and private medicine successes and our industrial progress of which we are so proud. They are aging, chronic disease,
radiological health, mental health, air and water pollution, rehabilitation,
and accident prevention. In fact, so serious has air and water pollution in
and around our large cities become that the national government, strongly
pushed by President Johnson, has in the last three years enacted several
new or enlarged grant-in-aid programs aimed at helping cities finance
remedial measures but these are just barely scratching the surface of the
problem.

*Waste
collection
and
disposal:*
            The collection and disposal of wastes is everywhere an important
municipal activity, although the job is done a good deal more effectively in
some cities than in others. Few people appreciate the fact that, counting all
kinds—ashes, inorganic rubbish, street sweepings, garbage, and sewage—a
city's wastes exceed a ton a day per capita. In every city of size, the task
of collecting and disposing of this is, therefore, immense and involves thousands of dollars and hundreds of functionaries. Collection does not pose any
particular problems by now except in the ghettoes but disposal is literally
as well as figuratively a mounting problem.

*1. Gar-
bage and
refuse*
            How can a city dispose of the garbage and inorganic refuse after it
is collected? The older methods of dumping garbage in a convenient
stream or burning it with other combustible refuse in an open dump are
no longer acceptable. River and lake water can cleanse itself of organic
waste matter but this ability is lost when the amount dumped into it is
too great—a situation that exists in most areas today. Open dumping
grounds can no longer be found within an economically feasible distance
without the fumes from them discommoding neighboring towns. The
sanitary landfill method is, therefore, becoming more popular. In addition
to its health advantages, economies result. The collection of garbage and
trash can be combined (and the ubiquitous tin can added) and otherwise unusable land can be reclaimed for public parks or sold for private
development, thereby adding either to the amenities or to the tax base.
Where land is not available, cities are turning to incinerators as the
second best method. Some localities, though, resist the added expense

unless forced. When the public health is affected, a state can intervene. New Jersey, for instance, prohibits the open dump as a means of municipal refuse disposal.

Sewage consists primarily of waterborne human effluvia from dwell- **2. Sewage** ings and wastes from many industrial plants such as laundries and slaughter- houses. More than other forms of waste, this bears the germs of disease; and proper collection and disposal have urgent importance for the health of the community. A prime municipal engineering activity is, therefore, the installation, operation, and maintenance of an adequate sewerage system consisting of trunk lines, lateral branches, and connections for every building used as a dwelling or for commercial or industrial purposes. The problem is not solved with the construction of a sewerage system, the chief purpose of which is to collect sewage and carry it off; there remains the question of final disposal. In cities on an ocean or a large lake or river, the matter may find ready solution but after a few years of this the water is ruined for all other purposes. Where, however, the same lake or river serves as the source of water supply for nearby communities, and where restoration of water purity is vital for human needs, different methods of disposal have to be found, or the sewage must be subjected to chemical treatment before it is turned into the lake or stream in question.

The contamination of the water in and about most of our cities has **Water** progressed to the point where only drastic action can restore our streams **pollution** to acceptable conditions. Of the significant sources of pollution, half were municipal sewerage systems in the early nineteen-sixties. Both the states and the national government have laws prohibiting stream pollution. The basic Water Pollution Act of the national government was passed in 1948, amended in 1956 and 1961. A separate division of the United States Public Health Service has been created to implement this law. The service issued its first enforcing order against a municipality in 1959. Prohibiting pollution may not be enough unless municipalities are also aided in constructing treatment plants. To this end, the same act in 1956 authorized $500 million and in 1961 an additional $570 million for matching grants to the states for municipal plant construction and other state antipollution activities. By 1967 over 1200 projects had been com- pleted or were under construction under this program. Preferences under the 1956 authorization were given to small plants; therefore, the situation in metropolitan areas was not particularly alleviated. Though providing that one half of the aid should go to communities of less than 125,000 people, the 1961 amendments raised the ceiling for individual projects to $600,000 and projects that would serve more than one community could receive aid up to $2.4 million for each one. Aids are still given for plant construction only; therefore, suburban extensions to existing city systems, an urgent need, have not yet been helped. Extension of these programs was made in the Housing and Urban Development Act of 1965. This act aimed at achieving integrated water supply and sewage disposal planning for metropolitan areas.

Sewerage districts

One approach that is finding increasing favor is the sewerage district. These districts are independent units of government established usually by the voters of the area under state enabling acts. A sewerage district can be created to serve an entire metropolitan area—the central city and its suburbs—or any portion of it where the need is greatest. Once created, these districts enjoy financial and administrative autonomy under state law. They are governed by boards appointed by the governor or other state official (such as a judge) or by local officials in the areas they serve. Sometimes part of a board membership is elected by the voters of the area but very rarely do the voters elect an entire board. These boards employ professional staffs, which are usually technically proficient. One of the oldest is the Metropolitan Sanitary District of Greater Chicago.

Water supply

Though water for domestic uses is only a very small part of the amount used in cities, the necessity for keeping it pure for drinking purposes makes its supply and distribution a public health concern. American urban communities use at least 100 gallons a day per capita, but a municipality has to be able to provide more than its average need. Demands for water fluctuate and on a maximum day 50 percent more than the average consumption may be needed and the maximum hourly demand may be two or three times the hourly average. The needs of domestic users and industry are making increasing demands. Population growth, technological advances that depend on water (such as air conditioning and home garbage disposal units) and new industrial processes that need a lot of water (such as the manufacturing of synthetic fibers) are depleting ground water levels and burdening surface sources. The American Waterworks Association reported in 1959 that $400 million is needed every year just to keep up with increasing population and expanding uses and that one out of every five public systems is deficient in supply. Sources are being found farther and farther away from the cities and sources formerly bypassed are being reconsidered. Fortunately, purification advances have made some of these relatively economical; however, it has been estimated that over 220 million Americans in the year 2000 may have to get by with the quantity now used by 100 million. About 30 inches of annual rainfall produce about 4,300 billion gallons of water per day of which about 600 billion gallons are usable; and whereas in 1900 only about 48 billion gallons were needed for all uses, today's requirements exceed 300 billion gallons of which about 10 percent is used in urban areas. The need to conserve this vital natural resource is leading to some interesting experiments. For instance, Oceanside, California, has adopted a program of reclaiming its entire sewage flow for reuse by industry, for irrigation, or for ground water recharging. The national government has in recent years been substantially increasing its financial and administrative commitment to solving the water supply problem.

TRANSPORTATION

About one-third of all the land in an average city is occupied by its streets and parking facilities. Though these streets comprise only 10 percent of the three million and more miles of highways in the United States, they carry one-half of the nation's traffic.

One of the major advances in street and highway design during the last few decades has been classification according to use. Streets and high- *Streets:* *1. Types* ways are now classified as local and residential streets, secondary thoroughfares, major boulevards and expressways, and limited access highways and freeways. Paving, width, and other elements of design should differ for each type, and the pattern of a city's arterial and access streets should be planned not only for present but for expected future use. Although breaks in paving occur because of poor drainage and extremes of weather, street paving does not often get a chance to wear out. Obsolescence is usually caused by traffic patterns that put streets to uses heavier than the ones for which they were intended.

Constructing and maintaining streets is extremely costly. Concrete *2. Cost* paving runs as high as $10 a square *yard,* including gutters and curbs. *and* Construction costs of municipal streets amount to more than $3 billion a *financing* year and this does not include the costs associated with land acquisition, demolition, and moving of utility lines. Maintenance has amounted to more than $1 billion annually in recent years. Not all this is financed from local sources, though most of it is. The states follow different patterns of help including direct state construction of city streets that are part of the state trunk system, financial aids, and shared motor fuel or other taxes. However, local dissatisfaction with rurally dominated state legislatures and highway administrations has led city officials to Washington. Since 1944, urban extensions of the primary and secondary federal aid system have been specifically provided for in national grants (even though the grants are still channelled through the states). A major portion of the system of interstate and defense highways authorized in 1956 is being built in urban areas. It will carry not only long distance traffic but a large number of urban and suburban commuters.

Though all this money is being spent on city streets, traffic con- *3. Prob-* gestion, as most people are aware, continues to plague the urban resident. *lems* This problem arises mainly because the effect of streets on other land uses has not always been taken into account. For instance, an improved or new street is supposed to relieve congestion by moving traffic faster; but if commercial activity is intensified along its length (which usually happens), more people are brought into an area and congestion is increased. Each year more cities are taking a critical look at their streets and traffic patterns in order to plan them as part of an overall land-use plan and to relate them to other public programs that are also changers of land use, for example, slum clearance, urban renewal, and recreational facilities.

Rapid transit

In the opinion of most experts, the decaying cores of our large cities can not be saved without dependence on transportation facilities that are more efficient carriers of persons and goods than the private automobile. One bus can carry 30 to 50 people, takes up only a little more street room, and rests in a terminal. Vehicles that run on tracks are even more efficient users of space. However, many, perhaps most, privately owned and operated transit systems are losing money. Deficits have been attacked by raising fares and letting facilities deteriorate; then fewer people use them. Threats of abandonment have brought city officials increasingly into the picture. Municipal ownership is one solution. In 1967, more than 65 cities owned transit systems. Other cities are considering buying or leasing private systems but there is less enthusiasm for this solution than formerly. More cities and states are experimenting with tax reductions and direct subsidies designed to alleviate the financial plight of the privately owned and operated systems. National subsidies have also entered the picture in the sixties. Revitalizing central business districts by relieving traffic congestion is not the only goal of these cities and states. Many commuters are dependent on this form of transportation.

Terminal facilities 1. Airports

Many cities own and operate terminal facilities, usually through a business agency such as a municipal utility. The two most common are airports and parking facilities for private automobiles. The situation in airports has been characterized succinctly in the phrase—everyone wants one for his city but not near his home. The national government has encouraged even small cities to build airports with financial aid for construction. Few cities are breaking even on the operation of their airports. Of the 7,700 cities and towns with airports in 1967, fewer than 10 percent were served by commercial airlines.

2. Parking

Parking a private automobile is sometimes a desperate undertaking. Most cities of any size meter curb space, provide municipal lots, or do both. More off-street parking facilities are being provided each year at a high cost for land acquisition in high value areas and a subsequent loss of tax base. Proportionately more parking spaces are provided by middle-sized cities. Each city must decide for itself whether it is better to discourage private cars from entering central business districts or encourage this by improving parking facilities.

A properly coordinated metropolitan transportation system that integrates mass transit facilities with streets and highways and parking facilities is recognized as a most important present need. Studies and plans of this kind are under way in the metropolitan areas of Washington, D. C., Pittsburgh and Allegheny County, St. Louis, New York, San Francisco, and many other cities.

EDUCATION

In the great majority of cities, education is not administered by the *Independ-* regular city government. While many school districts are coterminous (or *ent status* substantially so) with cities of various sizes, schools are usually in charge of a popularly elected school board endowed with independent power to levy taxes and appropriate school funds subject only to the requirements of state law. The objective in removing school affairs from the regular city government has always been to "keep the schools out of politics." Some also fear that city school systems would come off with diminished financial support. Educational activities are invariably the ones on which most money is spent whether the schools are an integral part of the city government or not. Much of the discussion is philosophical and no change has been made either way for many years. Most schools are well run by competent staffs and high-minded officials.

The last 40 years have seen a remarkable expansion of educational *Expansion* activities in American cities. These now include—over and above the *of educa-* regular work of instruction through the familiar 12-year gradation— *tional* medical, dental, and psychological examination of school children; opera- *activities* tion of low-priced or free lunchrooms; special classes for children found mentally or physically defective; evening classes for immigrants and illiterates; vocational preparation, including manual training, domestic science, skilled trades, and commercial courses; sometimes provision of junior colleges, or even of regular four-year collegiate institutions; and numerous other services—including driver education. In hundreds of cities, schoolhouses are made available for evening lectures and entertainments and as centers of neighborhood sociability. Many school yards, too, have been enlarged and transformed into general public playgrounds equipped with special apparatus, with children of the neighborhood not only permitted, but encouraged, to resort to them outside of school hours. Hundreds of schoolhouses throughout the country, also, are now used as polling-places on election day, and even some so-called conservative New England communities permit public meetings to be held in them, including political gatherings during electoral campaigns.

The last two decades have been serious ones for public education. *Current* They have witnessed efforts at desegregation of the races, high birth rate fol- *problems* lowed by a decline, Sputnik and the resulting reexamination of educational goals, and striking suburban expansion. The American Society of Planning Officials has estimated that 100 new families in a community means four new teachers and four new classrooms. For fast growing communities this has meant a new school every year. The most difficult problems are in secondary education to maintain interest, attendance, and effective instruction. A community that can support an adequate grade school at present standards may find that it is not large enough to support a high school. Many suburbanites are caught in a vise when city school systems or districts reverse their past practices of admitting tuition pupils. As enrollments mount, more schools (and they are usually high schools) have had to close their doors to nonresidents. For in the last decade, school enrollment in the United States rose by one million pupils every year and the rate of growth continues despite the falling birth rate, partly because more young people are remaining in school longer.

Under state school district organization laws, a district large enough for a modern high school can be formed by merging or consolidating smaller districts. Sometimes grade school districts are combined. Sometimes grade school districts join others that give instruction for the full twelve years. Where popular consent is required in the individual districts, mergers are exceedingly difficult to accomplish. Wealthier districts do not wish to merge with poorer ones, and vice versa, each certain that taxes will be raised. If a new building is required, each district wants it in its own areas. If an existing building is abandoned, the district owning it objects. These difficulties are not confined to high school organization but are more intense there, for the high school more than the grade school is the center of community activities. Nor are these difficulties confined to suburban areas, but they are intensified here if cleavages between old and new residents occur, the new residents wanting the "best of everything" and the former residents hurt and bewildered that what they have been proud of is not considered good enough. Only in those few states where the county is the unit for school administration are these problems somewhat alleviated. The growth of college-going in the past two decades has further pressed urban school systems. Many of our large cities have expanded their offerings to include post-high school opportunities either of the four-year collegiate type or two-year community college or vocational type.

PUBLIC WELFARE

Because of the development of programs by the nation and the states, the city's welfare responsibility has become simply that of providing general assistance or relief (indoor and outdoor) for persons not sufficiently provided for by the state, nation, and community chests. Such relief is usually financed in part by state grants-in-aid. Numerous other activities varying from city to city and frequently related to public health are also carried on, such as vocational guidance clinics, free legal aid for the poor, day care centers for children of working mothers, visiting nurse services, public baths, race relations advisement, and many other activities aimed at advancing people's physical, moral, and economic well-being.

PARKS AND RECREATION

Although considered by many part of the welfare program, recreational activities are becoming so important they deserve separate consideration. The shorter work week has given adults more leisure. The vacant lot for children's play has disappeared and the streets are no longer safe for them. The recognition of the relation between delinquency and idleness has stimulated a demand for more recreational activities. The old-time remedy, work, is no longer a cure-all. Compulsory school attendance laws and prohibitions of child employment have closed this door. The greatest need in this field is the need for space. The community that has enough park acreage available and has been able to keep its parks inviolate from through-traffic or has managed to acquire open land ahead of development is either lucky or unusually foresighted.

HOUSING AND URBAN RENEWAL

This is, typically, a city not a suburban activity. The national program provides financial assistance to local authorities for low-rent public housing and urban renewal and development projects. The keystone of the city government's responsibilities is urban renewal. By participating in this program, cities may acquire, clear, and prepare blighted areas for new construction and rehabilitation. Cleared land may be used for public housing or resold to private builders for redevelopment. To be eligible for aid, a city has to commit itself to the following program: adequate building and housing codes, effectively enforced; a comprehensive planning division; analysis of its blighted neighborhoods; assumption of responsibility for relocating displaced families; provisions for citizen participation in the program; and ability to finance its part and administer the program. These commitments are approved by the Department of Housing and Urban Development and are recertified annually. After the project is planned, it too must be approved. The objective of urban renewal is not only to clear hopelessly blighted neighborhoods and reverse incipient blight but to rebuild in such a way that future blight is prevented. In meeting project standards, cities have had the most difficulty with relocating families and businesses displaced by the projects. A special type of mortgage insurance (FHA) is available to assist communities and private builders to provide new housing or rehabilitate existing housing to accommodate people displaced by this program and other governmental action. However, some cities have had to undertake public housing projects they had previously shied away from and others have had to expand their public housing programs. The dis-

Slum clearance

placed families are not usually able to afford private housing that meets standards, either FHA or municipal.

It has been estimated that it would take the entire national product for one year to replace all the substandard buildings in the United States. The impossibility of such a task makes rehabilitation of existing housing necessary. Such rehabilitation also serves to reverse incipient blight. Municipal responsibility in this field is mainly discharged by the enforcement of various codes that set up building standards—health and sanitation codes, building codes, plumbing codes, fire codes, etc. The newest addition to this roster is the housing code. Unlike the older ones that mostly govern structural and material requirements, a housing code sets up occupancy standards. These are usually persons per dwelling unit, persons per bedroom, or floor area or combinations of these. This type of code tries to reach directly the basic cause of deterioration, which is the crowding of more people into a building than it was intended to house. Building codes have been subject, however, to severe criticism. The most common criticisms are outmoded structural requirements, uncoordinated enforcement, unnecessarily elaborate procedures for notification of violations and repair orders, costly and time-consuming court cases in the last resort, and fines too low to act as a deterrent. Needed repairs and alterations are either not made or are delayed while blight spreads through a neighborhood. Most cities could do more in this field, especially where relatively small areas of blight threaten otherwise good neighborhoods.

FINANCING THE SERVICES

Besides having to find the money to meet the new needs caused by the growth of our urban areas and the demands for better and more service by a prosperous citizenry, our cities have been hit by the high cost of living as has every other enterprise. School construction costs, for example, continue to rise, construction costs for streets and other public works increased more than 50 percent from 1950 to 1967 and advanced another 4½ percent in 1959, municipal employment increased 70 percent from 1946 to 1966 but payrolls rose 300 percent. Across the nation cities and suburbs alike have been feeling the pinch. The cities have suffered a loss of income from the movement out of their jurisdictions of the very people best able to pay—manufacturing and retail trade and the middle-income group. At the same time, cities have been under increasing obligations to provide streets and other services for nonresidents, and to rebuild an aging physical plant. The suburbs have the opposite difficulty. They have been building an entire physical plant in one generation, and at inflated prices. The suburbs for their part are not able to take advantage of large-scale economies and they pay the costs of independence in other ways, too—in duplication of services and inexperienced administration.

In 1967, the operating expenditures of all local governments totaled over $43.3 billion. More than 40 percent of the total was spent on education and the balance largely on health, safety, welfare, and transportation.

Local revenue comes from sources falling into a half dozen very unequal categories. At the top of the list, by a very wide margin, is the general property tax. In 1966, the property tax accounted for 40 percent of all general revenue received by city governments and was more than 50 percent of the revenue raised from their own sources. Before 1950, the main nonproperty tax resource of municipal governments was the gross receipts tax levied on public utilities. (Counties and school districts were still virtually limited to the property tax.) Since then, more local units have adopted general local sales taxes. By 1967, over a thousand municipal, county, and school sales taxes were being levied. In some municipalities—virtually all in Pennsylvania and Ohio—income taxes, personal or both personal and corporate are levied. Besides relieving the property tax, both these taxes reach the nonresident and force him to contribute to a government whose services he uses. Of the two, the sales tax is the more popular though both are regressive as used by local governments. Somewhat similar to taxes, but not of general application, are special assessments levied against benefiting property owners to meet part or all of the cost of pavements, gutters, sidewalks, or water and sewer mains which tend to improve property values in the neighborhood. Usually there also will be income from water rates and other utilities, such as street railways or electricity distributing plants. Charges for other services, such as care in municipal hospitals or extra street sprinkling have been common in the past also. Because of the sheer inadequacy of the property tax to support municipal services today, more places are resorting to these direct charges. The most common is the sewer rental charge. Municipalities also charge for services to outlying areas. Licenses and permit fees are extracted from a multitude of enterprises and pursuits, many of which are regulated, such as dance halls. Finally, and more important than anything else except taxes, are the proceeds of state-collected, locally shared taxes and grants-in-aid, the latter bringing cities substantial sums not only from the state treasury but, for certain purposes, for example, airports and highways, from the national treasury as well. In 1967, state and national money returned to local units accounted for 25 percent of all local revenue.

Revenue

Because a metropolitan area is not a legal entity, it is composed of many taxing and charging jurisdictions of unequal financial resources. These inequalities are intensified by local property assessment because it provides a means by which units can compete for desirable development, thus increasing a comparative advantage. However, equalizing assessments as described earlier would remove some inequalities. Reliance on the property tax as the main source of revenue in itself creates situations that have adverse effects on other parts of the area. In the first place, the temptation is almost irresistible for a unit to seek industry or to zone for

Financial resources in metropolitan areas

large lots only on the theory that these types of land development can
best pay for increased school enrollments and other services. Such activities
can result in premature or ill-advised land use that increases sewer, water,
and transportation costs for other units also. In the second place, if most
or all of a community's tax base consists of low value property, the burden
on it becomes intolerable. Inequality of financial resources is inevitable as
long as separate taxing jurisdictions remain, but when services are provided on an unequal basis because of it, a situation exists that demands
attention. We still do not have an acceptable theory of local taxation that
takes into account the metropolitan complex. Within a city, the ability to
support services differs from one neighborhood to another, yet police
and fire protection are not allocated on this basis. The resources of the
whole city are pooled. The only way at present that the resources of an
entire metropolitan area can be tapped to provide a minimum standard
of service throughout the area is the indirect one of state aid and shared
taxes and national aid. State aids and shared taxes are often criticized, however, for their maldistribution. Income taxes are usually distributed according to the residence of the taxpayer, which intensifies service inequalities.
It has been urged that they be distributed on the basis of need. State aids
are supposedly distributed on this basis but often the formulae used assume
that cities are wealthy places of high property values that need less, and
that municipalities generally do not need aid to give a minimum standard
of service, which is the main concern of the state. Neither of these assump-
tions are borne out by the facts in many metropolitan areas. For this reason
and the fact that metropolitan areas sometimes cross state lines and because
of the national interest in so many urban activities, national aid is becoming
an increasingly important revenue source for units in metropolitan areas.

Borrowing   City government debts have been increasing from the same causes as
expenditures. From a low of $13 billion in 1946, the local debt outstand-
ing in 1967 has mounted to more than $55 billion. (The total for all local
governments was $70 billion). In authorizing new indebtedness, a local
governing body usually operates under certain restraints. In the first place,
many charters or state laws require popular approval in a referendum
before new bonds can be issued; in the second place, in nearly all states, a
ceiling is fixed by the constitution or a statute. The effect of these restrictions has often been adverse. Rather than producing local economy they
have put local governments in a strait jacket to find ways to finance needed
improvements. Enterprises that pay their own way from their own revenues
commonly finance their extensions by issuing revenue bonds that need
neither voter approval nor are they subject to ceilings. The popularity of
special districts for providing services such as water supply and sewage
disposal and many others is in part traceable to this, for they finance their
capital programs this way. (And, incidentally, often charge for their
services directly instead of relying on property taxes for their operations.)
Commonly too, debt limits take no cognizance of overlapping govern-

mental areas. Consolidation of units is hindered if the combined debt limit is lower than the sum of the separate units. This sometimes occurs in school district reorganization. Because debt limits are stated in terms not of a fixed amount, but of some percentage of the jurisdiction's assessed valuation, they are not applied uniformly over an area because assessment ratios vary. This results in the same inequalities in resources that resulted from the local assessments in the first place (i.e., for taxation). For these reasons, and the fact that today needs are increasing faster than assessments, especially for schools, a different approach seems called for. One proposed suggestion is to use the total financial resources of the local government as the basis for a ceiling. Another is the approach used by North Carolina. A state administrative agency is authorized to handle each situation on its merits and to approve local debt proposals under broad discretionary authority.

REFERENCES

E. C. Banfield and M. Grodzins, *Government and Housing in Metropolitan Areas* (New York, 1958). Chaps. IV, V, VII.

H. Bartholomew, *Land Uses in American Cities* (Cambridge, Mass., 1955).

J. C. Bollens, *Special District Governments in the United States* (Berkeley and Los Angeles, 1957). Chap. VI.

H. E. Brazer, *City Expenditures in the United States* (New York, 1959), a statistical study of the effects of city size, density, and other factors on per capita expenditures.

G. D. Butler, *Introduction to Community Recreation* (New York, 1959).

F. S. Chapin, Jr., *Urban Land Use Planning* (New York, 1957).

H. S. Churchill, *The City Is the People* (New York, 1945).

R. M. Fisher (ed.), *The Metropolis in Modern Life* (New York, 1955).

R. A. Futterman, *The Future of Our Cities* (New York, 1961).

J. Gottmann, *Megalopolis* (New York, 1961).

A. M. Hillhouse and M. Magelssen, *Where Cities Get Their Money* (Chicago, 1946). 1949 supplement by A. M. Hillhouse. 1951 supplement by M. B. Phillips. 1956 supplement by H. F. Alderfer and R. L. Funk.

J. C. Ingraham, *Modern Traffic Control* (New York, 1955).

J. Jacobs, *The Death and Life of Great American Cities* (New York, 1961).

M. C. McFarland, *The Challenge of Urban Renewal* (Washington, D. C., 1958).

R. B. Mitchell and C. Rapkind, *Urban Traffic, a Function of Land Use* (New York, 1954).

R. S. Moulton (ed.), *Handbook of Fire Protection* (National Fire Protection Assoc., Boston, 1954).

Municipal Finance Officers Association, "Municipal Sales Tax in the United States and Canada," *Municipal Finance* (Feb., 1956). Entire issue.

R. E. Murphy, *The American City* (New York, 1966).

National Health Council, *Urban Sprawl and Health* (New York, 1959).

W. Owen, *Cities in the Motor Age* (New York, 1959).

————, *The Metropolitan Transportation Problem* (Washington, D. C., 1956).

The Police Year Book (Chicago), published annually by the Assoc. of Chiefs of Police.

J. Rannels, *The Core of the City* (New York, 1956).

L. Rodwin (ed.), *The Future Metropolis* (New York, 1961).

E. Rose, *The Public Library in American Life* (New York, 1954).

E. Saarinen, *The City: Its Growth, Its Decay, Its Future* (New York, 1943).

E. B. Schulz, *American City Government: Its Machinery and Processes* (New York, 1949).

R. A. Sigafoos, *The Municipal Income Tax: Its History and Problems* (Public Admin. Service, Chicago, 1956).

W. G. Smillie, *Public Health Administration in the United States* (3rd ed., New York, 1947).

J. R. Sour, *Cities in a Race with Time: Progress and Poverty in America's Renewing Cities* (New York, 1966).

R. Starr, *The Living End: The City and Its Critics* (New York, 1967).

Tax Institute, *Financing Metropolitan Government* (Princeton, N. J., 1955).

U.S. Conference of Mayors, *City Problems* (Washington, D. C.), annual publication.

R. Vernon, *The Changing Economic Function of the Central City* (Committee for Economic Development, New York, 1959).

O. W. Wilson, *Police Administration* (New York, 1950).

C. Woodbury (ed.), *The Future of Cities and Urban Redevelopment* (Chicago, 1953).

11

GOVERNMENT IN METROPOLITAN AREAS

The baffling thing about government in metropolitan areas is that there is none. Though a majority of these areas are contained within a single county, in no area is there a local government with authority to provide all the needed services for the entire area. There are cities that provide these for parts of areas; there are special districts that provide one or two services for an entire area. There are all sorts of unique combinations of service and area. The results as we have seen are: governmental complexity, unequal financial resources, unequal and inadequate provision of services, and lack of citizen control and political accountability. The ideal form for a metropolitan government would be a general purpose one with jurisdiction geographically corresponding to the metropolitan community. Under such a government there would be no duplication of services. There would be one tax system. And the government would receive its support from and be accountable to the people of the entire area. Most of the older methods for preventing or overcoming governmental deficiencies in urbanized areas assume that the city is the appropriate form to accomplish these ends. These methods included (1) extraterritorial jurisdiction and services by which a municipality provides services to or extends its controls over adjacent areas; (2) annexation by which a city physically extends its boundaries and, therefore, its jurisdiction; (3) city–county consolidation by which the area of the county is put under the city government for the provision of municipal-type services; and (4) city–county separation by which the urban area is separated from the rural area and consolidated under the city government. Today the problems are more complex and extend beyond the city's ability to encompass them. The methods most discussed today are (1) federating all the units in a metropolitan area into a supergovernment; (2) making

METROPOLIS—SIXTIES STYLE

Super metropolitan area along Eastern Seaboard, stretching from Virginia to New Hampshire, is shown in black.

SOURCE: *The New York Times.*

the county an urban government with municipal powers to provide urban services; (3) setting up special districts; and (4) providing services jointly.

EXTRATERRITORIAL JURISDICTION AND SERVICES

In most states, municipalities may extend their jurisdictions and services beyond their boundaries in a radius of from one to five miles. The most common types of jurisdiction extended are regulatory and involve the control of land use, such as extension of a city's zoning, planning, sub-division controls, into unincorporated territory. This allows the city authorities to control the fringe areas and assure that developments won't occur contiguous to the city that would put an unnecessary burden or future responsibility on the city that it would not be able or wish to assume. Another type of extraterritorial jurisdiction is the ownership of land by a city outside its limits for parks, airports, water supply, and the like. This is sometimes objected to by the residents of the area but the city's interest is limited to that of a proprietor.

Services are provided for areas outside a city by the city's selling particular ones. Some are sold to persons directly but the common practice is for the city to sell the service to another municipality which in turn bills the ultimate user. Sewage disposal and water distribution are the most common services sold. These practices may ease the pressure on the suburbs to find other methods for solving common problems. On the other hand, the city can use its services as a lever to obtain return advantages, such as eventual annexation. Sometimes a city is compelled to sell a service by the state. For instance, New York City must furnish water to the suburbs in the vicinity of its aqueduct in Westchester County.

ANNEXATION

In the latter part of the nineteenth century when the urban popula- *Current* tion was expanding with the new industrialization, American cities en- *use* gaged in frequent and large-scale annexations. A typical example is Pittsburgh, Pa., which grew from half a square mile to 28 square miles by 1900. City boundaries kept pace with and indeed often went beyond the urban area. From then until 1945–1948, annexations were fewer and fewer in number and in the amount of territory taken in. Since the end of the Second World War, the pace has accelerated but the amount of annexed territory is still small. The average amount taken in, in 1948 was less than half a square mile. In 1966 the total number of square miles annexed annually had increased over five times, but the average amount had only doubled. Many cities must make many separate annexations to acquire even a small amount of territory. For instance, Rockford, Ill., had to complete 53 separate actions to gain less than one and a half square miles. The use of this device is increasingly falling behind the rate of urbanization. The main reasons for this are that: (1) Many areas now contain numerous incorporated municipalities adjacent to the central city that resist annexation. (Some, like Minneapolis, Minn., are completely ringed. In older areas even incorporated suburbs are surrounded.) (2) Metropolitan areas have grown beyond state and county lines. (3) State laws are too cumbersome to apply, too stringent, and generally unworkable. Most of the recent sizable annexations have taken place in small, medium-sized, or fast-growing communities—mostly in Wisconsin, and in the South and Southwest, notably in Virginia, California, and Texas. The greatest legal difficulty is the requirement of most states that the residents of territory to be annexed must approve the action in an election. Even in the states with the most liberal annexation laws, voters in incorporated municipalities have this separate and controlling vote. It is notheworthy that none of the recent large anneaxtions (of ten square miles or more) has been of incorporated territory and none has required this separate vote. Most of them have been accomplished under one of the following five types of legal authorization: (1) The city council of the annexing city passed an ordinance. (2) The people of the city undertaking the annexation voted in favor of the proposal. (3) The election results in the city and the area to be annexed were counted together. (4) A state legislature passed a special law. (5) A court rendered a decision favorable to the annexation. Since the problems of metropolitan areas have the most effect on municipalities, most students feel that the ability of these areas to annex should be encouraged, that state laws should be liberalized, but that safeguards should exist to protect the public interest in the area as a whole.

State responsibility for local boundary changes

The experience of Texas, which has very liberal annexation laws and where the most amount of territory has been taken into the cities, points up the difficulties in purely local determinations of the wisdom and expediency of annexations. It also shows the relationship of annexation to incorporation. In Texas, any home rule city may write into its charter the procedure by which it will acquire additional territory that, however, must be unincorporated at the time of the proposed annexation. Most of them have taken advantage of this to write charters that permit them to annex such territory without the consent of the people in the area involved. This unilateral action has resulted in competitive actions by municipalities to acquire territory considered desirable while other areas have been neglected. It has also resulted in relay races of new incorporations to forestall annexation and premature annexation proposals to forestall new incorporations.

The states are beginning to modify the relevant laws to facilitate annexation and to limit incorporations in outlying parts of urban areas. When an area has a choice between annexing or incorporating, it is as doubtful if the merits of either can be decided in an election as it is that the local governing body can decide it. The broader aspects of local boundary changes should be considered by some procedure that takes into account the effects of the changes on the area as a whole. In Ohio, this is accomplished by having the county governing body consider proposals. In New Mexico, boards of arbitration consisting of city and fringe area residents consider proposals. The best alternatives, however, include the establishment of standards in state law and this is the current trend. In North Carolina, for example, a city council may annex territory on its own determination but has to follow certain legal standards and its action may be appealed. The application of standards by a state agency, however, is the preferred method. Virginia has been following this procedure for years and in this state annexation has had the most sustained use, possibly because of it. In Virginia, special annexation courts hear proposals that have been instituted by a city or by the governing body or residents in the area of the proposed annexation. The standards applied by the court are written into state law and include such items as the need of the city for this territory for its orderly growth and development, the need of the area under consideration for services, the financial ability of the annexing city, and the existence of a community of interest between the two. The city council may accept or reject an affirmative finding of the court and any decision may be appealed. The chief criticism of the Virginia system has been that special courts do not accumulate and use a sustained body of information and knowledge. It is also dubious whether the adversary system is applicable to the weighing of issues and policies involved in this type of action. For this reason, the creation of state administrative agencies to pass on the merits of each proposal is receiving more attention. Besides being able to consider the impact of a proposal on the area as a whole, in the light of public policy, such an agency can initiate actions and consider alternative proposals. Minnesota and Wisconsin, to take two examples, have similar agencies that consider annexations, incorporations, and consolidations. In Alaska, a Local Boundary Commission has been created in the executive branch of the state that will consider proposed boundary changes and establish procedures for adjustments. In addition, Alaskan boroughs (counties) may not create service districts in an area that can be served by an existing one, by becoming a city, or by annexing to one.

Regardless of changes in annexation laws and better procedures, many areas will be unaided. In the first place, quite a few cities are unable to assume additional burdens. (It has been estimated that a newly annexed area will not "pay its way" for ten years.) In the second place, annexations are limited to adjacent and as mentioned above, in practice, to unincorporated territory. Even cities that have annexed considerable territory still comprise only part of their metropolitan areas. For example, Dallas, Texas, which has annexed over 80 square miles in recent years, still includes much less than one-half of its metropolitan area.

CITY–COUNTY CONSOLIDATION

Next to annexation, the preferred method for reorganizing government in metropolitan areas was for many years city–county consolidation. This reform eliminates one level of government by combining the city and the county and is accomplished by extending the city's territory to the county boundaries and transferring county functions to the city. Not all

Characteristics and difficulties

city–counties are exactly coterminous in area with their respective counties and not all, or identical functions, have been consolidated. The county retains its identity and certain officials such as the coroner are commonly retained. The administration of justice usually continues to be a county function. But the pattern of consolidation has been different in each case. In the nineteenth century Boston, Philadelphia, New Orleans, and New York City were merged with their counties. The only city–county consolidations instituted in the twentieth century have been those of the City of Baton Rouge and the Parish of East Baton Rouge, Louisiana in 1949, Nashville, Tennessee and Davidson County in 1962, and Jacksonville, Florida with Duval County in 1967.

The following characteristics of these early consolidations are of special importance: (1) Except for the New York City consolidation, only one county was involved in each. (2) All were accomplished by state legislation. (3) Other units existing in the county were merged with the new unit. (4) Though the city area was expanded at the time of the consolidation, city–counties have been unable subsequently to enlarge. None of these city–counties now contains as much as one-fifth of its respective metropolitan area. Consolidation is still useful for small areas that embrace only one county and do not cross state lines but two main differences from the earlier situations limit its chances of success today. First, existing municipalities other than the city have commonly been retained in recent proposals. If they continue to be part of the county and, therefore, contribute to its support, they would in effect be relinquishing autonomy. Secondly, there are many more incorporated municipalities now in urban counties and to protect them state legislation today usually requires local referenda on proposals, the results of which are often counted separately in the city and in the rest of the county. At least 18 proposals for consolidations have been defeated at some stage in the twentieth century. The fact that other proposals for metropolitan reorganization have also been defeated in most of these areas shows that the common requirement of separate majorities in local referenda is the greatest single stumbling block. The Baton Rouge consolidation was accomplished by a single overall vote. Most of the negative votes occur in the suburban and rural areas. These areas with some justification feel that their taxes will be raised to provide municipal services they neither need or desire. There is a real difficulty in adjusting financial support for different levels of service in the hinterland outside the central city. The creation of service districts within the county with different tax rates obviates this difficulty and is one of the most promising recent developments. Since this is applicable to other forms of metropolitan reorganization, a closer look at the Baton Rouge consolidation plan which includes this device is in order.

Baton
Rouge

The City of Baton Rouge and the Parish (county) of East Baton Rouge were consolidated in 1949 pursuant to a 1946 constitutional amendment. The legal identities of the parish and the city are maintained and each has its own budget. The parish provides for the administration of justice and highways and bridges for the area. Certain parish officials are retained—the assessor, sheriff, coroner, district attorney, tax collector, and clerk of court. Functions not common to the two units are supported separately. (Schools are administered by a separate unit and welfare is a state responsibility.) The city and county are under one executive, an elective mayor–president, and the city council of seven members elected at large serves as the parish council with the addition of two members elected from the rural area. At the time of the consolidation, the boundaries of Baton Rouge were extended, almost tripling the size of the city, but a town and village were left undisturbed. Further incorporations are prohibited. To provide for the differences in service needs in the urban and rural territory, the parish is divided into three districts:

(1) The *urban service district,* in which the highest tax rate is paid. In this area, services are supplied by the city and include police and fire protection, garbage and refuse collection and disposal, street lighting, traffic regulation, and inspectional services.

(2) The *rural service district,* in which a minimum level of service is supplied at a lower tax rate by the parish. The only "urban" service is police protection. Other municipal-type services may be provided by the parish as need arises but only by creating taxing districts for them.

(3) The *industrial service district* where no residences are permitted in which municipal services are provided by the industries at their own expense. Additional ones may be provided by creating tax districts for them on petition of 90 percent of the property owners of the area.

One drawback apparent in the Baton Rouge division of the area into *Urban and* service and taxing districts is that changing land uses would make difficult *rural* readjustments necessary. In areas of mixed uses, drawing boundaries would *service* be so complicated as to make the plan unworkable. However, since this *districts* is one of the better ways to secure voter approval of reorganization proposals, it deserves serious consideration where applicable. The more common proposal is the creation of only two districts—a general one that would cover all the territory of the area and in which the common services at a minimum level would be provided, such as general police and fire protection, schools, parks, and recreation; and an urban service area or areas for extended services such as water and sewer mains, increased police and fire protection, street lighting, refuse and garbage collection. California, Alaska, Connecticut, Virginia, and Kentucky, for example, have authorized local governments to create these different taxing districts.

The Jacksonville–Duval consolidation was achieved by a countywide *The* referendum and the structure of government created was a mayor–council *Jackson-* system with the councilmen representing districts in the county. Elective *ville* officers including the school board were continued and service districts *program* similar to those in Baton Rouge were established. A few municipalities remain outside of the consolidated set-up for some functions. A similar consolidation of Tampa and Hillsborough County failed to receive approval by the voters. The earlier Nashville–Davidson County consolidation also replaced executive governments with a new one and also made district distinctions between the urbanized and the nonurbanized areas.

CITY–COUNTY SEPARATION

Limited use

Separation of a city from its county and the formation of the remainder of the county into a new or reconstituted county has been urged on different occasions as a means for city residents to avoid paying county taxes. There is something parochial about separation. The main benefit, a financial one, accrues to the city. City–county separation does not solve problems common to a whole area or provide an adequate answer to how to provide a minimum level of services throughout an area. It is not often urged today by students of the subject and two of the cities that were separated from their counties in the nineteenth century have since tried to institute other forms of governmental organization. As in the case of the consolidated city–counties, these separated cities were given land at the time of the separation but have been unable to annex any since. Denver is the only one that has annexed land and it still comprises only a small part of its metropolitan area.

City–county separation in Virginia

In Virginia a different situation exists. In that state separation is automatic for any city of 5,000 or more population and is complete for cities of 10,000 or more inhabitants. Virginia cities have been able to expand because of their system of annexation described above and so have avoided some of the problems of urban expansion experienced by other cities. In that state, however, the question of what happens to the remainder of the county if it becomes too small to give adequate services has not been solved. This has happened in Henrico County. A recent study group (1967) felt that the Virginia local units failed to solve areawide problems and recommended the creation of planning districts by the state to coordinate local efforts.

The Atlanta–Fulton County plan of improvement

The 1952 reorganization of the City of Atlanta and Fulton County, Georgia, has elements of city–county separation, consolidation, and annexation. As such, it is hoped that most of the knotty problems resulting from one or the other of these methods will be mitigated. At the time of the reorganization, 82 square miles of territory, mostly urban, were added to the city and in the following year ten more square miles were annexed. The county was excluded from performing municipal functions. The city provides water, sewage disposal, parks and recreation, and traffic engineering throughout the area. The county performs consolidated areawide services such as public health and rural services. Certain management functions have been merged, such as tax assessment and collection. The city health department was abolished and the county fire protection,

airport, refuse collection, parks and recreation were transferred to the
city. Incorporated units other than Atlanta were left untouched and some
functions still overlap; for instance, schools, law enforcement, and public
works are performed by both governments, but the plan has been considered a distinct step forward in improving metropolitan relationships.

FEDERATION

The obvious parallel between metropolitan areas with their sectional
interests and established governments and the national government with
its states has made the idea of metropolitan federation most intriguing to
students of the subject. Under this type of reorganization the individual
local units are retained to provide local services and meet diverse needs
and a new metropolitan "federal" government is created to provide areawide services. Citizen control of governmental decisions that affected
people where they work and also where they live would be enhanced.
A means would be provided for flexibility in meeting future problems. The
financial resources of the entire area would be pooled to provide a minimum level of service throughout the area and an areawide approach to
common problems would be possible. Though the home rule enjoyed
by the individual units would be diminished, the area as a whole would
find increased ability to stand on its own feet.

*Advan-
tages
and
present
use*

There are two types of federation possible: (1) the borough plan,
the prototype of which is London with its County Council, which provides common functions, and its 28 boroughs and the city, which take
care of more local affairs; and (2) the district plan. The only example of
a metropolitan federation in North America is Toronto. In 1953, the
legislature of Ontario created a supergovernment for this area that is six
times the size of the city. County functions were transferred to it and this
metropolitan government was given responsibility to provide the basic
areawide services. Local services remain the responsibility of the local
units—the city of Toronto and the suburban cities and townships. The
legislative body of 25 members is a metropolitan council composed of the
12 heads of the suburban governments, 12 officials from the city, and a
chairman appointed by the provincial government. The basic weakness of
this plan is this system of representation. In the first place, it is based on
political units, not on population. Each suburban unit has one representative regardless of size and the representation is weighted in favor of the
city since the most rapidly growing areas are on the outskirts. In the second
place the representatives have dual responsibilities—a legislative one to the
metropolitan government and an administrative and executive one to their
localities. For these reasons, recent proposals for federation in the United
States have recommended the district system of representation.

Because concessions are made to the local units, proposals for federa-

Obstacles to federation

tion have the most chance of lasting success and it would seem also of local approval. Such, however, has not been the case. More proposals have been defeated locally at the polls than at any other stage. A constitutional amendment is usually required before a local charter can be drafted but this is usually secured. The only exceptions have been one for Cleveland that was defeated by the voters of Ohio in 1958 and one for the St. Louis area that was defeated in Missouri in 1930. Some of the reasons for local charter defeats are the same as those for defeats of other types of reorganization—fear of rises in taxes, fear of big government, fear of loss of independence, and public apathy. In addition, proposals for federation need to have more details worked out than do other types of metropolitan reform. Decisions have to be made on the distribution of powers among the units involved and the method of representation on, and composition of, the governing body. The result is a long and complicated charter difficult to understand.

A federated county— Dade

The nearest approach to a federal system of metropolitan government in the United States is the one established in 1957 in Dade County (Miami), Florida. Following a constitutional amendment adopted in 1956 permitting Dade County to draft a home rule charter, a Metropolitan Charter Board appointed by the governor drew up a charter which was submitted to the voters and approved. The charter provides for a reorganized county government with a manager and the abolition of certain constitutional offices, such as the sheriff and coroner. The county is a union of 26 municipalities and Metro, which is the name given the reorganized county. Functions are being transferred to the county very gradually, though the charter gives the county control over sewage disposal, water supply, transportation, traffic, central planning, and other municipal functions to which areawide control may be applicable. All other municipal powers are reserved to the cities. The county may set minimum standards that the municipalities may raise, for instance, in zoning and subdivision regulation. The municipalities will retain responsibility for local services such as local streets. Difficulties were experienced from the outset in allocating these functions but Metro is still in existence and has received four distinct votes of confidence from the people. The governing body is a board of eleven commissioners (reduced to nine in 1963), five elected at large, five from districts, and one from the city of Miami. Other cities may have a representative when they reach 60,000 population.

Reasons for use of the county as a metropolitan government

THE URBAN COUNTY

The failures at the polls and the inadequacies of so many proposals for metropolitan reorganization have led to a reconsideration of the role of counties in urban areas. Over half of the metropolitan areas consist of one county and in quite a few others it is a major portion of the area. It is the only existing general purpose local government that approaches the areawide criterion for a metropolitan government. In addition, many counties in urban areas are already assuming functions that are in effect municipal. Though reorganizing county governments so they would be equipped to deal with urban problems more extensively is difficult, it may be easier than trying to abolish or bypass them.

At present most urban counties are not in a position to assume additional responsibilities. To transform a county into an efficient unit of government capable of performing urban functions requires first the internal reorganization outlined in an earlier chapter. Urban counties need, in addition, as we have mentioned, reconsideration of (1) their roles as agencies of their state governments and (2) the composition of their governing bodies. Counties are not municipal corporations in law. Though they are becoming more so in practice, the courts are still able to distinguish their powers from municipal ones. In some states, counties may adopt home-rule charters and a few have done so. It is difficult to see how a county can perform urban functions without municipal and ordinance making powers. In some areas, however, there are also nonlegal objections to extending county powers. The greatest benefit so far in expanding county activity has accrued to suburban residents in unincorporated areas and city residents do not particularly enjoy paying through their county governments for services for others that they provide for themselves in their own units. To meet this criticism separate taxing and service districts could be used. *Prerequisite—county reform*

When county services are extended to municipalities in its area, an additional set of considerations arises. The composition of the county governing body becomes important. Central cities, in particular, are commonly underrepresented on county boards. If the county is to extend its operations to cities (in order to eliminate duplication and provide areawide approaches to problems), it should be more representative. County governing bodies could be organized on a federated basis, and many of them are by having township supervisors sit with city and other municipal representatives. This usually results in too large a board and has the same drawbacks as the borough plan of federation. A small board, such as has been advocated for rural areas, is not appropriate either. Urban counties are not homogeneous and sectional interests need representation just as they do on city councils. This could be secured by district representation (Milwaukee County is an example) combined with election at large if that is desired (such as is in use in Dade County, Fla.). This can have the added advantage of relating representation to population.

When sweeping proposals have been submitted to the voters to reorganize counties and give them power to act as urban governments, they have usually been defeated. The most common method for reaching this goal is the *gradual* transference of municipal activities (with or without *Methods for increasing county functions* previous reorganization). Authorizations for this can usually be given by state enabling acts (instead of constitutional amendment) and can be accomplished then by contract between the units without voter approval. Each year additional states pass laws permitting counties to contract with municipalities to perform services for them. The actual use of this method has progressed furthest in California. A survey by the National Association of County Officials in 1958 revealed a pattern to this activity across the country. Only a very small number of urban counties reported no cooperative activity. Most formal agreements (i.e., contracts) were with cities. Functional consolidations accounted for the greatest number of these and the most common were in public health, prisoner care, and elections. Informal agreements were most common in police and fire protection. In the majority of agreements, fees were charged. The most common services provided free but under contract were public health services and tax assessment and collection. (Fees are not usually charged when the service is provided on an informal basis.)

The increasing use of the county to solve urban problems testifies to the popularity of this method. However, this should not be confused with metropolitan *government*. It represents rather an indication of an *emerging* metropolitan government in some areas. Although the list of urban county activities is long, it is not so impressive when compared with the problems still remaining.

SPECIAL PURPOSE DISTRICTS

Advan-
tages
The most widely used device for dealing with metropolitan problems has been the special purpose district, a quasi-municipal corporation established for the performance, usually, of a single governmental function. Created because older units have been or are inadequate for the purpose contemplated or because other proposals to meet urban problems have failed to get approval, urged by those who are concerned with (to them) an overwhelming need in one particular area, popular with the general public (by analogy with the familiar school district, they are considered to be "out of politics"), appealing to some groups because of their business methods and engineering proficiency, these special purpose districts are almost universally frowned on by scholars. However, they have advantages that are generally recognized. These are as follows: (1) A special district can be organized to include an area covering one or more local governmental units. All the devices studies so far are intracounty (with the exception of the consolidation that created New York City) either in conception or in practice and the legal and practical difficulties involved in using any of the other devices in interstate areas are or seem to be insurmountable. Special districts need not be limited to one county operation and they can be set up by interstate compact and international agreement. (2) These special districts can be established relatively easily compared to the

other solutions. They are authorized by state law, not by constitutional amendment. If local approval is needed, one overall vote is all that is usually required. (3) Once established, they have a flexible structure that can often be changed by amendment of state law without local approval, or amendment of an interstate compact, which would not require local approval in any case. In expanding their boundaries, they also enjoy flexibility. Such action can sometimes be taken under a simple court order, sometimes on petition of a small percentage of the voters or property owners in the area, sometimes by the district governing body acting alone. In a few states, expansion of the area is impossible or limited, but this is not the usual practice. (4) Their establishment does not disrupt or change the established governmental structure or affect local officeholders. (5) They do not usually suffer the financial restrictions imposed by state law on other local units. (6) In their relationships with the state legislature, they do not seem to labor under the antagonism cities do. (7) They can provide an areawide approach to an areawide problem. (8) Finally, the wide variety existing in their uses and organizational practices makes a tailor-made plan not only possible but probable. It is not surprising, therefore, that the numbers of special districts have increased rapidly since 1942 when rapid growth of urban areas has produced so many service needs. This has led to the suggestion that the uses of special districts could be increased and their functions expanded, but this necessitates an examination of their disadvantages and inadequacies.

The criticisms of the special district as a solution to problems in metropolitan areas revolve around their relationships with the other units of government in the area, the limitations on their activities, and their remoteness from the general public. The creation of a special district means that the number of units in an area is increased; local government is made more complex; and intergovernmental cooperation and planning is decreased by the withdrawal of a function from the responsibility of the general purpose governments. Of equal importance, when an expanded use of special districts is contemplated, are the limitations on their functions that result from their lack of general legislative power and their methods of finance. The types of districts we have been discussing in general have no ordinance-making power and there is no move apparent to increase this power as there is for counties. This usually debars them from regulatory activities and limits them to service functions. Their methods of finance—commonly special assessments, charges, rates, and rents—limit them to self-supporting activities. The effect of both these limitations so far has been that in suburban areas especially, water supply and sewage disposal are usually more adequately provided for than police and fire protection.

The most serious criticism of the special-purpose district, however, is its remoteness from the general public. This occurs because of one or more of the following practices: (1) Many of their governing bodies are appointed in whole or in part by state judges or governors. In the case of

*Inade-
quacies*

interstate districts, they are appointed by the respective governors. (2) Sometimes a district is organized in such a complicated fashion that the typical voter does not know what it is or what it does. (3) Often the governing bodies are not directly elected by the people, either in whole or in part, and in some instances franchise depends on property qualifications— a voting restriction virtually abandoned for other electoral processes. All these practices place the voter at one or more removes from the district government and lessen political accountability.

Can the special district be retooled?

It has been suggested by many observers of the metropolitan scene that special-purpose districts might be transformed or evolve into multi-purpose ones. In this case a very useful metropolitan government would result—provided that these districts could be made more responsive to the public. This would involve decisions on the composition and methods of selection of their governing bodies comparable to those encountered in plans for federation. It is not likely that many present single-purpose districts will evolve into many-purpose ones. Most districts at present are single purpose; a few provide related services such as sewage disposal and storm water drainage, but, even when a district is permitted by state law to give other services, the practice has been for districts not to expand their activities. Neither have these districts shown any inclination to *seek* authority to add to their responsibilities. The creation anew of a multi-purpose district to serve as a metropolitan government seems even more difficult to achieve than the other forms of metropolitan reorganization.

JOINT AGENCIES AND COOPERATIVE ACTIVITY

The conclusions on the possibilities of metropolitan government reached by many are that local units are incapable of creating broader mechanisms of government to solve the urban problems of an expanding population. Though more special-purpose districts will be created and more urban counties will undertake additional functions, other proposals have little chance of success. The stake of the national government in the economic and social vitality of our great metropolises and the legal responsibility of the states mean that they will undoubtedly participate more and more in solving metropolitan problems. On their own endeavors, however, the local units have made progress in cooperative arrangements. Sanitation, health, fire protection, water supply, airports, and library services are among the functions that with increasing frequency are being turned over by individual governmental units to joint agencies. Minnesota, Louisiana, Missouri, Georgia, New Jersey, and California are among the states that permit local units to perform jointly any function they may perform separately. The Municipal Authorities in Pennsylvania are an outstanding example of joint activity. The advantage of this form of endeavor is that it can be intercounty and interstate. The latest addition to cooperative activity among local units is metropolitan councils. These are associations of local officials who study the problems of their areas (with the help of professional staffs). They may make plans for their areas and recommend lines of action to their local units. The largest is the Metropolitan Regional Council for the New York area. Similar agencies are also functioning in Denver, Washington, D. C., and Wichita, Kansas. Of less broad scope are regional planning commissions such as those operating in the Twin Cities (Minneapolis and St. Paul), the Northeastern Illinois and Detroit areas. Though many avenues of approach can and should be taken simultaneously by the largest areas, probably the only all-inclusive methods possible for them on local government terms (short of the creation of city states) are these councils and commissions for discussion, study, and planning.

REFERENCES

Advisory Commission on Intergovernmental Relations, *Metropolitan America: Challenge to Federalism* (Washington, D. C., 1966).
——, *Metropolitan Councils of Government* (Washington, D. C., 1964).
G. E. Baker, *Rural vs. Urban Political Power* (New York, 1955).
J. C. Bollens, *Special District Governments in the United States* (Berkeley and Los Angeles, 1957). Chaps. I–V, VIII.
——, *The States and the Metropolitan Problem*. Report to the Governors' Conference of the Council of State Governments (Chicago, 1956).
B. Chinitz, *City and Suburb: the Economics of Metropolitan Growth* (Englewood Cliffs, N. J., 1964).
Conference on Metropolitan Area Problems, *Metropolitan Surveys Now in Progress* (New York, 1960).
R. H. Connery, *The Federal Government and Metropolitan Areas* (Cambridge, Mass., 1960).
T. R. Dye and B. W. Hawkins (eds.), *Politics in the Metropolis: A Reader in Conflict and Cooperation* (Columbus, Ohio, 1967).
V. Jones, *Metropolitan Government* (Chicago, 1942).
H. Kaplan, *Urban Political Systems: A Functional Analysis of Metro Toronto* (New York, 1967).
National Association of County Officials, *The Urban County Congress* (Washington, D. C., 1959).
New York Metropolitan Region Study (Cambridge, Mass., 1958–1960). Ten volumes. The following are especially appropriate:
    E. M. Hoover and R. Vernon, *Anatomy of a Metropolis.*
    R. Vernon, *Metropolis: 1985.*
    R. C. Wood, *1400 Governments.*
S. Scott and L. Keller, *Annexation? Incorporation?: A Guide for Community Action* (Univ. of Calif., Bur. of Public Admin., Berkeley, 1959).
B. Tableman, *Governmental Organization in Metropolitan Areas* (Ann Arbor, Mich., 1951).
Toronto Civic Advisory Council: Committee on Metropolitan Problems, *Final Report* (Toronto, 1951).

INDEX